THE COMING GOLDEN AGE

31 WAYS TO BE KINGDOM READY

DR. DAVID JEREMIAH

W PUBLISHING GROUP

AN IMPRINT OF THOMAS NELSON

To Dr. Richard Furman
Revered thoracic surgeon,
Cofounder of World Medical Mission, the
medical ministry of Samaritan's Purse,
Avid student of the Bible . . .
AND my once-a-week-talk-to-on-the-phone-FRIEND.

CONTENTS

CONTENTS

INTRODUCTION

I've been fascinated by biblical prophecy all my life, and nothing encourages me more than God's predictions about the future. But I don't make many predictions myself. The Bible is infallible; I'm not. Yet I'm going to predict right now that reading this book will make you feel like the farmer I read about in Kentucky.

We don't know his name—he hasn't divulged it, nor the exact location of his farm. But we know what he found. While digging in his cornfield last year, he saw a glint of gold. It was a coin. As the man wiped away the dirt, he was astonished to discover a twenty-dollar Double Eagle coin from the 1860s.

"After I flipped the first clump of dirt," he said, "over the next forty-five minutes to an hour, the coins kept coming. I knew it was hundreds."

In all, the farmer uncovered more than seven hundred Civil War era coins just beneath his corn patch. Most of them were minted between 1840 and 1863. A few were silver, but most of them were gold.

Someone long ago had buried the coins to protect them during the war. For reasons unknown, they were never retrieved until our nameless farmer literally struck gold. Experts say the old coins are worth millions of dollars today.[1]

I'm feeling kind of like that farmer. I've lived in my Bible for years without fully appreciating the hoard of golden coins lying just beneath the surface. Recently I've been digging them up—hundreds of verses about the coming Golden Age, the impending thousand-year reign of Jesus Christ on this planet. Some commentators say it is the single most mentioned subject in all of God's Word.[2]

Ten centuries when the world will be peaceful, prosperous, and under the power and authority of Jesus Christ!

This Millennium of time is ahead of us. It's the epoch between our Lord's return to this planet and the onset of the new heaven and new earth of the eternal age.

This knowledge is invaluable to us. It answers our questions and anticipates our future. If you're looking around the world right now, alarmed and afraid, I've got something wonderful to show you. If you think our planet is headed toward destruction, think again! The unfailing hand of the Lord Jesus Christ—the same hand that is guiding you—is directing the course of events on this earth.

It's time to cast discouragement out of your life. If you belong to Jesus Christ, you're included in the future He's designed. There is a coming Golden Age, and it gets even better after that!

In brief, this is what will happen. The Bible teaches that a great disappearance could occur any day now—the Rapture of the church from this planet. Jesus will come in the skies and call His people upward to be with Him (1 Thess. 4:13–18). The vanishing of millions or billions of people will traumatize the nations, leading to a global power shift and worldwide war (Rev. 6:1–8). A cunning one-world ruler will emerge, triggering seven years of Tribulation on our planet (Dan. 9:27; Rev. 6–18).

The final half of that period will be harrowing beyond anything known to history. God's wrath will fall on the earth in waves just as the Antichrist is gathering the nations against little Israel (Rev. 15:1; Zech. 14:2). Jesus called it a "great tribulation, such as has not been since the beginning of the world until this time, no, nor ever shall be" (Matt. 24:21).

All this will climax in the ultimate war in world history—the battle of Armageddon (Rev. 16:16). Just when Israel appears on the verge of annihilation, Jesus Christ will appear in the sky and destroy the hostile forces of the Antichrist (Zech. 14:2; Rev. 19:11–16). Our Lord will literally speak the victory, and He will deliver His people.

We'll be with Him. We'll see this happen!

Jesus will then descend to the earth and His feet will touch the Mount of Olives, the hilly ridge on the east side of Jerusalem (Zech. 14:4; Acts 1:11). He will gloriously enter the city of Jerusalem, assume the reins of world government, and reign for one thousand years (Rev. 20:4–6).

We call this the Millennium—the coming Golden Age. It's the kingdom to come, the fulfillment of all the promises God made to Israel in the Old Testament. It's also the bridge of time that will take us into the eternal enclaves of the new heaven, the new earth, and the everlasting capital of New Jerusalem.

Yes, there's a lot to unpack about all this, which we'll do in the following pages. But the general sequence is easy enough for us to grasp. This framework puts everything in its place so we can assemble the prophetic chronology in our minds.

First, the Rapture, which was the subject of my book *The Great Disappearance*.

Then a seven-year period of Tribulation, climaxing in the battle of Armageddon.

And then Jesus will come again and establish His kingdom promised throughout the Bible. That thousand-year age will condition and prepare us for our eternal home—heaven!

Rapture. Tribulation. Armageddon. Return. Millennium. Eternity.

Got it? This book is about that underappreciated millennial part of the sequence.

As I researched all this, one thought struck me more forcibly than any other. If the Rapture were to occur today, our world—including you and me—would be only seven years away from the most remarkable and glorious state we could ever imagine on this fallen planet. I felt exhilarated by that. The Lord wants us to think about it. He has scattered passage after passage about this throughout Scripture from Genesis to Revelation, and the amount of biblical truth is massive when it comes to this future Golden Age.

In fact, the sheer amount of prophetic Scripture on this subject could be overwhelming. To make it as simple as possible, I've broken it down into thirty-one millennial facts from the Bible. If you read one chapter a day for just a month, it'll help you become kingdom ready!

In this book, you'll discover the world you've always wanted, where . . .

- a new and improved Golden City of Jerusalem will become the capital of the world;
- the earth will be characterized by holiness and global peace;
- sickness will be rare, and people will live for centuries;
- fierce animals will become as gentle as house pets;
- worship will be spontaneous, continuous, and glorious;
- the nation of Israel will become the world's leading travel destination;
- Satan won't be around to bother us;
- Jesus will literally reign over the world from His throne in Jerusalem, and He will be accessible to His people.

If all that sounds fantastic to you, it's because it *is* fantastic. But it is also true—it's all there in the Bible. There is nothing too hard for God, and He always keeps His promises. He has made a lot of them to Israel, especially through the Old Testament prophets and in the book of Revelation. He has a plan for our world, and He hasn't forgotten it. He has a prophetic love for Israel, and He will bring to pass every word He has spoken.

Things may seem bleak today. Depressing headlines. Breaking news. Virulent evil. Roller-coaster politics. Rampant antisemitism and religious persecution. Personal fears and worries. But just ahead of us, perhaps little more than seven years from now, all that will change by the power of our risen and reigning and righteous Lord Jesus Christ.

Just seven years after the Rapture! That's less than two US presidential terms.

Join me in the fruitful fields of Scripture and let's dig up the cache of golden verses waiting for us just beneath the surface. As we learn more of what God has ahead for us, we'll anticipate tomorrow with fresh enthusiasm. We'll await our Savior with greater longing. And we'll relish the coming Golden Age with increased expectancy.

When you see what the Bible has to say about the future, you'll stop frowning in frustration and you'll start shouting for joy.

There's gold in this book! Golden Bible verses about a golden age! So let me restate my opening prediction. I think you'll find enough treasure in the following pages to feel just like the wealthy person you really are in Jesus Christ.

CHAPTER 1

IMAGINE

For just one day, wouldn't you like to see the world as it should be? War zones turned into ceasefire zones. Politicians making godly decisions. Crime nonexistent. Laughter filling our homes. Worshipers filling our churches. Can you picture it?

For just one day, wouldn't you love to be on a planet without a single natural disaster? Imagine what it'd be like to have a one-day suspension of the devil's power. Of evil's grip. Of temptation's pull. Of anxiety's torment.

Wouldn't it be wonderful if doctors' exam rooms were empty on that day? If no funerals occurred? If police officers had absolutely nothing to do? If broadcasters had only good news to report?

Let's not stop at a single day. What if that utopia-like state lasted an entire week?

Now imagine fifty-two thousand such weeks, all in a row—one thousand years of universal peace, prosperity, and cheer. Ten centuries of happiness, free from war and worry.

No one can count the number of summit meetings, diplomatic negotiations, or peace treaties that have come and gone over the centuries, from antiquity till now. The whole world craves peace yet seems in constant turmoil. Even today, turning on the news is like taking a trip to the land of anxiety and alarm.

But Jesus is coming, and He will change that. I'm eagerly awaiting His imminent return; and just seven years after the Rapture He will come again to our tempestuous earth to make it right. This has become so real I can almost visualize it. There's no study in Scripture that will satisfy your heart in the exact way this topic will. As I'll show you later, this thousand-year period is the transition between time and eternity, between the old earth and the new one, between the momentary and the everlasting.

Yes, things will get worse before they get better. After the Lord catches us up in the air to be with Him, the world will descend into seven years of Tribulation that will feel like all the wars and famines and disasters of human history combined. It will reach fever pitch with the battle of Armageddon.

Our Lord will shut down that war the moment He returns, and He will bind Satan with chains that are padlocked for a thousand years. During this time, the atmosphere of earth will be free from satanic static. Demons and the principalities and powers of darkness will be silenced and banished. Imagine the weight removed from our shoulders when we no longer have to be aware of the snares of the devil or the prince of the power of the air!

The Lord will then proceed to do what He did in the Gospels—heal people. Not just one or two here and there, but everyone. The Lord Jesus will be "the Sun of Righteousness" who arises "with healing in His wings" (Mal. 4:2).

Even if you're not sick, you'll feel a strength and wellness you've never before known. Life expectancy will be measured by hundreds of years, and perhaps you'll even have enough lung power to blow out all 790 candles on your birthday cake (Isa. 65:19–20).

Think of how wonderful you'll feel to be rid of aches and pains, chills and pills. No more cancer, no heart disease, no diabetes, no artificial joints. "The lame shall leap like a deer, and the tongue of the dumb sing. For waters shall burst forth in the wilderness, and streams in the desert" (Isa. 35:6).

You'll feel like traveling the world—and you will!

The primary destination of the nations will be the land of Israel. The Bible says, "People from nations and cities around the world will travel to Jerusalem. The people of one city will say to the people of another, 'Come with us to Jerusalem to ask the LORD to bless us. Let's worship the LORD of Heaven's Armies. I'm determined to go.' Many peoples and powerful nations will come to Jerusalem to seek the LORD of Heaven's Armies and to ask for his blessing" (Zech. 8:20–22 NLT).

Can you imagine the conversations you'll have on that day? You'll say to a friend, "Come, let us go up to the mountain of the LORD, to the house of Jacob's God. There he will teach us his ways, and we will walk in his paths" (Isa. 2:3 NLT).

We'll no longer need to invest so much effort and spiritual energy into evangelism. Instead, we'll have much greater opportunities to build one another up in the Word of God. We'll not need to teach our neighbors, saying, "You should know the Lord." For everyone from the least to the greatest will already know Him (Jer. 31:34).

You'll travel to a much-enlarged Israel on a regular basis with no jet lag or terrorist threats. You'll walk the Highway of Holiness to the city of Zion with a song in your heart (Isa. 35:8). There you'll find a gleaming and glorious metropolis on a heightened elevation, bursting with luxurious accommodations. The new millennial temple will take away your breath—how massive, how beautiful! Its courtyards and gateways, its altars and priests, its offerings and celebrations will be the delight of the earth (Ezek. 40–45).

You'll hear music everywhere, for "joy and gladness will be found there. Songs of thanksgiving will fill the air" (Isa. 51:3 NLT).

Most of all, Jesus Christ will be there, physically and personally and visibly. He will teach His truth to the peoples and rule among the nations (Mi. 4:1–3; Isa. 9:7). Don't you believe He will somehow have enough time for everyone who wants to see Him? He'll teach us so much more about Himself and His ways, and He will direct the nations in their courses. He will be both King and Priest (Zech. 6:13).

The land of Israel will become the center of the earth, and the people of Israel will become examples of godliness for all the world. "All who remain in Zion will be a holy people—those who survive the destruction of Jerusalem and are recorded among the living. The Lord will wash the filth from beautiful Zion and cleanse Jerusalem of its bloodstains. . . . He will provide a canopy of cloud during the day and smoke and flaming fire at night, covering the glorious land" (Isa. 4:3–5 NLT).

Jerusalem will also be the financial capital of earth as merchants from the seven seas bring the wealth of many nations to the Holy Land. Ships from the ends of the earth will dock at the ports of Israel, bringing Jews home and carrying silver and gold (Isa. 60:5–11). Jerusalem's gates will always stand open; they will never be closed (v. 11).

Old people will walk through Jerusalem's boulevards and plazas with strength, and the city will be filled with boys and girls playing in the streets (Zech. 8:4–5). Look! There's a horse and carriage rumbling through the streets, and on the horse's harness bells are the words "HOLINESS TO THE LORD" (14:20).

No longer will the Jewish people be the punching bag of the world. Antisemitism will be a distant memory, and the nation of Israel will be paramount on earth. When people encounter a Jewish person anywhere on the globe, they will grab his arm and ask for a blessing (Zech. 8:23).

Day and night, the air will be filled with songs praising our God and our Messiah, Jesus Christ. In that day, Jerusalem will be called by many names: "The city of our God" (Ps. 48:1), the city of God's delight (Isa. 62:4), "THE LORD IS THERE" (Ezek. 48:35), "the City of Truth" and "the Holy Mountain" (Zech. 8:3), and Mount Zion, "the perfection of beauty" (Ps. 48:2; 50:2).

The land of Israel will be a symbol and source of blessing for all the earth (Zech. 8:13).

Can you visualize that Golden City with its glorious canopy covering it—the clouds above it, a wall of fire around it, and the glory of God in its midst (Zech. 2:5)? Everyone there will be filled with the Holy Spirit (Ezek. 39:29). The Lord will take delight in His people and rejoice over them with singing (Zeph. 3:17).

To the south of Jerusalem, you'll enjoy visiting the breadbasket of the world—an area of former desert hills now turned into a garden of Eden by the crystal river gushing from the temple precincts (Isa. 51:3). At some points you'll see people wading in that river, and in other areas they'll be swimming (Ezek. 47:3–6). You'll no longer have to settle for floating in the Dead Sea because the slimy residue of the centuries will be flushed away. The inflowing living waters of the crystal river will turn the Dead Sea into one of the most beautiful lakes in the world. It will be a fisherman's paradise (Ezek. 47:9–10).

This entire area will be called "the garden of the LORD" (Isa. 51:3).

What vineyards you'll see, watered by showers of blessing (Ezek. 28:26)! The hills will drip with sweet wine; grain and grapes will grow faster than they can be harvested (Amos 9:13). The orchards and fields will yield bumper crops, and everyone will live in safety, sitting under arbors and fig trees (Ezek. 34:27). Gardening and farming will be a joyful task, unhindered by weeds, drought, or pests. The entire land of Israel will blossom like a lily and spread out like an olive tree (Hos. 14:5–6).

Even earth's wildlife will be transformed. Lions and lambs will lie down together, and children will play with tigers and bears the way they now play with puppies and kittens. Imagine that!

The Pentagon, if it's still standing, will become a worship center or a biblical seminary. Military bases will be vacated. People will no longer kill, steal, or destroy. Hospitals will be torn down. Prisons leveled. Slums transformed. People will forget about locking their doors at night or carrying a weapon for protection.

You and your loved ones in Christ will enjoy a thousand-year prelude to an even greater future blessing—eternal life in the new heaven and new earth and the city of New Jerusalem. You'll have an entire millennium to prepare and condition you for eternity.

Does this seem too good to be true? The Lord will say to us something like, "All this may seem impossible to you now, but is it impossible to Me?" The Lord's implied answer is no, because for Him nothing is impossible (Zech. 8:6; Luke 1:37).

If the God who created the world long ago is truly in charge, how else do you think His story of redemption on earth—what we should rightly call *His story*—would conclude? The work of the Lord never ends in tragedy but in triumph. Jesus didn't die for the world only for it to end in a man-made nuclear holocaust or biological disaster. Those things may appear, but they're not the end of His plan for us.

There's coming an appointed hour when our Lord Jesus Christ will return as He promised and descend in glory clouds to the Mount of Olives to establish His kingdom and fulfill all His promises to Israel and to the world. And in that coming Golden Age, "the earth shall be full of the knowledge of the LORD as the waters cover the sea" (Isa. 11:9).

Imagine what a time that will be!

CHAPTER 2

THREE GOLDEN TRUTHS

In the midst of World War I, the American Red Cross recruited young men to travel to Europe to help the suffering masses there. One farm boy from Missouri caught the vision. He was too young to apply for the US Army, but he forged the date on his birth certificate and managed to join the American Red Cross. He became an ambulance driver in France.

While there, he fell in love with the charm and elegance of French design and architecture. He took it all in—the ornate chambers of the palaces, the gardens of Versailles, the paintings in the galleries. It animated his imagination like . . . well, like magic.

Later, young Walt returned to Europe with his wife and continued to dream of creating worlds of fantasy, lands filled with kings and queens, castles and palaces, heroes and villains, and enchanted kingdoms. Today if you visit one of Walt Disney's theme parks, you'll see royalty everywhere:

- King Mufasa
- King Triton
- Queen of Hearts
- Prince Charming
- Princesses Snow White, Cinderella, Ariel, Jasmine, Mulan, and Moana

People call Disney theme parks the happiest places on earth—but that's not quite true. There are also expensive tickets, long lines, and frazzled parents trying to manage exhausted youngsters. Yet it's interesting that even children believe there should be a place where royalty is good, kings are needed, and happiness rules the day.

Christian author C. S. Lewis believed our longing for these mythological worlds indicated a true desire in the human heart for a world where everything would be as it should be. Behind the myths, he said, is an ultimate reality that pulls us onward and upward.[1]

In other words, we dream about a Golden Age for this world because there truly is a better world available. Somehow, we know that in our hearts.

We know it from our Bibles too!

I want to tell you about a coming Golden Age with a great and glorious King ruling over a happy planet filled with noble people. Scripture describes this wonderful era in many places and in many ways, as we'll see throughout these pages. But the central passage is found in Revelation 20:

> Then I saw an angel coming down from heaven, having the key to the bottomless pit and a great chain in his hand. He laid hold of the dragon, that serpent of old, who is the Devil and Satan, and bound him for a thousand years; and he cast him into the bottomless pit, and shut him up, and set a seal on him, so that he should deceive the nations no more till the thousand years were finished. . . .
>
> And I saw thrones, and they sat on them, and judgment was

committed to them. . . . And they lived and reigned with Christ for a thousand years. (vv. 1–4)

When we study biblical prophecy today, we focus a lot of attention on the second coming of Christ—and rightly so—which Jesus said will take place like a flash of lightning (Matt. 24:27). But most of us haven't heard much about His subsequent reign on earth, which will last for a thousand years.

The Millennium is no postscript in Scripture. Instead, it is the crux of the matter. The critical climax of history. We're going to spend many chapters exploring and examining what the coming Golden Age will be like, including all the wonders we'll experience—and all the terrors we'll avoid! But for now, I'd like to start by focusing on three simple truths about the coming millennial kingdom that will serve as a helpful foundation for that exploration.

A KINGDOM GROUNDED IN TIME

Revelation 20 is the Bible's definitive text on the Millennium. In the first seven verses, the phrase *thousand years* is repeated six times. The apostle John was clear in recording the details of his vision, and he was particularly careful to emphasize and reemphasize the precise length of time the millennial kingdom will be established on earth.

In fact, not only do those verses repeat the phrase *thousand years*, but they do so in a way that emphasizes six different characteristics of the Millennium. Here's what I mean:

- Verse 2 describes the specific amount of time Satan will be bound in the bottomless pit.
- Verse 3 describes the length of time the nations on earth will be free from Satan's deception.

- Verse 4 explains how long saints martyred during the Tribulation period will reign with Christ once the Tribulation period has ended.
- Verse 5 refers to the amount of time "the rest of the dead" (referring to those who are unsaved) will wait until their resurrection and judgment.
- Verse 6 refers to the amount of time saints who will take part in the "first resurrection" (the Rapture) will reign with Christ.
- Verse 7 describes the amount of time that will elapse before Satan is released from his prison.

So we have six mentions of a thousand-year period in seven verses, with each of those instances referring to an idea or event that is specific and concrete. In the words of theologian Leon J. Wood, "In six different ways, [we are told] that the duration [of this period] will indeed be of this length."[2]

When the Bible describes the Millennium as a period of one thousand years, that's exactly what it means.

A KINGDOM GOVERNED BY CHRIST

The second basic truth about the Millennium is that it will be a physical extension of God's kingdom here on earth. This coming Golden Age will not be a purely spiritual reality. Meaning, we will not be floating around on clouds while strumming harps. The millennial kingdom will be established here on earth.

Let's focus for a moment on that word *kingdom*. The Bible contains several references to "the kingdom of God" or "the kingdom of heaven," and it's easy to assume that those passages refer to the same thing. However, that is not correct. Many of those passages point to God's dominion and sovereign rule over the universe or the spiritual kingdom that exists in heaven. But many other passages speak of a concrete, earthly kingdom over which Jesus will reign as King of kings and Lord of lords.

One famous example is found in Daniel's prophetic explanation of King Nebuchadnezzar's dream: "And in the days of these kings the God of heaven will set up a kingdom which shall never be destroyed; and the kingdom shall not be left to other people; it shall break in pieces and consume all these kingdoms, and it shall stand forever" (2:44).

That kingdom is the Millennium. It will be a direct manifestation of God's sovereignty and authority—not in heaven but here in our world.

It is during this period—this Golden Age or kingdom age—that God will fulfill the many prophesies recorded in the Old Testament regarding the restoration of Israel, the rule of the Messiah from Jerusalem, and the establishment of a utopian kingdom defined by justice, compassion, and prosperity. We will explore several of those prophecies (along with many others) in the pages to come.

For now, it's helpful to understand the Millennium as a restoration and expansion of the garden of Eden. In that famous garden, God was physically present with humanity. He walked and talked with Adam and Eve in the cool of the day. At the same time, Adam and Eve functioned as God's stewards—they were given dominion over creation and expected to manage it well.

A similar dynamic will be established during the Golden Age. Yet instead of a single garden, God's kingdom will take root throughout every nation, region, and continent. Even the natural world will be restored. In the words of the apostle Paul, "For the earnest expectation of the creation eagerly waits for the revealing of the sons of God. For the creation was subjected to futility, not willingly, but because of Him who subjected it in hope; because the creation itself also will be delivered from the bondage of corruption into the glorious liberty of the children of God" (Rom. 8:19–21).

A KINGDOM GUARDED AGAINST INIQUITY

You may wonder, *How can the Millennium be such a glorious and golden period on this planet when our world has been corrupted by sin?*

The answer to that question can be found by looking once again at Revelation 20: "Then I saw an angel coming down from heaven, having the key to the bottomless pit and a great chain in his hand. He laid hold of the dragon, that serpent of old, who is the Devil and Satan, and bound him for a thousand years" (vv. 1–2).

The third basic truth about the Millennium is that Satan will be completely removed from our world. He will be literally locked away for ten centuries—he and his demons with him. That means for a thousand years, human beings will not strive against "principalities, against powers, against the rulers of the darkness of this age, against spiritual hosts of wickedness in the heavenly places" (Eph. 6:12). We will be free from the spiritual influence of evil.

More than that, our world will be filled with the presence and the Spirit of Christ. The prophet Isaiah foresaw this wonderful reality when he wrote, "Here is my servant, whom I uphold, my chosen one in whom I delight; I will put my Spirit on him, and he will bring justice to the nations" (42:1 NIV).

Can you imagine a world in which Satan and all demonic influence have been removed? Better still, can you imagine a world focused on the preeminence of Christ and completely pervaded by His Spirit? That will be our reality during the Golden Age.

Importantly, the Millennium will not be perfect. It will not be heaven because it will not be completely sinless—a truth we will explore more deeply in later chapters.

"The Millennium is the precursor of the eternal state. It will be different than life as we know it today, but it will still fall short of the absolute perfection of the eternal state."[3]

It's helpful to think of the Millennium as a transition period between the old earth (what we are experiencing now) and the new earth (what we will experience for eternity). The Golden Age will be a foretaste of the incredible wonder and joy that will characterize our eternal state in the New Jerusalem, which is our true heavenly home.

In 2020, Jay Speights experienced a preview of the Golden Age—we could call it a foretaste of the foretaste. Speights was researching his family's DNA when he made a surprising discovery: he is a prince. Specifically, he is related to a former king in the West African nation of Benin.

That discovery started Speights on an amazing journey, both literally and figuratively. One morning, he received an email from the current king and queen of Benin that read, "We are smiling as we read this. You are related to the ninth king of Allada. Dear prince, we invite you to come home. . . . And we're waiting for you to come. And we'll have a big party for you."

The native of Rockville, Maryland, wasn't about to turn down such an interesting invitation, so he booked a ticket to Benin. From the moment he arrived at the airport and saw a large crowd waiting to greet him, Speights realized his life would never be the same.

"People were just clapping, chanting, cheering," he said. "It was an unbelievable moment. I almost cried. I did cry later because it was overwhelming. There were many tearful moments. . . . When we got in front of the palace, I just sat there for a moment. Just like, 'Wow. This is too much to take in.'"

Speights spent the next several days touring the wonders of a kingdom he had never known. He walked around the palace three times as a ritual that signifies a return. He toured ancient shrines and a village that was more than one thousand years old. He received clothes from the queen and sat in his family lodge. He was formally enthroned as a prince. He was even given a new name by the king: Videkon Deka, which means "the child who came back."[4]

Eventually, Speights returned home to his regular life in Maryland. But what used to seem ordinary has now been touched with the wonder of his place in a kingdom far away.

That should be a familiar feeling for followers of Jesus. We, too, have a place in a kingdom. God's kingdom. We, too, are royalty, adopted by our heavenly Father and appointed to be coheirs with Christ. We, too, will experience the thrill of leaving behind our mundane lives and stepping into something grand and majestic and magnificent in every way.

Yet our first taste of that eternal kingdom will be grounded in time, governed by Christ, and guarded against iniquity here in our own world. The Millennium will be the glorious foyer of our Father's house—one in which we will abide for centuries. Therefore, let us prepare today for the blessed promise of tomorrow.

CHAPTER 3

SCRIPTURE'S GOLDEN PROMISES

The world's largest puzzle contains an incredible sixty thousand pieces. In actuality, it is sixty separate puzzles, a thousand pieces each, that can be combined to form one enormous scene. The finished product, which depicts a world map surrounded by famous landmarks, is eight feet tall by twenty-nine feet wide and weighs a whopping ninety-four pounds.

Nina Grasse wanted to tackle that puzzle, but not alone. "I knew that it would be fun, but I knew that it would take me forever," she said. Then she had an idea. As the owner of a funeral service, she wondered if her community might get involved. "We thought with the funeral home having meal rooms where there's tables, people could easily come and help build the puzzle."

So, she made the purchase. Then she started sending invitations to her local community of Reedsburg, Wisconsin. And the people responded! More than a hundred volunteers pitched in over a period of weeks. Some worked for an hour here and thirty minutes there. Others spent whole days perusing, picking, and placing pieces.

Pretty soon the entire town of Reedsburg was paying attention. People were excited to keep track of the puzzle's progress. Even local TV stations and newspapers offered updates as each new section was completed.

Finally, on February 12, volunteers gathered with excitement to complete the sixtieth section of the puzzle. The final moment in the massive project.

There was just one problem, and I bet you can already guess what it was: a single piece was missing. After weeks of work, the community had 59,999 pieces placed in perfect position—but one maddening little gap threatened to ruin the accomplishment.

Thankfully, the puzzle's manufacturer heard about the issue and sent a replacement. The crisis was averted, and the project was finished.[1]

There are a number of Bible readers who consider the Millennium to be a New Testament–only phenomenon. Indeed, many cast doubt on the reality of the Millennium by saying that it appears in only one chapter of Scripture: Revelation 20.

Such criticisms are not correct. The promise of the Millennium is present throughout Scripture, including large portions of the Old Testament. In fact, trying to make sense of the Old Testament without a proper understanding of the Millennium would be like trying to construct a puzzle that is missing a major piece.

In the words of seminary professor J. Dwight Pentecost, "A larger body of prophetic Scripture is devoted to the subject of the Millennium, developing its character and conditions, than any other one subject."[2]

You may be wondering, *Why did God include the Millennium in His prophetic plans for the end of the age? Why not just move humanity directly from the Tribulation into the eternal state?*

The simplest answer to those questions is that God keeps His promises. As we'll see in this chapter, there are many promises contained in the Old Testament that point directly to an earthly kingdom in which God's people literally reign with Christ and thrive in a period of bliss for a thousand years. As we study those promises over the next few pages, you'll notice that they fit into two major categories: the promise of a coming King, and the promise of His future kingdom.

THE PROMISE OF A KING

Biblical prophecy is filled with predictions of the coming day when King Jesus will rule over the earth—an incredible promise. More incredible still, we who follow Jesus as Lord in this life will rule with Him as coregents in that future kingdom.

The first time Jesus stepped into our world, He came to redeem us—but the world rejected Him. When He comes the second time, He will rule this world in righteousness. During this period, the great predictions of His earthly kingdom will be fulfilled.

Here are a few examples of those predictions:

- "He shall have dominion also from sea to sea, and from the River to the ends of the earth. Those who dwell in the wilderness will bow before Him, and His enemies will lick the dust. The kings of Tarshish and of the isles will bring presents; the kings of Sheba and Seba will offer gifts. Yes, all kings shall fall down before Him; all nations shall serve Him" (Ps. 72:8–11).
- "He shall speak peace to the nations; His dominion shall be 'from sea to sea, and from the River to the ends of the earth'" (Zech. 9:10).
- "Also your people shall all be righteous; they shall inherit the land forever, the branch of My planting, the work of My hands, that I may be glorified" (Isa. 60:21).

When Jesus establishes His earthly reign, kings will fall down before Him. Nations will serve Him. He will establish His kingdom with justice and judgment. His people will be righteous, and Israel will inherit her land. War will be suspended, and the Lord's dominion will stretch from sea to sea.

Perhaps the most powerful prophecy regarding the Millennium came in the form of a promise from God to King David regarding his future legacy. God told David, "Your house and your kingdom will endure forever before me; your throne will be established forever" (2 Sam. 7:16 NIV).

God proclaimed that a literal, historical descendant of David would sit on Israel's throne and that the rule and reign of that future king will endure forever. That King is Jesus.

Isaiah confirmed that promise through another prophecy:

> For unto us a Child is born, unto us a Son is given; and the government will be upon His shoulder. And His name will be called Wonderful, Counselor, Mighty God, Everlasting Father, Prince of Peace. Of the increase of His government and peace there will be no end, upon the throne of David and over His kingdom, to order it and establish it with judgment and justice from that time forward, even forever. The zeal of the LORD of hosts will perform this. (9:6–7)

This is the same promise the angel Gabriel quoted to Mary about her miracle child in Luke 1:32–33: "He will be great, and will be called the Son of the Highest; and the Lord God will give Him the throne of His father David. And He will reign over the house of Jacob forever, and of His kingdom there will be no end."

Jesus has not yet reigned as the acknowledged King over the house of Jacob, but that will change when He returns at the end of the Tribulation. That will change during the Millennium when God fulfills His promise of an earthly kingdom under the lordship of Christ.

THE PROMISE OF A KINGDOM

Major sections of the Old Testament prophetic books are given over to the theme of the millennial kingdom. In Isaiah, entire chapters are devoted to this subject, two of which I quoted earlier.

Before Isaiah, David wrote these beautiful prophetic lines describing God the Father gifting the kingdom to His Son, Jesus Christ: "Yet I have set My King on My holy hill of Zion. I will declare the decree: The LORD has said to Me, 'You are My Son, today I have begotten You. Ask of Me, and I will give You the nations for Your inheritance, and the ends of the earth for Your possession. You shall break them with a rod of iron; You shall dash them to pieces like a potter's vessel'" (Ps. 2:6–9).

Some of the most vivid prophecies of the kingdom age are found in the writings of the prophet Daniel. In chapter 2 of his book, Daniel sees the whole course of human history revealed in the dream of the pagan Gentile king Nebuchadnezzar. This dream presented the future of the Gentile nations through the vision of a gigantic, man-shaped statue made from different materials. As Daniel understood, the succeeding world empires were portrayed by this statue. His vision culminated when a stone was used to cut down the statue by an unseen hand.

Here is Daniel's explanation of this vision: "And in the days of these kings the God of heaven will set up a kingdom which shall never be destroyed; and the kingdom shall not be left to other people; it shall break in pieces and consume all these kingdoms, and it shall stand forever" (2:44).

In a later vision, Daniel saw the King coming to take His kingdom:

I was watching in the night visions, and behold, One like the Son of Man, coming with the clouds of heaven! He came to the Ancient of Days, and they brought Him near before Him. Then to Him was given dominion and glory and a kingdom, that all peoples, nations, and languages should serve Him. His dominion is an everlasting dominion, which shall not pass away, and His kingdom the one which shall not be destroyed. (7:13–14)

In the book of Revelation, the seventh trumpet sounds, and this is the message that accompanies it: "The kingdoms of this world have become the kingdoms of our Lord and of His Christ, and He shall reign forever and ever!" (11:15).

This will be a great day of promises fulfilled. It will also be a terrible and frightening day of reaping what's been sown. The apostle John made that clear in Revelation 19: "Now out of His mouth goes a sharp sword, that with it He should strike the nations. And He Himself will rule them with a rod of iron. He Himself treads the winepress of the fierceness and wrath of almighty God. And He has on His robe and on His thigh a name written: KING OF KINGS AND LORD OF LORDS" (vv. 15–16).

In this passage, John tells us how the King will arrive and begin His reign. He will come as a conqueror, taking back His world. As the Old Testament prophets indicate, there is a close connection between our Lord's victory at the battle of Armageddon and His reign over all the earth.

Here are the words of the prophet Zechariah: "Then the LORD will go forth and fight against those nations, as He fights in the day of battle. . . . And the LORD shall be King over all the earth. In that day it shall be—'The LORD is one,' and His name one" (14:3, 9).

Part of Jesus' mission immediately preceding the Millennium will be the removal of Satan. Christ must rid the earth of its evil usurper before He can establish His reign. We've already been given a front-row seat to those events because of Revelation 20, which we will explore more deeply in another chapter. But it's important for us to remember that Christ's earthly kingdom will be focused more on the presence of our Savior than the absence of our Enemy.

As one scholar has written, "The central focus of the Millennium is not Satan; it is the Savior, the Lord Jesus Christ. It is His time of manifestation, His time of revelation. Christ, in all of His glory, will institute His reign of righteousness and peace. During the Millennium, the unveiled glory of Christ will shine forth in all of its fullness."[3]

Alva J. McClain, the founder of Grace Theological Seminary, described Christ's kingship this way:

> The age-to-come, as [Jesus] liked to call it, will be ushered in by the exercise of His immediate power and authority. He has all power now; He will take this power and use it to the full when He returns. The age-long silence of God, the taunt of unbelief, will be broken by the transition and resurrection of the church, by the unloosing of judgment long withheld, by the visible and personal presence of the Mediatorial King, and by the complete establishment of His Kingdom on earth for a period specified by our Lord as "1000 years." . . . During this period every aspect of the Kingdom as set forth in Old Testament prophecy is realized upon earth. Truly the golden age of the world, children will be born, life goes on, men work and play, but under ideal conditions.[4]

May 6, 2023, was a day of ceremony and symbolism unlike any other in our world for sixty years. That was the day Charles III was crowned king in the city of London.

The coronation festivities began with a formal procession to Westminster Abbey, with the future king and queen riding in a luxurious state coach. The procession moved slowly past nearly four thousand invited guests, with thousands more gathered at special viewing areas along the route.

Once inside Westminster Abbey, Charles was greeted by another twenty-two hundred people representing more than two hundred nations from around the globe. He wore special regalia signifying his power and authority as the sovereign of the realm.

The coronation itself included several priceless artifacts. The sovereign's orb, for example, is a golden globe topped with a cross of diamonds that dates back to 1661. The sovereign's scepter houses one of the largest diamonds in the world. The coronation chair was originally crafted in the year 1300, and the crown itself—St. Edward's Crown—had touched the heads of only six monarchs prior to King Charles III. The ceremony involved several stages, including the oath, anointing, investiture, and enthronement.[5]

In many ways, the royal ceremony on that day was the most glorious moment our world could produce.

Yet the coronation of any earthly king will be nothing in comparison to the glorious return and promised rule of Christ, the true King of kings, at the beginning of the coming Golden Age.

CHAPTER 4

THY KINGDOM COME

Gerald Ford, his head bowed in reverence, was reciting the Lord's Prayer when he learned he was about to become president of the United States. He had gathered for a weekly prayer meeting in the office of John Rhodes, minority leader of the House of Representatives. Also present were Minnesota congressman Albert Quie and Secretary of Defense Melvin Laird. This group gathered each Wednesday to pray for the nation and for one another, but today was tense. They were on the cusp of an unprecedented moment in American history: the resignation of an embattled president. After each of the men had prayed individually, they offered in unison the Lord's prayer: "Your kingdom come. Your will be done on earth as it is in heaven."

Suddenly Rhodes's secretary entered the room and said, "I know I'm never supposed to interrupt this meeting, but considering the circumstances I think I should. The White House just called and said Jerry Ford should come down to the White House right away."

No one needed to ask why. Congressman Quie asked, "Jerry . . . What if, when you have a press conference, somebody should ask you, 'Where were you and what were you doing when you found out that you were going to be the president?'"

"Nobody's going to say that," said Ford on his way out the door.[1]

The Watergate Scandal is only one of thousands of crises that have jerked the history of the world like a rag doll. Think of other unexpected events that have upset the trajectories of the human story—the fall of Babylon in the days of Daniel; the sack of Rome by the Visigoths in AD 410; the victory of William the Conqueror in England in 1066; the assassination of Austrian archduke Franz Ferdinand that sparked World War I; the Japanese attack on Pearl Harbor in 1941; the collapse of the Soviet Union in 1991; the terrorist attacks on September 11, 2001.

It seems history is lurching along with no rhyme or reason, subject to the blowing of the wind or the falling of the dice, and the world is destined to end in the ashes of ultimate catastrophe. Historian Henry Steele Commager said, "History is a jangle of accidents, blunders, surprises, and absurdities, and so is our knowledge of it."[2]

But never forget the Lord reigns! His throne is secure in the heavens, and He rules behind the scenes and beneath the surface of the tides of history. Like a river that flows beneath the ground then surges to the surface for all to see, His rule will burst forth with cascading power when Jesus comes again.

I want to impress upon you this fact: the millennial kingdom of Jesus Christ will be the great fulfillment of the prayer taught to us by Jesus: "Your kingdom come. Your will be done on earth as it is in heaven" (Matt. 6:10).

Every day, millions of Christians say that prayer in hundreds of languages in thousands of diverse settings and situations. It has been so for the last two thousand years. No prayer has been more frequently uttered, more meaningfully offered, and more urgently needed. Even now, as you read these words, someone, somewhere, is praying the sixty-six words of the Lord's Prayer.

I want to suggest that when we pray, "Your kingdom come," we're praying for two parallel realities. There are two phases of the kingdom of our Lord Jesus. The first is the present reality of the kingdom of grace, the church of the Lord Jesus, which is growing in the world right now. Jesus is the King over the hearts of millions of people who are following Him in their homes and to the ends of the earth.

But the ultimate fulfillment of this second petition of the Lord's Prayer will be answered as soon as Christ returns and sets up a visible, geopolitical kingdom headquartered in Jerusalem. That kingdom is the subject of this book.

THE KINGDOM OF GRACE

I want to introduce you to a phrase Bible scholars use to describe the kingdom of God: *already but not yet.* Have you heard that? This phrase was coined over a hundred years ago by Princeton theologian Geerhardus Vos and made popular by another scholar, George Eldon Ladd, in the 1950s. The idea is that the kingdom of heaven is *already* here, *but* it has *not yet* come in its fullness.

Ladd wrote, "The Word of God does say that the Kingdom of God is a present spiritual reality. . . . At the same time, the Kingdom is an inheritance which God will bestow upon His people when Christ comes in glory. . . . The Kingdom is a present reality (Matthew 12:28), and yet it is a future blessing (Romans 14:17). It is an inner spiritual redemptive blessing (Romans 14:17), which can be experienced only by way of the new birth (John 3:3), and yet it will have to do with the government of the nations of the world (Revelation 11:15)."

Ladd continued, "Therefore, what we pray for is 'Thy Kingdom come; thy will be done on earth as it is in heaven.' This prayer is a petition for God to reign, to manifest His kingly sovereignty and power, to put to flight every enemy of righteousness and of His divine rule, that God alone may be King over all the world."[3]

Those of us who know Jesus Christ as our Lord are currently—at this moment—citizens of the kingdom of God on this earth. We are walking models of those who have allowed the Lord to reign on the throne of our hearts. We are kingdom people, infiltrating the earth for His purposes.

Jesus began His preaching ministry with the news of the imminent appearing of the kingdom of God. He said, "Repent, for the kingdom of heaven is at hand" (Matt. 4:17). He also said, "Let the little children come to Me, and do not forbid them; for of such is the kingdom of God" (Mark 10:14). In Luke 17:21, He said, "The kingdom of God is within you."

When Jesus stood before Pilate, He said, "My kingdom is not of this world. If My kingdom were of this world, My servants would fight" (John 18:36).

When the Holy Spirit descended on the 120 disciples in the upper room in Jerusalem shortly after the ascension of Jesus Christ, the church came into sudden and sublime existence. The word *kingdom* means the king's domain; so, those who acknowledge Jesus Christ as Lord are His people, His possession. We are a spiritual kingdom in a physical world. Our Lord told us in Matthew 12:28, "But if I cast out demons by the Spirit of God, surely the kingdom of God has come upon you."

Paul wrote, "For the kingdom of God is not eating or drinking, but righteousness and peace and joy in the Holy Spirit" (Rom. 14:17). In Colossians 1:13, he added, "He has delivered us from the power of darkness and conveyed us into the kingdom of the Son of His love."

When you pray for God's kingdom on earth, you are praying for the spread of the gospel and the expansion of the church. When you pray for the missionaries God places on your heart, when you engage in mission trips around the world, when you give to ministries that are reaching the globe, when you intercede for your own local churches— you are echoing the prayer of Christ. You are asking God to let His kingdom come to all the earth.

THE KINGDOM OF GLORY

Yet the Lord had much more in mind when He told us to pray, "Your kingdom come." This petition cannot be totally fulfilled by the present era of the church. When asked about His return, Jesus told the parable of the fig tree. Just as the budding of the fig tree heralds the coming of summer, the signs of the times will herald His return. "So you also, when you see these things happening, know that the kingdom of God is near" (Luke 21:31).

In the upper room, He told His disciples, "I bestow upon you a kingdom, just as My Father bestowed one upon Me, that you may eat and drink at My table in My kingdom, and sit on thrones judging the twelve tribes of Israel" (22:29–30).

British preacher J. C. Ryle wrote, "By His kingdom we mean first, the kingdom of grace which God sets up and maintains in the hearts of all living members of Christ, by His Spirit and word. But we mean chiefly, the kingdom of glory which shall one day be set up, when Jesus shall come the second time, and all men shall know Him from the least to the greatest."[4]

Thomas Watson, one of the greatest of the Puritan writers, said, "The kingdom of grace is nothing but the beginning of the kingdom of glory. The kingdom of grace is glory in the seed, and the kingdom of glory is grace in the flower."[5]

When the seventh trumpet sounds in the book of Revelation, loud voices in heaven will shout, "The kingdoms of this world have become the kingdoms of our Lord and of His Christ, and He shall reign forever and ever!" (11:15).

One day the Lord Jesus will be King over the earth and reign for a glorious cycle of a thousand years. That kingdom will be more than His citizens embedded among hostile nations as we see it now. It will be a geopolitical kingdom with Jerusalem as the royal capital.

Psalm 145 says, "They shall speak of the glory of Your kingdom, and talk of Your power, to make known to the sons of men His mighty acts, and the glorious majesty of His kingdom. Your kingdom is an everlasting kingdom, and Your dominion endures throughout all generations" (vv. 11–13).

The prophet Obadiah wrote, "The day of the LORD is near for all nations. . . . But on Mount Zion will be deliverance; it will be holy, and Jacob will possess his inheritance. . . . And the kingdom will be the LORD's" (vv. 15, 17, 21 NIV).

We should think of this whenever we look at a map. Right now, the brooding nation of Russia spreads from central Europe to farthest Asia; beneath it is Mongolia, then China. Nearby is India. The global south is composed of Africa, Australia, and South America. The United States and its familiar boundaries rest between the Atlantic and Pacific, with Canada above and Mexico below. Among the smallest nations is tiny Israel—only about ten miles across at its narrowest point, and a mere 263 miles from north to south.

Yet one day soon, the boundaries of Israel will stretch from the Mediterranean to the Euphrates (Josh. 1:4), and Zion (Jerusalem) will be the capital of the world (Ps. 2:6). Jesus will reign from His throne, and all the nations will fall into place under His authority. Peace will reign, His holy people will populate the government, and a scepter of righteousness will be the scepter of His kingdom (Heb. 1:8).

The venerable J. Vernon McGee put it in his own simple way: "The Millennium is God's answer to the prayer, 'Thy kingdom come.' When we pray . . . the Lord's Prayer, we say, 'Thy kingdom come . . . in earth, as it is in heaven' (Matt. 6:10). That is the kingdom which He is going to establish here on earth, and it is called the Millennium."[6]

Just as the angels in the invisible realms honor and quickly obey their King, so will it be on this planet. And so it should be with you and me now.

THREE PRAYERS FOR YOU TO OFFER

The Bible gives us three prayers connected with the coming end of this age. The first is the one I've emphasized in this chapter and is taken from the Lord's Prayer. Jesus said, "Your kingdom come. Your will be done on earth as it is in heaven" (Matt. 6:10).

The second prayer is a one-word term I learned early in life because I grew up using the King James Version of the Bible. The apostle Paul closed his first letter to the Corinthians with the word "Maranatha" (16:22 KJV). This is a direct English translation of a Greek word meaning, "O Lord, come!" It was Paul's exclamatory request to heaven for the prompt return of Jesus Christ to set up His kingdom.

Very similarly, the final prayer of the Bible is Revelation 22:20: "Even so, come, Lord Jesus!"

How many times have you looked toward heaven and offered these three prayers in recent weeks? They should be on our lips as we observe the troubling headlines of earth. They should come to our minds when we face trials and temptations of all kinds. They should sound from our hearts whenever we see a beautiful sunrise and from our mouths as the sky explodes in color with the setting of the sun.

We should always make these prayers very personal, especially when we say to the Lord, "Your will be done." It's gripping to notice how that phrase appears at the beginning and ending of our Lord's ministry. In His inaugural sermon in Matthew 6, as we've seen, Jesus taught us to pray, "Your will be done on earth as it is in heaven" (v. 10). And amid blood and tears, He prayed on the last night of His natural life, "Nevertheless, not as I will, but as You will" (Matt. 26:39).

Because Christ surrendered Himself to the Father's will in Matthew 26, we can pray with confidence and anticipation these glorious prayers that point toward His coming Golden Age: "Maranatha! Even so, come, Lord Jesus! Your kingdom come. Your will be done on earth as it is in heaven."

In his book *Praying Circles Around Your Future*, Mark Batterson wrote, "Your prayers have the potential to change the course of history. In the grand scheme of God's story, there is a footnote behind every headline. The footnote is prayer. . . . Never underestimate the power of a single prayer."[7]

If you want to start drawing circles around your future right now—and that of the whole world—then take a moment with me to pray this prayer:

Maranatha!
Even so, come, Lord Jesus!
Your kingdom come. Your will be done
on earth as it is in heaven.

CHAPTER 5

THE CURSE REVERSED

America and Europe are under invasion, and the enemy troops are deadly, aggressive, and ugly—so ugly they look like movie aliens from outer space. They are colonizing the earth. Recently, Australia was invaded. Even China is under assault.

These deadly armies are red fire ants, and they're spreading all over the world. Each colony can contain multiple queens and millions of ants. The queens can live as long as seven years and lay up to five thousand eggs per day. The fiery insects can dig multiple underground tunnels that extend from their mounds by thirty feet. In a flood, the entire colony bands together to form a raft and float to safety to reestablish itself.

Fire ants are easily angered. They can bite, but their sting is worse. Their sharp syringes inject venom into their victims without mercy. If a colony is disturbed, the ants can swarm and attack the offending animal or person. More than eighty people in the world have died this way.[1]

Fire ants are hard to kill. You know that if you've ever had to deal with multiple mounds in your backyard! They're also on the move in unprecedented ways. Recently, squadrons were found on Italian soil. One researcher said, "Finding this species in Italy was a big surprise, but we knew this day would come."[2]

I'm afraid fire ants will be with us until another day comes—the day when nature itself will be changed. I'm speaking of the day of Christ's return and the start of His millennial reign.

When God created the universe in Genesis 1, He made everything good—even fire ants. The Bible says, "God made the wild animals according to their kinds, the livestock according to their kinds, and all the creatures that move along the ground according to their kinds. And God saw that it was good" (v. 25 NIV).

So what happened?

Sin happened, and with it came a curse that affected all of nature and humanity.

THE CURSE IS ANNOUNCED

When Satan tempted Adam and Eve, the first couple listened to his crafty words and disobeyed the Lord. The results were tectonic and tragic. In Genesis 3:14, God said to the serpent, "Because you have done this, you are cursed."

God then told Eve, "I will greatly multiply your sorrow and your conception; in pain you shall bring forth children" (v. 16).

Then He said to Adam, "Because you have heeded the voice of your wife, and have eaten from the tree of which I commanded you, saying, 'You shall not eat of it': Cursed is the ground for your sake; in toil you shall eat of it all the days of your life. Both thorns and this-tles it shall bring forth for you. . . . In the sweat of your face you shall eat bread till you return to the ground, for out of it you were taken" (vv. 17–19).

Notice the expanding elements of the curse. The serpent was cursed, pain was injected into the process of childbirth, the ground—the created physical order—was cursed, and death entered the human story. The entire world was affected by the sin of Adam and Eve. And we've been living with the consequences ever since.

Isaiah spoke of this when he wrote, "The earth mourns and fades away, the world languishes and fades away. . . . The earth is also defiled under its inhabitants, because they have transgressed the laws. . . . Therefore the curse has devoured the earth" (24:4–6).

As a result of the fall, animals became predatory, insects became pests, humanity became sinful, and death became universal. This set the tone for all of human history, which has been characterized by pride, selfishness, fighting, anger, endless wars, and ceaseless funerals.

THE CURSE IS ABATED

You'd think the return of Jesus Christ to this world to establish His kingdom would change that curse, wouldn't you? You would be right! Many of the chapters in this book describe how the power of Christ's presence will permeate the earth and roll back many of the effects of the curse. First of all, that old serpent, the devil, will be bound in shackles and imprisoned in the bottomless pit for a thousand years.

Second, the Lord Jesus will rule and reign, and people will relish His teachings. He will judge between the nations, and they will engage in war no more.

Third, the land will yield its harvests, and the reapers will follow sowers at double speed. Wolves and sheep will graze together, and even the snakes (and fire ants!) will lose their loathsome venom. The earth will be filled with the knowledge of the Lord as the waters fill the sea. The climate will be wonderful, the weather agreeable, the gardens productive, the air clean, the plagues gone.

Dr. J. Dwight Pentecost wrote, "The original curse placed upon creation will be removed, so that there will be abundant productivity to the earth. Animal creation will be changed so as to lose its venom and ferocity."[3]

Many people enjoy Isaac Watts's famous hymn "Joy to the World," but did you know the words of that song actually refer to our Lord's second coming and to His millennial reign? We'll take a deeper look at that hymn in a later chapter, but the relevant verse for this topic is:

> No more let sins and sorrows grow,
> Nor thorns infest the ground;
> He comes to make His blessings flow
> Far as the curse is found.

You may wonder, *Is it true that no thorns will infest the ground, or is that just poetic license?* Well, Genesis 3:18 says "thorns and thistles" are part of the curse. But in speaking of the millennial age, Isaiah said, "Instead of the thorn shall come up the cypress tree, and instead of the brier shall come up the myrtle tree" (55:13).

In other words, when the Lord Jesus returns, He will extend natural and physical blessings into the universe to the furthest boundaries of the curse. Most aspects of the curse, especially those connected with nature, will be relieved.

The apostle Paul wrote about this in Romans 8:19–21, saying, "All creation is waiting eagerly for that future day. . . . Against its will, all creation was subjected to God's curse. But with eager hope, the creation looks forward to the day when it will join God's children in glorious freedom from death and decay" (NLT).

Imagine the change if millennial conditions suddenly swept over the earth tomorrow! But it's almost impossible to imagine the contrast the coming Golden Age will present after the nightmare of the seven-year Tribulation. It will certainly seem as if the curse is lifted— and much of it will have been.

But remember, the thousand-year reign of Christ is a transition between history and eternity. It's the passageway between the old universe and the new heaven and new earth and the New Jerusalem. While the curse will be wonderfully eased and lessened during the Millennium, part of it will still remain. Animal deaths will occur as fish are harvested in the restored Dead Sea (Ezek. 47:10–11) and sacrifices are offered at the millennial temple (40:41). People will still die, though rarely (Isa. 65:20). And, yes, Satan will be bound, but he will not yet be cast into his final destination of eternal hell (Rev. 20:1–10).

THE CURSE IS ABOLISHED

Does that mean we will always endure the consequences of the fall? By no means! The curse, which was enacted in Genesis 3 and will be eased at the return of Christ, will be fully ended, abolished, and canceled when we arrive at the eternal state.

Remember, the coming Golden Age will encompass a thousand years of blissful life on earth under the rule and reign of Jesus Christ—but those thousand years will not be heaven. Not yet. The last two chapters of the Bible describe our postmillennial home, where God will create a new universe and a new planet Earth. The Golden City of New Jerusalem will descend from the heavens to become our forever capital.

The throne of God will reside in the heart of that city. Notice the words I've emphasized in Revelation 22:3: "There shall be *no more curse*, but the throne of God and of the Lamb shall be in it, and His servants shall serve Him."

My friend Dr. Tim LaHaye wrote, "During the 1000-year millennial kingdom, there will be a partial lifting of the curse and the consequences of original sin. There will still be death (for those who entered the Millennium in their natural bodies), and the complete effects of the fall will not be lifted until the creation of the new heavens and new earth in the eternal state after the Millennium."

But, LaHaye added, "The coming literal kingdom of Christ to this earth will be the most blessed time this world has known since the Garden of Eden. In fact, many Edenic features will characterize it. All those who rebelled against God will be gone. Satan will be bound so he cannot tempt man, and Christ will enforce righteousness with the help of His holy angels and the church. . . . The curse on the earth will be lifted, and the ground will bear incredible harvests."[4]

I've waited until the end of this chapter to share with you the most glorious teaching of all about the reversal of the curse: Only one Person can do it—and He did it at a cost greater than we can comprehend. Our Lord Jesus Christ *became Himself a curse to reverse the curse.*

At the very moment of the fall in the paradise of Eden, almighty God was standing there with the gloating serpent on one side and the ruined pair on the other. He spoke, and His words began the entire sequence of biblical prophecy. He told Satan in Genesis 3:15: "And I will put enmity between you and the woman, and between your seed and her Seed; He shall bruise your head, and you shall bruise His heel."

This is the first prophecy of the Bible, and all the other messianic prophecies are compacted inside it just like a forest of oak trees are contained in a single acorn. The Seed of the woman—the Messiah Jesus—would crush Satan's head, although in the process a nail would pierce His heel. That promise was given at the same time as the curse was issued.

Galatians 3:13 says, "Christ has redeemed us from the curse of the law, having become a curse for us (for it is written, 'Cursed is everyone who hangs on a tree')."

Randy Alcorn wrote, "The removal of the Curse will be as thorough and sweeping as the redemptive work of Christ. In bringing us salvation, Christ has already undone some of the damage in our hearts, but in the end he will finally and completely restore his entire creation to what God originally intended (Romans 8:19–21). Christ will turn back the Curse and restore to humanity all that we lost in Eden, and he will give us much more besides."

He added, "The Curse is real, but it is temporary. Jesus is the cure for the Curse."[5]

The world watched in horror when the Notre Dame cathedral caught on fire in 2019 in Paris, France. The roof, the spire, and most of the interior were destroyed. Incredibly, most of the historic stained windows withstood the heat and flames. But they were heavily covered with smoke, lead dust, and soot.

Glass manufacturers from all across France set to work, trying to clean the windows. This involved gently rubbing each segment of glass with cotton soaked in water and ethanol. The experts discovered the windows were charred by more than the terrible fire. Centuries of human breath and candle soot had also diminished the colors and light of the intricate windows.

Some of those glass panels date back to the twelfth century, and the windows cover nearly 1,100 square feet of Notre-Dame's massive walls. Many scenes depict Bible stories so that worshipers can learn the truth of Scripture by gazing at them. When the restoration work is over, experts say the windows will dazzle worshipers with all their original glory.[6]

In a similar way, God created this universe as a colorful window displaying His glory, but it was blackened in the fires of sin and through the soot of the curse. Jesus Christ is the great Restorer—the Redeemer—who dabs and wipes each piece and each person with a cloth dampened in His blood. When He is finished, the result will overpower us with its beauty—a mosaic of redeemed people. We can glimpse it now in our testimonies, we will see it more fully during the coming Golden Age, and we will see it eternally in the New Jerusalem.

The curse, which was decreed in Eden and will be decreased during the Millennium, shall be dissolved and eradicated in the eternal state.

But let me tell you one final thing. Between now and then, the Lord can perform a parallel work in your life. Two verses in the Bible talk specifically about how God turns curses into blessings.

In Deuteronomy 23:5, Moses reminded the Israelites how the false prophet Balaam tried to curse them. He said, "But the LORD your God turned the curse into a blessing for you, because the LORD your God loves you."

Nehemiah 13:2 recalls that incident, saying, "However, our God turned the curse into a blessing."

Jesus can reverse the curses that befall us in this life! He does it because He loves us.

You may feel Satan is tempting and trying you; the world seems against you; the burdens may be rolling over you right now. But Jesus, your Redeemer and Restorer, knows how to turn curses into blessings. He can cause everything to work together for the good of His blood-cleansed children. He can shine His glory through us, even when we're in the smoke and fire.

Entrust your cares to Him, rely on His promises, and let Him bring the atmosphere of the coming Golden Age into your heart right now. Praise Him as the great Curse Reverser.

Doing so will make you want to sing for joy—to the world!

CHAPTER 6

ARMAGEDDON

Seventy-two minutes! That's all the time you'll have to get yourself right with God should a nuclear war erupt. Annie Jacobsen, a national security expert, has written a bestseller in which she describes a minute-by-minute sequence of events between the first missile launch and the end of the world in the event of a nuclear war.

In her hypothetical scenario, North Korea launches an intercontinental ballistic missile (ICBM) at the Pentagon and another missile from a submarine at a nuclear reactor in California. The American president has only six minutes to decide how to respond while at the same time being evacuated from the White House.

The president orders ICBMs launched at North Korea, but these must fly over Russia, whose leaders assume *they* are the target. The Kremlin launches a retaliatory strike, and within seventy-two hours, billions of people are killed and the remainder are left starving in a poisoned world where the sun no longer shines and food no longer grows.[1]

The time between a completely normal day and the total devastation of planet Earth: one hour and twelve minutes.

This isn't science fiction. Annie Jacobsen interviewed dozens of national security experts, and her account is factual and realistic. This *could* happen to our world at any minute.

I do indeed think the world is facing an existential danger, but I don't expect it will happen exactly as Jacobsen imagines. The Bible presents another scenario, and the prophetic passages of Scripture tell us exactly what will happen during the world's last great war, which we commonly call the battle of Armageddon. This conflict will be so destructive, so cataclysmic, that it will make all other wars in human history seem like minor skirmishes in comparison.

Ultimately, the battle of Armageddon will draw the final curtain on modern civilization as we know it. When concluded, Jesus' victory in that battle will usher in the coming Golden Age.

Let's take a deeper look at what the Bible reveals about the where, when, what, and why of Armageddon.

THE *WHERE* OF ARMAGEDDON

Revelation 16:16 says, "They gathered them together to the place called in Hebrew, Armageddon." The term translated as "Armageddon" is actually *Harmagedon*, which is "Mount Megiddo" or "the hill of Megiddo." This terrible battle will occur on the vast hills and plains near Megiddo, located about sixty miles north of Jerusalem. Those plains have been the location of many large battles over the course of human history, hosting the armies of Egyptians, Assyrians, Greeks, Romans, and more.

From this area in north central Israel, the armies of the world will occupy the promised land and descend on Jerusalem. The prophet Zechariah said, "I will gather all the nations to Jerusalem to fight against it" (14:2 NIV). This will be Satan's last attempt to destroy the Jewish people.

All around us today we see the plague of antisemitism, which runs like a black ribbon through history. It will reach its high-water mark at this battle.

THE *WHEN* OF ARMAGEDDON

As Zechariah indicated, all the nations of the world will be involved in the battle of Armageddon. Revelation 16 adds that the world rulers will be under the influence of demonic forces: "They are demonic spirits that perform signs, and they go out to the kings of the whole world, to gather them for the battle on the great day of God Almighty" (v. 14 NIV). This will be a truly global conflict, including armies from every group of people present on our planet during the Tribulation. Most fearsome of all, many of those armies will be led by the Antichrist.

Let's get some context on how the events of the Tribulation will lead up to this terrible battle at Armageddon.

THE DEAL WITH ISRAEL

After the Rapture, the world will be in chaos. Obviously, the removal of so many people all at once will cause a huge amount of physical and economic damage. More importantly, the removal of all godly residents will leave the remaining population in a spiritual vacuum. The presence of the Spirit-filled church on earth, which currently helps restrain evil, will be gone.

The Antichrist will rise to fill that vacuum. He will start by manufacturing peace in the Middle East, including the establishment of a treaty with Israel. The prophet Daniel told us that "he shall confirm a covenant with many for one week" (9:27). In prophetic language, this means a week of years, so this covenant will be made with Israel for seven years.

On the heels of that covenant, this self-appointed world ruler will begin to strengthen his power by performing amazing signs and wonders, even including a supposed resurrection from the dead

(Rev. 13:3). Then, with his grip on the world greatly enhanced, he will boldly take the next step in his arrogant defiance of God: "Then the king shall do according to his own will: he shall exalt and magnify himself above every god, shall speak blasphemies against the God of gods" (Dan. 11:36).

Step-by-step, the Antichrist will promote himself from a European leader, to a world leader, to a tyrannical global dictator, and finally to a god.

THE DECISION TO FIGHT

The Antichrist's grip on global power will not last long. Major segments of the world will begin to assemble their own military forces and rebel against him. An unnamed "king of the South" and his armies will be the first to come after the Antichrist, followed by additional armies from the North: "At the time of the end the king of the South shall attack him; and the king of the North shall come against him like a whirlwind, with chariots, horsemen, and with many ships" (Dan. 11:40).

The Antichrist will put down these first attempts at rebellion. But before he can celebrate his victories and move on toward his goal of destroying Israel and Jerusalem, he will be attacked by an army out of the East.

THE DISTURBING NEWS

Daniel prophesied that "news from the east and the north shall trouble him [the Antichrist]; therefore he shall go out with great fury" (11:44).

The Bible leaves no doubt as to the source of the news that so disturbs and enrages the Antichrist: "Then the sixth angel poured out his bowl on the great river Euphrates, and its water was dried up, so that the way of the kings from the east might be prepared" (Rev. 16:12).

The Euphrates is one of the greatest rivers in the world. It eventually unites with the Tigris to become the Shatt Al-Arab and finally empties into the Persian Gulf. Today, the entirety of the Euphrates flows through Muslim territory. In Genesis 15 and Deuteronomy 11, the Lord specified that the Euphrates would be the easternmost border of the promised land. It serves both as a border and a barrier between Israel and her enemies.

It's no wonder, then, that the Antichrist will be disturbed and frustrated. Having put down a rebellion against him, he will break his treaty with Israel and move to destroy the Jewish people (Dan. 9:27). But just when it appears that the Antichrist is about to gain control of everything, he will receive word that the Euphrates River has dried up and massive armies from the East are crossing it to come against him.

Just how large is that army? Look at what John tells us: "Now the number of the army of the horsemen was two hundred million; I heard the number of them" (Rev. 9:16). Suddenly the Antichrist must divert the major portion of his attention to defending himself against an amassed force the size of which the world has never seen.

In our world today, both China and India could produce an army of this size. When this unprecedented army crosses the bed of the Euphrates against the Antichrist, the greatest war of all history, involving hundreds of millions of people, will be set in motion. The major battleground for that war will be the land of Israel.

THE *WHAT* OF ARMAGEDDON

If you are a follower of Christ, what happens next may evoke an urge to stand up and shout like a football fan watching the star quarterback come onto the field.

> Now I saw heaven opened, and behold, a white horse. And He who sat on him was called Faithful and True, and in righteousness He judges and makes war. His eyes were like a flame of fire, and on His head

were many crowns. He had a name written that no one knew except Himself. He was clothed with a robe dipped in blood, and His name is called The Word of God. And the armies in heaven, clothed in fine linen, white and clean, followed Him on white horses. Now out of His mouth goes a sharp sword, that with it He should strike the nations. And He Himself will rule them with a rod of iron. He Himself treads the winepress of the fierceness and wrath of Almighty God. And He has on His robe and on His thigh a name written: KING OF KINGS AND LORD OF LORDS. (Rev. 19:11–16)

The great Lord Jesus—the captain of the Lord's hosts, the King over all kings—will descend to defend and protect His chosen people and put a once-and-for-all end to the evil of the Antichrist. But He will not come alone.

First, Jesus will be joined by His saints. The book of Jude says, "Behold, the Lord comes with ten thousands of His saints" (v. 14). All those who have died in the Lord, along with those who were raptured before the years of the Tribulation, will join with the Lord and participate in the battle to reclaim the world for the rule of Christ.

Second, He will be joined by His angels. Jesus Himself told us, "When the Son of Man comes in His glory, and all the holy angels with Him, then He will sit on the throne of His glory" (Matt. 25:31).

According to Zechariah, the Lord will "go out and fight against those nations, as he fights on a day of battle," descending to the Mount of Olives, which will split in two, providing an escape route for the besieged residents of Jerusalem (14:3–4 NIV).

THE *WHY* OF ARMAGEDDON

We've seen the "where," the "when," and the "what" connected with Armageddon. Now let's explore the "why." What are God's reasons for permitting this terrible war?

This question is important because of the way our sensibilities revolt when we read about the carnage that will take place during and after this battle. For example, "And the rest were killed with the sword which proceeded from the mouth of Him who sat on the horse. And all the birds were filled with their flesh" (Rev. 19:21).

Why such terrible violence? What is God doing? In answer, there are at least three divine purposes for the battle of Armageddon.

The first purpose is for God to *finish His judgment of Israel*. Remember that the Tribulation period will be a time of divine indignation against the people of Israel—the people who have rejected their Messiah time and time again. It's no accident that this future period is often referred to as "the time of Jacob's trouble" (Jer. 30:7).

A second purpose of Armageddon is for God to *finalize His judgment against the nations that persecute Israel*. Those nations will be gathered together on the plains of Megiddo, giving God the perfect opportunity to deal with them finally and decisively. The prophet Joel wrote, "I will also gather all nations, and bring them down to the Valley of Jehoshaphat; and I will enter into judgment with them there on account of My people, My heritage Israel, whom they have scattered among the nations; they have also divided up My land" (3:2).

Finally, a third purpose for Armageddon is to deliver God's *formal judgment against all those who reject Him*. The apostle John wrote, "Men were scorched with great heat, and they blasphemed the name of God who has power over these plagues; and they did not repent and give Him glory. . . . Now out of His mouth goes a sharp sword, that with it He should strike the nations" (Rev. 16:9, 19:15).

The Bible is clear: one of these days, God's judgment will fall on the world's wicked nations and wicked individuals. Justice will prevail. Then, with evil out of the way, Satan will be bound, and the Lord Jesus Christ will begin the process of inaugurating His golden kingdom.

I began this chapter by telling you about Annie Jacobsen's book that gives the world only seventy-two minutes between the first missile launch and the virtual destruction of the world. She's not the only one harboring those kinds of doomsday fears. A new simulation by researchers at Princeton's Program on Science and Global Security found that within the first hours of the start of a nuclear war between America and Russia, 34.1 million people could die and another 57.4 million could be injured. But that's only the beginning of the death toll. The radioactive fallout and climate changes would put billions at risk.

The researchers said, "The risk of nuclear war has increased dramatically in the past two years. . . . There is no sane plan once a nuclear weapon is launched."[2]

You and I could spend all our time worrying about that. But I have a better plan. Let's center our thoughts on the Lord Jesus Christ, who is waiting to return for His church and, as the battle of Armageddon rages, will come again in power and great glory. He will appear through the skies with His saints and angels. He will slay the wicked by the words of His mouth, and He will bind Satan for a thousand years. From Jerusalem, He will rule and reign in this world and bring to fulfillment not our worst fears but all our best hopes.

Let's look up, for our redemption is drawing near!

CHAPTER 7

THE GOLDEN CITY

Eliezer Ben-Yehuda and his new wife, Devora, sailed wide-eyed into the port of Joppa, overwhelmed that their Jewish dream was coming true—setting foot on the Holy Land. They arranged transport from Joppa to Jerusalem by overnight horse cart and approached the city just as the sun was rising. The large gate into the Old City was closed, but just then the gate began to creak open.

"A miracle!" whispered Eliezer as he and Devora entered the city they had dreamed about since childhood. But everything disoriented them—the foul smells, the filth, the impoverished sights, and the suspicious Arabs.

They thought, "This was Jerusalem the Golden? Where were their own people? Where was the spirit of holiness they had expected? Was this the city which had seen so many centuries of conflict, siege, plunder, massacre, and misery? Was this the city which men from all corners of the globe had fought over? Was this the city in which the prophets had preached . . . which had been destroyed and reconstructed eighteen times and had suffered two long periods of desolation and had passed from one religion to another six different times?"[1]

The year was 1881. Eliezer and Devora were among the first wave of Zionist Jews returning to the land that would later once again be called Israel. In the years to come, Ben-Yehuda would almost single-handedly do the impossible—resurrect the Hebrew language from antiquity and make it the language of the Jews once again. His son, Ben-Zion, was raised hearing and speaking only Hebrew, which kept him from playing with other children. But Ben-Zion became the first native speaker of Hebrew in modern times. Eliezer believed if his own son could do it, then an entire nation could.

Ben-Yehuda didn't live long enough to see the modern state of Israel appear on the map in 1948. But like so many Zionists, he saw it in his dreams. His funeral was attended by thirty thousand people, and you'll find his grave on the Mount of Olives. Today, one of the most popular streets in Jerusalem is Ben Yehuda Street.

What drew the Zionists back to Jerusalem, which at the time was populated by Arabs and controlled by the Ottomans? Why is this city so strangely magnetic? Why is it that even today visitors weep when they see Jerusalem's golden walls rising from the plateau?

Let's find some answers as we focus for the next two chapters on the city of Jerusalem, including its role in history and its elevation during the Golden Age.

A CONFLICTED CITY

For three thousand years, Jerusalem has been at the forefront of geopolitical struggles, biblical history, and prophetic aspiration. Even today, it's the centerpiece of the world's three major religions and ground zero for international political maneuvering. For generations, Jerusalem has been a place of pilgrimage and pillaging, miracles and mayhem. Perhaps no piece of land on the planet has been as revered, disputed, or disrupted.

The longtime mayor of Jerusalem, Teddy Kollek, said,

Jerusalem has been the center of Jewish hope and longing. No other city has played such a dominant role in the history, culture, religion, and consciousness of a people as has Jerusalem in the life of Jewry and Judaism. Throughout centuries of exile, Jerusalem remained alive in the hearts of Jews everywhere as the focal point of Jewish history, the symbol of ancient glory, spiritual fulfillment, and modern renewal. This heart and soul of the Jewish people engenders the thought that if you want one simple word to symbolize all of Jewish history, that word would be "Jerusalem."[2]

As Jewish author Elhanan Leib Lewinsky once wrote, "Without Jerusalem, the land of Israel is as a body without a soul."[3]

A CHOSEN CITY

Why does this desert city bring so much charm and challenge to the world?

Jerusalem was chosen specifically by God for her role in the history of Israel, in the life of Jesus, and in the events of His return. The Bible says, "Since the day that I brought My people out of the land of Egypt, I have chosen no city from any tribe of Israel in which to build a house, that My name might be there, nor did I choose any man to be a ruler over My people Israel. Yet I have chosen Jerusalem, that My name may be there" (2 Chron. 6:5–6).

Because it is God who established the city of Jerusalem as His dwelling place, it's known as the city of God: "O city of God, what glorious things are said of you!" (Ps. 87:3 NLT).

Jerusalem is mentioned in the Bible 811 times, and to be born in Jerusalem is a signature blessing from God: "But someday the highest honor will be to be a native of Jerusalem! For the God above all gods will personally bless this city. When he registers her citizens, he will place a check mark beside the names of those who were born here" (Ps. 87:5–6 TLB).

A CHRIST-LOVED CITY

Jesus first visited Jerusalem as an infant when He was dedicated to the Lord on the temple grounds where Anna and Simeon uttered prophecies about Him. As a twelve-year-old, Jesus visited Jerusalem during the Passover and didn't want to return home. It took three days for His alarmed parents to locate Him (Luke 2:41–50).

After His baptism, Jesus was taken to Jerusalem by Satan, to the highest point of the temple (Luke 4:9–12). John recorded four visits of Jesus to Jerusalem (John 5:1–47; 7–10; 12–20), and the other Gospels add important details, particularly regarding the events of Passion Week. Jesus' death, resurrection, and ascension all took place in and around the city of Jerusalem.

Jesus loved Jerusalem, and He mourned over her unbelief, saying, "O Jerusalem, Jerusalem, the one who kills the prophets and stones those who are sent to her! How often I wanted to gather your children together, as a hen gathers her chicks under her wings, but you were not willing!" (Matt. 23:37).

Though Jesus died there, don't forget that Jerusalem was also the city of His resurrection, and the nearby Mount of Olives was the place of His ascension into heaven. Here, to this mountain, He will come again. The first place to feel the soles of His feet will be Mount Olivet on the eastern side of the Golden City.

A CAPITAL CITY

That brings us to the Millennium. The Golden City will be our Lord's home and headquarters throughout the Golden Age. For a thousand years, the greatest city on earth will not be Rome, Paris, Beijing, or Washington, DC.

It will be Jerusalem.

Jerusalem first became Israel's capital by decree of King David more than three thousand years ago. It has remained Israel's capital ever since. Though other nations conquered and settled in the land of Israel, none ever declared Jerusalem their capital. For many years, American public opinion spoke in favor of moving the United States Embassy from Tel Aviv to Jerusalem, and politicians agreed. In October 1995, the US Congress called for the move to occur by May 1999.

Finally in June 2017, the US Senate unanimously passed a resolution (90–0) that reaffirmed the 1995 Congressional decision and called on the president to implement it. Six months later, Jerusalem was declared to be Israel's capital, and the United States embassy moved from Tel Aviv to Jerusalem.

With that event, I believe another key has been turned in the grand lock of biblical prophecy. In the future, every nation will acknowledge Jerusalem as the world capital and will want their embassies there. Christ the King will rule and reign from there, and the people of the nations will stream through its streets, approach its vast temple, and hear the words of truth from the King.

The prophet Jeremiah said, "At that time they will call Jerusalem The Throne of the LORD, and all nations will gather in Jerusalem to honor the name of the LORD" (3:17 NIV).

The prophet Zechariah was full of this theme, writing, "Many nations shall be joined to the LORD in that day, and they shall become My people. And I will dwell in your midst. Then you will know that the LORD of hosts has sent Me to you. And the LORD will take possession of Judah as His inheritance in the Holy Land, and will *again choose Jerusalem*" (2:11–12).

Randall Price wrote, "Jerusalem is the city at the center. It is the center of mankind's hopes and God's purposes. God loves it, Satan hates it, Jesus wept over it, the Holy Spirit descended in it, the nations are drawn to it, and Christ will return and reign in it. Indeed, the destiny of the world is tied to the future of Jerusalem."[4]

A CONTINUING CITY

Almost all the Christ-centered events in the future will take place in Jerusalem. Without Jerusalem, these events would be impossible. But that's only the beginning. The everlasting capital city of Jesus throughout eternity will be Jerusalem—but a different city to be sure. Our eternal capital is "the New Jerusalem."

Earthly Jerusalem, to which Jesus will return and from which He will reign a thousand years, is the prelude to another Jerusalem—a city with ethereal foundations whose builder and maker is God (Heb. 11:10). New Jerusalem is the Celestial City, currently existing in the highest heaven, which will descend to its rightful place on the new earth at the dawning of the eternal state.

This is the city anticipated by Abraham (Heb. 11:16), promised by Christ (John 14:28), and awaited by the saints (Heb. 13:14). This is "the city of the living God, the heavenly Jerusalem" (Heb. 12:22). This is the "Jerusalem that is above" (Gal. 4:26 NIV).

The city of New Jerusalem is the place Jesus is preparing for us (John 14:1–6), and the Bible draws to a close with a breathtaking description of the city's dimensions, streets, vast river, wondrous throne, translucent gold, and glittering light. (We will take a closer look at New Jerusalem in a separate chapter near the end of this book.)

Frederick Buechner describes life in this city like this: "Everything is gone that ever made Jerusalem, like all cities, torn apart, dangerous, heartbreaking, seamy. You walk the streets in peace now. Small children play unattended in the park. No stranger goes by whom you cannot imagine as a fast friend."[5]

A CHALLENGING CITY

I want to end this chapter by showing you how Jerusalem challenges you and me right now. Namely, what does Jerusalem mean for Christians today? How should we view it or respond to it?

Over the last few years, and especially during the last few months, I have considered this question, and I want to conclude this chapter with two challenges.

DETERMINE TO LOVE ISRAEL

First, we should determine to love Israel and its capital city. The psalmist wrote, "Pray for the peace of Jerusalem: 'May they prosper who love you. Peace be within your walls, prosperity within your palaces.' For the sake of my brethren and companions, I will now say, 'Peace be within you.' Because of the house of the LORD our God I will seek your good" (122:6–9).

God will prosper those who love Jerusalem and seek her peace.

Let's pray for the international safety of Israel and Jerusalem. Modern Israel has been forced to maintain a continual state of warfare. Someone described it as living in a very nice house in a very bad neighborhood. That nation, that city, and her residents require our prayers.

DETERMINE TO LEARN FROM ISRAEL

Second, we can also learn so much from this city and its people.

Each year a research-based report is released as the *World Happiness Report*. It ranks the 150 nations of the world on the basis of their "happiness." The researchers used a "ladder with steps numbered from 0–10." The top of the ladder represents the best possible life for you, and the bottom of the ladder represents the worst possible life for you. Those who participated in the survey were asked to rank where they considered themselves to be.[6]

The Israelis—specifically those living in modern-day Israel—more than any other people in the world, placed themselves on the best possible part of the ladder.

Think about that for a moment: Israel is a country surrounded by enemies determined to wipe them from the face of the earth. Every citizen under forty, whether male or female, is automatically in the military. The average apartment in Israel costs 150 times the average salary. The cost of living in Tel Aviv is more expensive than anywhere else on earth. And Israel is a country inwardly divided in ways that few can explain and fewer can understand. There are hawks and doves; Jews from the East and Jews from the West; Jews and Arabs; modern Jews and Orthodox Jews; friendly Palestinians and hateful Palestinian enemies.

How could such a nation be considered one of the happiest nations in the world? Here's what I discovered. Every year in America, families gather on the fourth Thursday of each November to feast and to offer thanks. It's Thanksgiving Day in the United States.

In Israel, they don't do this every year. They do it every week! Every Friday afternoon at the beginning of Shabbat (the Sabbath), Jewish homes gather to feast and offer thanks. They have Thanksgiving every single week. According to one source, "The celebration includes singing, blessings for the children, prayers and a well-set table of foods. At this meal, you will find not only whole households but grown children and their families . . . extended families as many members who can be accommodated."[7]

No matter what is happening in their world, every Friday these families pause to be with one another and to express their gratitude to God. Even on the Friday after the atrocities of October 7, 2023, Shabbat was celebrated.

Senator Joe Lieberman, who died while I was writing this book, was one of the most congenial and respected leaders in America. Lieberman, a Jew, wrote a book entitled *The Gift of Rest: Rediscovering the Beauty of the Sabbath*. He said, "I love the Sabbath and believe it is a gift from God that I want to share with everyone." He said that although the Jews keep the Sabbath, the real truth is that the Sabbath has kept the Jews.[8]

Oh, how much we can learn from the original people of God—our Jewish friends!

CHAPTER 8

JERUSALEM REARRANGED

Here in California where I live, we're familiar with earthquakes. People often speculate about a possible "Big One" in our future. One community in my state has capitalized on this existential danger: Hollywood.

The 1974 movie *Earthquake*, starring Charlton Heston, is about an earthquake that destroys Los Angeles, leaving survivors wandering around devastated. *The Great Los Angeles Earthquake* is a 1990 movie in which a seismologist tries to warn officials that LA is about to be flattened. The 1997 movie *Volcano* features a massive earthquake beneath Los Angeles that triggers a dormant volcano under the La Brea Tar Pits. The 2015 movie *San Andreas* is about an earthquake that destroys San Francisco.

These and many other earthquake movies are scripted to keep moviegoers on the edge of their seats. But is there something more that draws us toward disaster films? Perhaps there's something in the human heart that warns us of coming convulsive changes to our world.

Jesus predicted an increase in the severity of earthquakes and other natural disasters in the last days (Matt. 24:7). After the Rapture of the church, horrendous natural and supernatural disasters will shake the globe. The last half of the Tribulation will see unprecedented natural catastrophes and cataclysms. The Bible tells us that during the great Tribulation, a worldwide earthquake will destroy the grand cities of the world—including the capital city of the Antichrist (Rev. 16–18).

None of these disasters will stop the Antichrist. Not yet. As we discussed previously, the armies of the world will defiantly converge around Jerusalem in Satan's final attempt to destroy the nation of Israel. Jerusalem will be surrounded and attacked. All will seem lost.

That's the moment when Christ will return. His feet will descend upon the Mount of Olives—the very place where He ascended into heaven in Acts 1. He will save His people, destroy His enemies, and establish His kingdom.

I want to tell you about three incredible topological changes that will occur when Jesus returns. These three changes will establish the geography for the messianic kingdom.

CHRIST'S RETURN WILL TRIGGER AN EARTHQUAKE

When our Lord's feet touch the ridge of the Mount of Olives, His very presence will trigger an earthquake in Israel that will literally change the topography of the Middle East. This is spoken of several times in the Bible, but let's begin with the prophet Zechariah, the next-to-last book in the Old Testament.

According to Zechariah 14:4, "On that day his feet will stand on the Mount of Olives, east of Jerusalem, and the Mount of Olives will be split in two" (NIV).

The Mount of Olives is a 2.2-mile-long ridge on the eastern flank of Jerusalem. Every time I've taken groups to the Holy Land, we stand on the Mount of Olives and look out over the Kidron Valley at the walls surrounding the Old City. It's one of the most famous views in the world. We gaze at the ancient site of the Jewish temple, now occupied by the Islamic Dome of the Rock.

Large olive groves used to cover the sides of the Mount of Olives. Some still exist. On the lower slopes is the garden of Gethsemane, where Jesus was arrested. Its name in Hebrew means "oil press."

King David fled over this ridge when his son Absalom led a coup against him (2 Sam. 15:30). A thousand years later, David's great descendant, Jesus of Nazareth, sat on this mount to deliver His great sermon about the end of the age in Matthew 24 and 25.

After the Lord's resurrection, He spent forty days appearing periodically to His disciples, then He ascended into heaven from Mount Olivet as His disciples watched in amazement (Acts 1:11–12).

Ever since the days of Zechariah, the Jewish people have expected the Messiah to descend to the Mount of Olives, and that's why today the slopes of the ridge are covered by an outspread Hebrew cemetery. Pious Jews want to be buried near the place of the Messiah's coming.

The prophet Zechariah described the battle of Armageddon with details we find nowhere else in Scripture. As we've seen, the Tribulation will end with a climactic battle in which the Antichrist will seek to destroy once and for all the Hebrew people and the Jewish state. This man of lawlessness will lead the forces of the world against Israel, encircle Jerusalem, and attack the Jewish capital.

Here is Zechariah's description of that moment in its fuller context:

> I will gather all the nations to Jerusalem to fight against it. . . . Then the LORD will go out and fight against those nations. . . . On that day His feet will stand on the Mount of Olives, east of Jerusalem, and the Mount of Olives will be split in two from east to west, forming

a great valley, with half of the mountain moving north and half moving south. You will flee by my mountain valley.... You will flee as you fled from the earthquake in the days of Uzziah. (14:2–5 NIV)

CHRIST'S RETURN WILL UNLEASH A RIVER

But that's not all! The earthquake that forms an escape route for the besieged Jews in Jerusalem will also unleash vast underground aquifers that will erupt and form a river. Zechariah 14:8–9 says, "On that day living water will flow out from Jerusalem, half of it east to the Dead Sea and half of it west to the Mediterranean Sea, in summer and in winter. The LORD will be king over the whole earth" (NIV).

This river will divide at some point south of Jerusalem. Half will flow into the Mediterranean Sea, but the other half will replenish the Dead Sea and transform the ecology of the Judean desert.

The prophet Ezekiel devoted an entire chapter to describing this perpetual river that will flow from beneath the Temple Mount in Jerusalem. He said, "I saw water coming out from under the threshold of the temple toward the east" (47:1 NIV). According to Ezekiel, this river will grow stronger and wider and deeper as it heads south toward the Negev Desert: "This water flows toward the eastern region and goes down into the Arabah [the Jordan Valley], where it enters the Dead Sea. When it empties into the sea, the salty water there becomes fresh. Swarms of living creatures will live wherever the river flows. There will be large numbers of fish, because this water flows there and makes the salt water fresh" (vv. 8–9 NIV).

I've been visiting the Dead Sea for decades. It's the lowest spot of elevation on land on the planet. Except for scant rainfall, the only source of water for the Dead Sea is the Jordan River, the waters of which are now being diverted for domestic use. That's why the Dead Sea appears to be, well, dying. The water level is lower every time I see it.

This strange lake has no outlet, which means the water simply evaporates in the intense desert heat, leaving behind all its minerals. Its mineral levels are so high that humans can float on the surface like corks. Nothing can live in this thick brine except a handful of microscopic aquatic organisms. Casting your fishing line into the Dead Sea is useless.

But all this will change when Christ comes to establish His kingdom.

According to Ezekiel, "Fishermen will stand along the shore; from En Gedi to En Eglaim there will be places for spreading nets. The fish will be of many kinds—like the fish of the Mediterranean Sea. . . . Fruit trees of all kinds will grow on both banks of the river. Their leaves will not wither, nor will their fruit fail" (47:10, 12 NIV).

The prophet Joel also chimed in: "In that day . . . all the ravines of Judah will run with water. A fountain will flow out of the LORD's house and will water the valley of acacias" (3:18 NIV).

The rugged, blistering Negev Desert will become a paradise watered by the river unleashed at the return of Christ.

Oh, one other thing about this river: it's a preview of the crystal river that flows from beneath the throne of God in New Jerusalem, watering and invigorating the entire new earth (Rev. 22:1–2). So much of what we see in the Millennium is a preview of eternity.

CHRIST'S RETURN WILL LIFT A CITY

But there's yet more! The power of Christ's return will trigger an earthquake, unleash a river, and precipitate a geological change in the altitude of Jerusalem. The entire city will be lifted up even as the surrounding area becomes a level but lower plain. This may seem fantastic, but remember—"Before the mountains were brought forth, or ever You had formed the earth and the world, even from everlasting to everlasting, You are God" (Ps. 90:1–2).

For God to change the topography of an entire city is not a heavy lift.

Isaiah hinted at this when he said, "Now it shall come to pass in the latter days that the mountain of the LORD's house shall be established on the top of the mountains, and shall be exalted above the hills; and all nations shall flow to it" (2:2; see also Micah 4:1–2).

The prophet Zechariah gave more specifics:

The whole land, from Geba [six miles north of Jerusalem] to Rimmon [thirty miles], south of Jerusalem, will become like the Arabah [desert regions]. But Jerusalem will be raised up high from the Benjamin Gate to the site of the First Gate, to the Corner Gate, and from the Tower of Hananel to the royal winepresses, and will remain in its place. It will be inhabited; never again will it be destroyed. Jerusalem will be secure. (14:10–11 NIV)

Dr. George Klein, in his commentary on Zechariah, wrote,

[These verses] overview the dramatic changes the Lord will bring to Jerusalem and her surrounding regions on that great eschatological day. . . . God will elevate the city of Jerusalem while leveling her environs. Geographically, Jerusalem sits nestled beneath the gaze of mountains on every side. These mountains offered the city limited defensive advantages. . . . Since the city will no longer need any defense other than the Lord, God will remove its natural fortifications. Miraculously, the Lord will transform Zion from one of the most vulnerable locales on earth to the most secure.

Klein goes on to say, "The Lord will lower the elevation of these sites [outside Jerusalem] so that they would become 'like the Arabah' [desert regions]. . . . The distinguishing feature of the Arabah is its flatness. . . . Analogous to the lowering of the surrounding cities, the Lord promises to elevate Jerusalem."[1]

Nathaniel West wrote, "Jerusalem and Mount Zion, by means of physical convulsion and geological changes suddenly effected through disruption, depression, fissure, and elevation, at the Lord's coming, shall be exalted or lifted high above the surrounding hills, and the adjacent region be reduced to a plain."[2]

In other words, the very geography of the promised land will be altered at the second coming of Christ. The Mount of Olives will be fractured at the end of Armageddon, opening a wide and accessible lane for the residents of Jerusalem to flee the besieged city for safer places. The foundations of that city will shift to such a degree that rivers of healing water will flow through it. The elevation of the city will rise as the surrounding countryside levels out.

Why such changes? Because the King has returned. Jerusalem will no longer be a fortress set amid rugged terrain. Instead, it will be a beacon on a hill elevated over large, flat plains—an invitation to come and see the King. It will be the capital of the earth with masses of people coming and going. It will be "beautiful in elevation, the joy of the whole earth . . .the city of the great King" (Ps. 48:2).

CHRIST'S RETURN CAN SHAKE YOU UP

In September 2023, a massive earthquake struck Morocco. Ancient towns were destroyed, and remote settlements were devastated. One man named Haytham, age thirty, had been asking questions about Christianity in the days before the quake. He communicated with a Christian satellite television network, saying, "I am from a different background, and I want to know if the Christian religion is real or not."

A counselor for the network made sure he had a Bible and urged him to read it. But before Haytham could dive into the Scriptures, the earthquake upended his life. As soon as possible, the counselor reached out again, and Haytham responded, "People are exhausted and afraid to leave their homes. We're currently sleeping outside the house."

Later the network contacted Haytham again. This time he said, "I started reading the Bible. I accepted Jesus Christ as my Saviour and Lord. I am quite happy, and I believe that my life is improving." He told them he had joined a local church and was soon to be baptized.[3]

Remember the jailer in Philippi in Acts 16? An earthquake also led to his salvation.

Let me suggest that, in a spiritual sense, these coming events can be real right now in your heart. When Jesus shakes up our lives and we let Him come and reign in our hearts, He is elevated. He is lifted up. He rules as King of our lives. And what does He do? He unleashes rivers of living water that flow from our lives to the dry and thirsty society around us.

That's what we read in John 7:37–39: "Jesus stood and said in a loud voice, 'Let anyone who is thirsty come to me and drink. Whoever believes in me, as Scripture has said, rivers of living water will flow from within them.' By this he meant the Spirit, whom those who believed in him were later to receive" (NIV).

Let Jesus shake you up. Then make sure you lift Him up and let Him make you a river of blessing for others by His Holy Spirit.

CHAPTER 9

KING JESUS

Queen Elizabeth II was the longest-reigning monarch in British history. She was a legendary figure, which is why all the world paused when word came of her death.

Queen Elizabeth spoke openly about her faith in Christ, especially during her annual Christmas messages to England. In her 2011 Christmas broadcast, she said, "Jesus was born into a world full of fear. The angels came to frightened shepherds with hope in their voices: 'Fear not,' they urged, 'we bring you tidings of great joy, which shall be to all people. For unto you is born this day in the City of David a Saviour who is Christ the Lord.'"

In that same message, the queen said, "It is through this lens of history that we should view the conflicts of today, and so give us hope for tomorrow."[1]

I would like to change one word in that sentence. I want to suggest that "it is through this lens of *prophecy* that we should view the conflicts of today, and so give us hope for tomorrow."

Our history is important. The Christian faith is grounded in historical facts like the birth, death, and resurrection of Jesus Christ. But anyone can look backward. The only ones who can truly peer into the future are those of us who study what God has said in Scripture. In the Bible, He tells us what will happen in the coming days.

The same Jesus who died and rose from the dead will come again and reign in this world, and He will reign far longer than Elizabeth, who occupied the throne for a remarkable 70 years and 214 days. Imagine a King who will occupy His throne on this planet for one thousand years!

Understanding the return of Christ and His millennial reign is what helps us understand the conflicts of today, and it gives us hope for tomorrow.

When we see what's happening today in America and Europe, in Russia and China, and especially in Israel and the Middle East, we realize the history of our day is moving in a prophetic direction. Perhaps sooner than we realize, this world will be under the political control of one King: Jesus. The Bible presents Him not just as Savior, not just as Messiah, but as a King who at this very moment is already sitting at the right hand of the throne in heaven.

Let's talk about the glory and majesty, the power and authority of our King and His kingdom!

THE REDEEMING KING

Jesus' first incarnation in our world was primarily a redemptive mission. In His own words, "The Son of Man did not come to be served, but to serve, and to give His life a ransom for many" (Mark 10:45).

Even so, Jesus did not enter our world as a prophet or a teacher or a shepherd or even a carpenter. He came as our redeeming King. We can see that in the royal titles ascribed to Him throughout the Scriptures.

KING OF THE JEWS

He is first of all *King of the Jews*. During two periods of His life Jesus was called the King of the Jews: His birth in Bethlehem and the end of His life in Jerusalem. Oddly, this phrase occurs nowhere in the Old Testament, nor do we find it in the epistles. It occurs only in the Gospels at the birth and death of our Lord.

At Jesus' birth, the wise men inquired, "Where is He who has been born King of the Jews?" (Matt. 2:2).

That leads us to the death of Christ. When Jesus stood before Pontius Pilate, the Roman governor asked Him, "Are You the King of the Jews?" Jesus replied, "It is as you say" (Matt. 27:11). Addressing the mobs before him, Pilate shouted, "Do you want me to release to you the King of the Jews?" And, "What then do you want me to do with Him whom you call the King of the Jews?" (Mark 15:9–12).

Their response: "Crucify Him!" (v. 13).

Pilate handed over Christ for crucifixion, along with a strange order for the executors. A sign was nailed to the top of the cross bearing the words: "THE KING OF THE JEWS" (v. 26). This was our Lord's title in birth and in death—one uttered by the magi, the magistrates, the mob, the markings over His cross, and by the Master Himself.

KING OF ISRAEL

In a similar way, Jesus is called the *King of Israel*. The first person known to have recognized this was the disciple Nathanael, who said in John 1:49, "Rabbi, You are the Son of God! You are the King of Israel!"

Approximately three years later at the Lord's triumphal entry on Palm Sunday, large numbers of people celebrated His arrival in Jerusalem, saying, "Hosanna! 'Blessed is He who comes in the name of the LORD!' The King of Israel!" (John 12:13).

Five days later, as Jesus suffered on Golgotha, one of His enemies shouted sarcastically, "If He is the King of Israel, let Him now come down from the cross, and we will believe Him" (Matt. 27:42). According to these and other scriptures, Jesus Christ is the only rightful everlasting heir to the throne of David.

I've been to Israel many times, and so far I've never seen a throne anywhere in Jerusalem. But its design is already in the mind of God, and one day the streets will again be filled with people shouting, "Hosanna! Blessed is He who comes in the name of the Lord! The King of Israel!" I want to see that with my own eyes; don't you?

KING OF KINGS

Jesus is also known as the *King of kings*. This is our Lord's ultimate title of royal honor, as we learn in Revelation 19: "On his robe and on his thigh he has this name written: KING OF KINGS AND LORD OF LORDS" (v. 16 NIV).

Yes, we live in a disturbed world. But remember, none of today's politicians, leaders, villains, or rogues will ever gain supreme authority. Not even the coming Antichrist. All will falter and fail, for only Jesus is the King of kings and Lord of lords. One day every knee will bow before Him, and every tongue confess that He is Lord (Rom. 14:11).

KING OVER THE WHOLE EARTH

The prophet Zechariah added another title to our Lord when he described His return to earth with these riveting words: "The LORD will be *king over the whole earth*. On that day there will be one LORD, and his name the only name" (14:9 NIV).

If you've had the opportunity to travel, you know our world is huge. There are so many landscapes and bodies of water and people groups that nobody could possibly visit everything interesting in a single lifetime this side of the grave. Yet Jesus will rule over every inch, every grain of sand, and every ocean drop.

KING OF GLORY

The last royal title I'll mention is the wonderful phrase found in Psalm 24. Jesus is the *King of glory*.

We know Psalm 22 as the Crucifixion Psalm, which predicts in vivid detail our Lord's brutal execution.

Psalm 23 is the Shepherd Psalm, in which we exalt in the Lord as our Shepherd.

And Psalm 24 is the Coronation Psalm, which describes the King of glory ascending to heaven and taking His seat on the throne to await the moment of His return: "Lift up your heads, O you gates! And be lifted up, you everlasting doors! And the King of glory shall come in. . . . Who is this King of glory? The LORD of hosts; He is the King of glory" (vv. 7, 10).

Jesus is King of the Jews, King of Israel, King of kings, King over the whole earth, and King of glory.

THE REIGNING KING

Among the famous figures of history, only a few have been known as "the Great." These characters are like monuments on the pages of time—kings who wielded extraordinary power or left an unusual mark. From the biblical era, we have Cyrus the Great, Darius the Great, Xerxes the Great, and Herod the Great. Between the Old and New Testaments, the world was changed forever by the meteoric rise of Alexander the Great. Europe also came under the sway of Charlemagne, often known as Charles the Great.

Most of these men were not as great as they thought. They were full of failure and sometimes guilty of heinous crimes.

But here's the interesting thing: the greatest King in history isn't among them. Jesus was never called "Jesus the Great" or "Christ the Great." He *is* great, of course, and greatly to be praised. But His greatness isn't derived from comparison with other kings. He's in a class by Himself. He stands alone in history.

Christ is the King whose power is absolute, whose reign is infinite, and whose throne is unconquerable. He is an indescribable King, for He reigns eternally without beginning of days or ending of life. He is the epitome of humility, yet the Bible calls Him "the ruler over the kings of the earth" (Rev. 1:5).

Yes, Christ is our Messiah, our Intercessor, the Compassionate

Servant, the Humble Teacher, and the Selfless Savior. But never forget He is Christ the King! Without His supreme and sovereign rule, our lives would sink into chaos. Nothing can stabilize our emotions like remembering His royal reign. He commands and He controls, and nothing is exempt from His preeminent power. That's why so many people rely on Him as the anchor of their souls.

Robert Strauss was a brilliant political strategist who served under several presidents from Jimmy Carter to George H. W. Bush. He's quoted as saying, "Everybody in government is like a bunch of ants on a log floating down a river. Each one thinks he is guiding the log, but it is really just going with the flow."[2]

The same can be said of all the rulers of history. All have died or will die, and none has risen from the dead. All of them have dominated the headlines for a period, but none has divided history in two. The rulers of this world enjoy limited authority for a limited time. Only Jesus possesses infinite authority for all eternity. Many rulers have improved the quality of life for their subjects, but only One gives eternal life.

This is what we're looking forward to! The only way we can make sense of our world and find hope for today is to remember what the Lord has promised about tomorrow. Except for King Jesus, all leaders are flawed. Many have unleashed wars, triggered riots, annihilated opponents, bankrupted treasuries, and acted as fools.

Others have exhibited great courage and demonstrated legendary leadership. After Abraham Lincoln died, the secretary of war, Edwin Stanton, looked down at him on his deathbed and said, "Now he belongs to the ages."[3]

But only One belongs to eternity. Jesus reigns peerless in time and eternity. He is the King of an endless empire. He rules above the stars and within the heart. He's the King of kings and Lord of lords.

As our politics and democracies have evolved, the world has deteriorated. One global think tank issued a report in December 2023 that said, "2024 will be a year of ballots and bullets. The elections held in more than 70 countries will serve as a stress test for the democratic system. . . . The erosion of international norms is more acute than ever, and events . . . more unpredictable."[4]

However, there is one event we can predict with certainty. One day the world's throne will be occupied by Jesus Christ—King of the Jews, King of Israel, King of kings, King over the whole earth, and King of glory. Remember, it is through the lens of biblical prophecy that we should view the conflicts of today and find our hope for tomorrow.

A travel magazine recently ran an article for people who want to visit the seven most beautiful thrones in the world. Two of them are in India, one in Iran, another in Russia, and there's the Dragon Throne in China. The sixth is St. Edward's Chair at Westminster Abbey in England, and the seventh is the Silver Throne in Sweden. The Silver Throne is designed to express purity, and it's a stunning sight with its silver, blue, and white trappings. You can find it in the Hall of State at Stockholm Palace.[5]

None of these seven thrones is very significant in the scope of history. Some are used for ceremonial occasions, and the others are simply for tourists to see. The glory has faded, and the power has seeped away.

But I want to end this chapter by describing another throne. It's the one that matters most right now. It's the throne God has placed in our own hearts.

Of all the kingly titles possessed by Jesus Christ, the one that is most personal to you and me is when we say, "Lord, You are *my* King. I vacate the throne of my heart and give it to You. I want You to rule and reign in my life. Under my own control, I make too many mistakes and messes. Forgive me for ever thinking I could be my own monarch and chart my own destiny. In the words of an old hymn, I say 'King of my life, I crown Thee now. Thine shall the glory be.'"

The moment we receive Jesus Christ as Lord, a coronation takes place inside us. Jesus becomes the King of our lives, and we give Him the glory. I urge you to let Jesus Christ rule and reign on the throne of your heart today.

CHAPTER 10

PRINCE DAVID

From the moment of his birth, he has been the most famous prince in the world. Perhaps even the most famous prince in human history. That fame reached a new level when, as a teenager, he endured the shockingly public divorce of his mother and father. It elevated to a fever pitch only a year later when his mother was killed in a tragic car accident.

I am of course referring to William Mountbatten-Windsor, who is best known as Prince William of the British royal family.

That is far from his only title, however. The young royal has officially been recognized with the following titles:

- Prince of Wales
- Duke of Cambridge
- Duke of Cornwall
- Duke of Rothesay
- Earl of Strathearn
- Earl of Chester

- Baron Carrickfergus
- Commodore-in-Chief of Scotland
- Colonel of the Welsh Guards
- Colonel-in-Chief of the Mercian Regiment
- Colonel-in-Chief of the Army Air Corps

Wow! Each of those titles comes with official duties and responsibilities, which means Prince William has quite a lot on his plate. Of course, with the elevation of his father, Charles III, to the station of king following the death of Queen Elizabeth, Prince William is now the heir to the throne in Great Britain.

Perhaps surprisingly, in spite of all his titles and privileges and expectations, Prince William seems to be a genuinely good man. Following his university education, he spent seven years in the Royal Air Force training for and performing the role of search-and-rescue pilot. He later became the first British royal to hold a job in the private sector when he served as a rescue pilot for the East Anglian Air Ambulance. He even donated his salary to charity.[1]

As we've already discovered, the coming Golden Age will feature a monarch unlike any other in human history: King Jesus. He is the King of kings and Lord of lords. He is the Ruler not only of our world but of all worlds.

Jesus will reign supreme during the Millennium, but He will not reign alone. He'll be supported by another worthy prince who also happens to be a wonderful man—a man after God's own heart. That man is David, the former king of Israel and the future prince of Christ's millennial kingdom.

DAVID'S REGAL CHARACTER

David is well known as one of the "founding fathers" of the Jewish people and a major force within the pages of the Old Testament.

What you may not realize is that David is also one of the most important people in the New Testament. In fact, he is mentioned more in the New Testament—fifty-six times—than any other Old Testament figure.

Not only that, but David likely has the most complete biography of any person present in the pages of God's Word. Abraham is certainly a critical character, but there are only fourteen biblical chapters dedicated to the story of his life. David's story is spread over an amazing sixty-two chapters, making him a central pillar in God's Spirit-inspired revelation.

Like all God's children, David has a story that is far from finished. He has a specific role to play in the coming Golden Age that will be second only to Christ Himself:

> The absolute monarchy of the Messiah will extend to Israel as well as to the Gentile nations. But directly under the Messianic King, having authority over all Israel, will be the resurrected David, who is given both titles of king and prince. He will be a king because he will rule over Israel, but he will be a prince in that he will function under the authority of the Messiah. Just as all the Gentile nations will have kings, so will Israel. The difference is that the Gentile kings will all have their natural bodies, while David will have his resurrected body.
>
> There are several passages that speak of David as being king over Israel and prince under King Messiah, with Jeremiah 30:9 being one of them: "But they shall serve Jehovah their God, and David their king, whom I will raise up unto them." Not only will the Jewish people in the future serve God, but they will also serve David their king.[2]

What makes David worthy of such a lofty elevation in both the past and the future? Let's take a closer look at three specific elements of David's greatness.

HIS CHARISMA

David may not have been physically imposing, but he possessed strength and agility that rivaled even the mightiest warriors. With his quick feet and powerful arms, he could scale walls and outrun armies. His accuracy and force with a sling were unparalleled, making him a formidable foe. Despite being too small for Saul's armor as a youth, David was able to kill a bear and a lion with his bare hands.

But it wasn't just his strength and athleticism that set David apart. He was also blessed with a ruddy complexion, sparkling eyes, and a confidence that captured attention wherever he went. Many scholars believe David was blessed with unusual hair—golden or reddish in color—which set him apart from his Jewish family and friends. He was a striking individual.

Scripture describes David as "skillful in playing, a mighty man of valor, a man of war, prudent in speech, and a handsome person; and the LORD is with him" (1 Sam. 16:18). The king of the Philistines said of David, "I know that you are as good in my sight as an angel of God" (29:9).

David was a man of the people. One text mentions that "all Israel and Judah loved David, because he went out and came in before them" (1 Sam. 18:16). He seemed to have a hand in everything that was important to the culture of his day. He was a working-class shepherd but also a king. He was a heroic soldier but also a poet. The man was comfortable at war or at peace.

David was gifted with great ability, and he chose to use that giftedness to glorify God and raise the fortunes of His chosen people.

HIS CREATIVITY

Not only was David a gifted athlete, but he was also a talented musician. Despite the long-standing rivalry between these two passions in his life, David excelled at both.

While attending school, I struggled to balance my love for basketball with a brief stint playing the baritone in the band. I thought I could strike a chord between them (pun intended), but eventually I gave up the horn.

David was a master in all he touched. His gift for creative expression extended beyond music and into writing as well. In fact, seventy-three of the psalms in the Bible's hymnbook were written by David. He is the founder of hymnody as we know it today. And while there were other influential musicians in the ancient world, none of their work can compare with the depth and beauty that mark David's writing.

From songs praising God to introspective hymns reflecting his own struggles, David's words and melodies continue to inspire and uplift us today.

HIS CHOSENNESS

Do you know how David became king in the Old Testament? God did it. God chose him. Looking down at King Saul's disobedience, God essentially declared, "I'm done with Saul. It's David's time."

But long before that, according to the record of the Scripture in 1 Samuel 13:14, we are told the Lord sought for David. In Psalm 89:20, we are told the Lord found David. In Psalm 78:70, we are told the Lord chose David. Again in 1 Samuel 13:14, we are told the Lord commanded David. And in 1 Samuel 16:1, we are told the Lord provided David.

You can't help but get caught up in those five verbs. God *sought* him, He *found* him, He *chose* him, He *commanded* him, and because of that, He *provided* him. God provided David to His people—both in the past and in our future.

David was chosen of God. That's the reason above all the other reasons for his greatness. When he was far from the palace as an exile, God was with him. When he sat upon the throne of that great kingdom, ruling in majesty and might, God was with him. When he stood as a young boy with a slingshot in his hand before that mighty giant, God was with him. And when he took his pen to write the great hymns which we enjoy as we worship our Lord, God inspired him.

There are no human ways to describe the greatness of this man, David, except simply to proclaim he was the choice of almighty God.

DAVID'S REIGN AS COREGENT

You've likely heard of Steve Jobs and Steve Wozniak, the cofounders of Apple Computers. But have you heard of Ron Wayne? He was the third partner who helped launch Apple as an organization. In fact, he designed the company's first logo and wrote up its first contract.

After several weeks, though, Ron stepped away. He held a 10 percent share in Apple, but he sold it back to Jobs and Wozniak for $800. He later received an additional $1,500 to finalize the dissolution. Basically, Ron Wayne accepted $2,300 for 10 percent of a company that is literally worth *trillions* in today's market.

Fortunately, Ron maintained a healthy perspective in spite of Apple's success. "I was 40 and these kids were in their 20s," he said. "They were whirlwinds—it was like having a tiger by the tail. If I had stayed with Apple I probably would have wound up the richest man in the cemetery."[3]

It's vital for partners to be on the same page in any venue, but that's especially true for high-pressure situations, as Mr. Wayne discovered. Thankfully, we can be certain that the partnership between King Jesus and His coregent, David, will function smoothly and effectively throughout the coming Golden Age.

Let's take a deeper look at what David's role in that partnership will involve.

PRINCE DAVID WILL SHEPHERD HIS PEOPLE

David began his professional career as a shepherd—a watchman over his father's flocks. In a similar way, David will serve as an official watchman over the Jewish people during the Millennium.

God Himself confirmed that reality in the book of Ezekiel: "I will establish one shepherd over them, and he shall feed them—My servant David. He shall feed them and be their shepherd. And I, the LORD, will be their God, and My servant David a prince among them; I, the LORD, have spoken" (34:23–24).

The intimacy of the repeated word *feed* in this passage is powerful. In the same way that a shepherd provides sustenance for every individual sheep, even in the most rugged wilderness, David will exercise the authority of Christ in supporting and sustaining the Jewish people during the Millennium.

PRINCE DAVID WILL SHAPE HIS PEOPLE

In ancient Israel, a king was supposed to be more than a head of state or a commander-in-chief. Israel's kings were called to be spiritual leaders over God's chosen people. They were expected to lead the way in worshiping God, obeying His Word, and submitting to His will.

David took that responsibility seriously during his reign as king in Jerusalem, and he will continue to shape the spiritual lives of the Jewish people during his reign as prince throughout the coming Golden Age.

Ezekiel declared, "David My servant shall be king over them, and they shall all have one shepherd; they shall also walk in My judgments and observe My statutes, and do them" (37:24).

The prophet Hosea added, "Afterward the children of Israel shall return and seek the LORD their God and David their king. They shall fear the LORD and His goodness in the latter days" (3:5).

PRINCE DAVID WILL SAFEGUARD HIS PEOPLE

For generations upon generations, the Jewish people have longed for the peace and protection they enjoyed during the reign of King David—a time in which Israel's enemies were defeated, her borders expanded, and her people supported. Such a season will indeed be repeated, and this time for a thousand years.

According to Jeremiah, "In those days and at that time I will cause to grow up to David a Branch of righteousness; He shall execute judgment and righteousness in the earth. In those days Judah will be saved, and Jerusalem will dwell safely. And this is the name by which she will be called: THE LORD OUR RIGHTEOUSNESS" (33:15–16).

Of course, the Jewish people will not have enemies during the Millennium. There will be no Haman. No Hitler. No antisemitism of any kind. Even so, Prince David will stand vigilant as a protector under the authority of Christ.

I recently read something interesting about the statue of David created by the great Michelangelo during the sixteenth century. Apparently, Michelangelo—who was only twenty-five at the time—wasn't the first person selected for the job. Or the second! Thirty-five years earlier, an artist named Agostino di Duccio accepted the commission and selected a huge block of marble for the carving. After starting work, however, he determined the marble was too flawed to be of any use, and he gave up. Ten years later, another sculptor attempted to salvage the commission, but he also threw in the towel, claiming the marble was worthless.

Michelangelo came along a full twenty-five years later and, by choosing to work with the supposed flaws of the stone, created the world's most famous sculpture: *David*.[4]

Don't you love the idea of something deemed worthless being turned into something extraordinary under the loving hands of a master?

God the Father did that with David more than three thousand years ago. Yes, David was a flawed human being; he had many faults, and he succumbed to grievous sins. Scripture plainly records the worst elements of David's humanity.

Yet under the loving hands of a divine Master, David was shaped into something magnificent. He is still being shaped—even now, even at this moment, he exists in the presence of the Father. And in the coming Golden Age, he will regain his rightful place as prince in Jerusalem.

Let me end this chapter by reminding you that the same divine Master who shaped David into a man after God's own heart wants to do the same with you. Yes, you're imperfect. Yes, you've failed many times. Yes, just like me, you are a flawed human being. But God is the potter and we are the clay. Let Him mold you and make you after His will. Let Him have His way in your life, and He will remold you from a lump of clay to a vessel fit for the Master's use.

CHAPTER 11

NO DEVIL

Sitting on thirty-seven acres of land southwest of Colorado Springs, ADX Florence is the most secure prison in America. If you could walk its corridors, you'd pass a who's who of archvillains, including Zacarias Moussaoui, who masterminded the 9/11 attacks; Terry Nichols, who helped plan the 1995 Oklahoma City bombing; James Marcello, the notorious Chicago crime boss; El Chapo, the Mexican drug kingpin; and until recently, Theodore Kaczynski, the Unabomber. Kaczynski was found dead in his cell in 2023.

Superspy Robert Hanssen also died in his cell there. In fact, most of those in the Florence supermax will never leave the place alive. The prisoners have extremely long sentences, and they're largely kept in solitary confinement with little or no time outside their cells.

Each unit is seven by twelve feet, with a stool and desk made of poured concrete, a concrete bed with a foam pad, and a toilet with a sink at its top. The cells are soundproof, and multiple cameras monitor each prisoner twenty-four hours a day. Only a narrow slit of a window lets in light, and the slits are designed so prisoners cannot ascertain where they are in the complex.[1]

There's never been an escape from ADX Florence.

I know of only one penitentiary more secure than America's supermax complex in Colorado. Designed by almighty God for the worst of the evil agents in the unseen realm, that prison is known as *the bottomless pit* or *the abyss*.

According to Revelation 20, when Jesus returns to set up His millennial kingdom, an angel will come from heaven. John described him as "having the key to the bottomless pit and a great chain in his hand. He laid hold of the dragon, that serpent of old, who is the Devil and Satan, and bound him for a thousand years; and he cast him into the bottomless pit, and shut him up, and set a seal on him, so that he should deceive the nations no more till the thousand years were finished" (vv. 1–3).

So far in these pages we have mostly been laying the groundwork for the concept of the Millennium. We've seen the way Scripture promises the coming Golden Age in both the Old and New Testaments. We've explored what will happen at the battle of Armageddon, why Jerusalem is critical to the Millennium, and the roles of King Jesus and Prince David during that thousand-year period.

Over the next several chapters, we're going to shift directions and examine what life will be like during the coming Golden Age. And one of the most significant facts about that period is the total absence of Satan. The world will be free of his provocations for 365,250 days—a thousand devil-free years!

I want to point out three things about these opening verses in Revelation 20: the person of the devil, the prison of the demons, and earth's period of deliverance from Satan's schemes.

THE PERSON OF THE DEVIL

In Revelation 20:2, the apostle John used four different words or titles for this person of evil. We're told a powerful angel from heaven will lay hold of "the dragon, that serpent of old, who is the Devil and Satan."

What's behind these four terms?

THE DRAGON

First, John referred to the devil as a dragon. This image occurred earlier in Revelation 12, where John saw a "great, fiery red dragon" who sought to destroy the Messiah at the time of our Lord's first coming (vv. 1–5) and who will dominate the events around His second coming.

We also see this dragon in the Old Testament. Isaiah 27:1 says, "In that day the LORD with his hard and great and strong sword will punish Leviathan the fleeing serpent, Leviathan the twisting serpent, and he will slay the dragon that is in the sea" (ESV). Similar to other prophets, Isaiah pictured the evil that came against Israel as a sea monster or Leviathan.

Here, in Revelation 20, John identified the ultimate version of this dragon as Satan.

THE SERPENT OF OLD

Revelation 20:2 goes on to mention "that serpent of old." This takes us all the way back to Genesis 3, when the serpent appeared in the garden of Eden to tempt Eve and Adam into doubting and disobeying God. As we've just seen, a similar image occurs in Isaiah 27:1, where our Enemy is described as a fleeing, twisting serpent.

While researching for this book, I read that scientists recently discovered the largest species of snake ever recorded. The discovery was made while actor Will Smith was filming a travel documentary for *National Geographic*. The newly named northern green anaconda species is massive—over twenty feet long and weighing as much as a thousand pounds. Popular Dutch biologist and thrill seeker Freek Vonk swam alongside one of the snakes, and the video gave me the chills![2]

Then I remembered that the largest and deadliest serpent in history isn't an anaconda. It's the devil, who slithered his way into our human family, infected us with his toxins, and who has proven to be as mean as—well, as a snake.

If the devil gives you the shivers as well, don't worry. He's going into the abyss at the dawn of the Millennium.

THE DEVIL

In Revelation 20:2, John gave us a third title for this evil personage: "the dragon, that serpent of old, who is the Devil." Our English word *devil* comes from the Latin *diabolus*, which itself comes from the Greek word John used here—*diabolos*. The root meaning is "one who accuses or slanders."

In Genesis 3, the devil slandered God in front of Adam and Eve. In the centuries since, he has delighted in accusing God's children before the throne, pointing out our faults and making accusations against us as he did about Job (Job 1:9–11), Joshua (Zech. 3:1), and the entire family of believers (Rev. 12:10–12). His efforts are thwarted because we're covered with the precious blood of Christ, though that doesn't stop his accusations.

SATAN

In Revelation 20:2, John's final word was *Satan*. "He laid hold of the dragon, that serpent of old, who is the Devil and Satan." That term comes straight from the Greek word *satanas*, which means "adversary." This word occurs more than thirty times in the New Testament, and what an awful association we find when tracing it through Scripture. Satan tempts us (1 Cor. 7:5), takes advantage of us (2 Cor. 2:11), buffets us (12:7), hinders us (1 Thess. 2:18), provokes us to lie and to deceive (Acts 5:3), and tries to steal the Word of God from our hearts (Mark 4:15).

Thomas A. Tarrants, president emeritus of the C. S. Lewis Institute, wrote, "We can safely say that [Satan's] goals are to reclaim or at least neutralize God's people, to destroy the church, to overthrow the kingdom of God, to displace God as King of creation and to become the object of all worship. This helps explain much of the evil and suffering that rages on earth."[3]

If you have ever felt unusually tempted, buffeted, taken advantage of, hindered, provoked, or weakened toward the Word, it's likely the adversary was plying his arts on you.

Oh, to be rid of him!

And, oh, we will be!

THE PRISON OF DEMONS

Now let's look at the opening verses of Revelation 20 again and notice the prison to which the devil is destined: "Then I saw an angel coming down from heaven, having the key to the bottomless pit and a great chain in his hand. He laid hold of the dragon, that serpent of old, who is the Devil and Satan, and bound him for a thousand years; and he cast him into the bottomless pit, and shut him up" (vv. 1–3).

The term "bottomless pit" is better translated as "abyss" because the Greek word John used was *abyssos*, meaning "a very deep place." This is God's supermax prison for evil spirits. It isn't hell. That will be the devil's final destiny. But for a thousand years, Satan will be banished from earth and imprisoned in this mysterious penitentiary.

The book of Jude says, "And the angels who did not keep their positions of authority but abandoned their proper dwelling—these he has kept in darkness, bound with everlasting chains for judgment on the great Day" (Jude v. 6 NIV). For reasons only God knows, He allowed the devil and some of the evil spirits to travel around earth's atmosphere and cause trouble, but in mercy to us He imprisoned some of these principalities and powers in the abyss.

Remember when Jesus cast the demons out of the man in Luke 8? Those demons "begged Jesus repeatedly not to order them to go into the Abyss" (v. 31 NIV). It was a place they dreaded. During the trumpet judgments in Revelation 9, an angel will open the shaft leading down to the abyss and release these malignant and heinous demons. They will swarm the earth, terrorizing its inhabitants. This will happen during the Tribulation. Thankfully, after those seven years, all demons will be reincarcerated in the abyss along with Satan himself.

John told us in Revelation 20 that the devil will be bound with chains he cannot escape and consigned to a prison he cannot avoid for a thousand years.

THE PERIOD OF DELIVERANCE

During that time, John said, Satan will "deceive the nations no more till the thousand years [are] finished" (Rev. 20:3). During the millennial reign of Christ, we who live and govern with Him on earth will be delivered from Satan's tyranny. As Swiss theologian René Pache wrote, "What change shall take place when the tempter is no longer able to seduce the nations! That will be better than it was in Eden, for Satan caused our first parents to fall."[4]

This doesn't mean there won't be sin on the earth. Those with mortal bodies will still battle their fallen nature, and the blessed eternal state of the new heaven and new earth is yet to come. (More on that in a later chapter.) But think of it like this. Today we have three great enemies of the soul: the world, the flesh, and the devil. Consider how different it will be without the Enemy to bedevil us.

The Bible says, "We know that we are children of God, and that the whole world is under the control of the evil one" (1 John 5:19 NIV). Paul said the devil is "the god of this age" (2 Cor. 4:4). During the coming Golden Age, he will lose his dominion here.

Gone will be Satan's ability to amplify sexual temptation and marital infidelity (1 Cor. 7:5). While we may be tempted, we'll not have to confront the supercharged enticements of Satan (Matt. 4:1–10). We'll not have to contend with being sifted as wheat by his evil designs (Luke 22:31). Nor will he fill our hearts to lie to one another as he did Ananias in Acts 5:3. We'll be able to better forgive one another because we'll be free from Satan's devices (2 Cor. 2:11).

He'll not swoop down on listening souls and snatch the Word out of their hearts (Mark 4:15). Nor will he hinder the workers of God as he hindered Paul in 1 Thessalonians 2:18. Nor will he physically and spiritually bind people as he did the poor woman in Luke 13:16 or oppress the poor and needy as he did in Acts 10:38.

Gone will be his ability to plague us with demonically caused natural disasters, family tragedies, illnesses, and physical attacks (Job 1:13–2:8). We'll be freed from his ability to hinder the work of the Lord on this planet.

No longer will he create agitation among the nations or prompt rulers to wage wars, commit genocide, and oppress the innocent (Dan. 10:13–14). His power to influence the leaders of the world to sin will be shelved for a thousand years (1 Chron. 21:1). Revelation 20:3 specifically says, "He should deceive the nations no more till the thousand years were finished."

Satan was "a murderer from the beginning" (John 8:44), so we would expect murders to be virtually nonexistent during the Golden Age of Christ. He "has sinned from the beginning" (1 John 3:8), so we would expect the Golden Age to exhibit moral character and righteousness. He was "puffed up with pride" and coaxed others to the same (1 Tim. 3:6), so we would expect the millennial age to be humbler and gentler.

Today, the devil makes many people take leave of their senses and do his will (2 Tim. 2:26). The coming Golden Age should be a time of wisdom and sensibility. The devil delights in throwing God's children into prison and persecuting them in all manner of ways (Rev. 2:10), so we would expect the reign of Christ to rejoice in the free expression of the gospel with little or no opposition.

In another chapter, we'll deal with the final doom of Satan, the moment in which he will be forever consigned to hell. But for now, the thought of his being bound is comforting. This is especially true because, for strange reasons I don't fully understand, we're enduring a resurgence of interest in Satan in our culture.

In 2023, *Newsweek* published a major article entitled, "Satan Is

Getting Hot as Hell in American Pop Culture." The writer, Paul Bond, who covers cultural trends for *Newsweek*, wrote, "The Devil is front and center in movies, TV shows, podcasts, and even children's books. . . . On Netflix alone there are dozens of titles dealing with hellish demons."

Bond quoted Carlos Martins, host of *The Exorcist Files*, as saying that humans crave spirituality. Church and synagogue attendance has been declining in the United States. To fill the void, many people are embracing "a rejection of received social customs and expected behavioral norms in favor of embracing 'me-first' pleasure. . . . The adoption of Satan as a figurehead is merely another 'shock' ceiling through which the movement has broken through."

Bond added, "More Americans are opening the door for Satan to enter their lives."[5]

As frightening as that is, remember, we may only be seven years away from the moment when God will throw Satan into the abyss and slam the door after him. The knowledge of that future promise should comfort us today. Though Satan is active, he cannot overcome the power of the cross of Jesus Christ and our Lord's resurrection. Even now, we're to live in victory.

For half a millennium now, Christians have been singing Martin Luther's great hymn "A Mighty Fortress." Let's anticipate the day when the prince of darkness will be banished by just a word or two from our Savior's lips:

> And though this world, with devils filled,
> Should threaten to undo us,
> We will not fear, for God has willed
> His truth to triumph through us.
> The prince of darkness grim,
> We tremble not for him;
> His rage we can endure,
> For, lo! His doom is sure;
> One little word shall fell him.[6]

CHAPTER 12

WELL DONE AND JUST BEGUN

Billboard is a magazine founded back in 1894 that's become a standard in the music and entertainment industry. In 2011, the magazine began presenting a prestigious award to singers who have had an outsized impact on the music industry. As of this writing, only three of these awards have been given—to Beyoncé, Whitney Houston, and Britney Spears.

Do you know what the magazine calls this presentation?

The Billboard Millennium Award.

If I could talk to the magazine's executives, I'd tell them about the real Millennium awards, which will be handed out at the beginning of the thousand-year reign of Christ. True, the recipients likely won't be world-famous superstars or successful entertainers, but Jesus said this about those who neglect Him for the sake of worldly gain: "Truly I tell you, they have received their reward in full" (Matt. 6:2 NIV).

Thankfully, Jesus also said, "Whoever gives one of these little ones only a cup of cold water in the name of a disciple, assuredly, I say to you, he shall by no means lose his reward" (10:42).

Any of us can do that. Each of us *should* do that! All of us can serve the Lord in ways great and small every day. Jesus said, "Love your enemies, do good, and lend, hoping for nothing in return; and your reward will be great" (Luke 6:35).

The psalmist said, "Surely there is a reward for the righteous" (Ps. 58:11).

The apostle Paul told the Colossians, "From the Lord you will receive the reward of the inheritance; for you serve the Lord Christ" (Col. 3:24).

As followers of Jesus, the reward we long to receive is hearing Him say those wonderful words: "Well done, good and faithful servant" (Matt. 25:21). Amen and amen! We will hear those words as we transition from this life to the Golden Age. But that will be just the beginning of our reward in the kingdom of Christ.

WELL DONE!

The *Las Vegas Sun* sponsors an annual award named for its founder, and in 2023, the Hank Greenspun Lifetime Achievement Award was presented to a former probation officer named Ed Cheltenham.

Years before, Ed had worked with a certain troubled teenager at a camp for delinquent youths. But when the time came for the boy to reenter society, he had nowhere to go. Ed and his wife, Sonya, took in the young man, and they went on to become foster parents for almost a dozen kids over the course of three decades. As a probation officer at the camp, Ed has helped hundreds of children while personally opening his home to those who had nowhere else to turn. For his decades of dedicated service, Ed Cheltenham received a lifetime achievement award that is well deserved.[1]

If you're like me, you feel a tug at your heart when an emergency responder, caregiver, schoolteacher, church volunteer, or good Samaritan is honored for their humble acts of valor. The Bible tells us to give "honor to whom honor" is due (Rom. 13:7).

Whom will Jesus honor at the beginning of the Millennium? Well, church ushers who showed up every week, took their places with a smile, welcomed people to worship, helped others find a seat, and made newcomers feel at home. Teenagers who delivered meals on their bicycles to senior adults or who invited their friends to a life-changing weekend retreat. Parents who prayed relentlessly for their wayward children. Persecuted Christians who were beaten for their faith, rejected by their families, and oppressed by their governments.

Surely God will have a special place for all those who, like Stephen, died for their commitment to Christ. When Justin Martyr was being slain for his faith, he said, "I ask nothing more than to suffer for the cause of my Lord Jesus Christ. If I can do this, then I can stand in confidence and quiet before the judgment seat of my God and Savior."[2]

Also to be rewarded is the bivocational pastor who worked all day in a factory and then burned the midnight oil preparing his sermon for Sunday. The Sunday school teacher who taught fifth graders for many years, falling in love with each new class of youngsters and never growing complacent in the work. The missionaries who labored in primitive conditions for a lifetime, while sometimes seeing little outward success for their labors. The high school and university students who believed God placed them on their campuses to share the gospel and to start an awakening of students for Christ, though they suffered ridicule at times. The senior adults who, when they could do little else, gave themselves to a ministry of prayer, and even when their resources were sparse, gave their widows' mites with joy to support the work of Christ around the world.

That's why 2 Chronicles 15:7 says, "But you, be strong and do not let your hands be weak, for your work shall be rewarded!"

In this life, there's nothing more satisfying than finding our purpose in serving the Lord and His kingdom, though we might not feel worthy of ever being rewarded for what we've done. The Lord, who knows our hearts and sees every hidden act of kindness, will bless all our selfless efforts given for the cause of His glory.

JUST BEGUN!

What reward will we receive at the beginning of the Millennium? In a word, *service*. Each and every believer who experiences the wonders of God's millennial kingdom will be given the opportunity to serve within that kingdom as a coregent (or representative) of Christ.

Earlier I quoted Matthew 25:21, when Jesus said, "Well done, good and faithful servant." But the Lord had more to say in that verse: "Well done, good and faithful servant; you were faithful over a few things, I will make you ruler over many things. Enter into the joy of your lord."

How wonderful to discover that when we've finished our loyal service for the Lord in the church age, we're not done! We've just begun! We'll have meaningful jobs to do in the Golden Age; then, afterward, during the endless realms of eternity, we'll find even more purposeful work to do. Revelation 22:3 says that in the new heaven and new earth, "His servants shall serve Him."

Randy Alcorn said,

Service is a reward, not a punishment. This idea is foreign to people who dislike their work and only put up with it until retirement. We think that faithful work should be rewarded by a vacation for the rest of our lives. But God offers us something very different: more work, more responsibilities, increased opportunities, along with greater abilities, resources, wisdom, and empowerment. We will have sharp minds, strong bodies, clear purpose, and unabated joy.[3]

Importantly, the work we enjoy during the Millennium will be directly connected with the "works" we engage in during the present age. The Bible teaches that when we serve the Lord here on earth as Christians, we will be rewarded in the kingdom with the opportunity to serve in new and special ways. Some of these rewards will involve political office and governmental authority. Remember, the coming kingdom isn't just spiritual; it is geopolitical. It involves a governmental structure that will span the globe.

Isaiah 9:6 says, "For unto us a Child is born, unto us a Son is given; and the government will be upon His shoulder."

Zechariah 14:9 says, "And the LORD shall be King over all the earth."

Who will serve as leaders over the nations, regions, provinces, and cities in the global kingdom of Christ? The answer is, those who are faithfully serving the Lord Jesus now, during our earthly lifetimes. Could you imagine yourself on the city council of a great metropolis where everyone is happy? What would it be like to serve as president or prime minister over a nation that feared no war and suffered no civil disturbances? What if you were the secretary of the treasury for a nation that had more money than it needed? It's hard to imagine, isn't it?

I don't want to speculate beyond the impressions we get in the Bible, but this seems to be what Daniel had in mind when he wrote: "But the saints of the Most High shall receive the kingdom, and possess the kingdom forever, even forever and ever. . . . And the time came for the saints to possess the kingdom. . . . And the greatness of the kingdoms under the whole heaven, shall be given to the people, the saints of the Most High" (7:18, 22, 27).

There will be a hierarchy of rulers and judges in the Millennium. We have noted David's high-ranking role and the lower role of the ruling saints. Between these tiers of authority will be the twelve apostles, who have already been given their assigned thrones for the purpose of judging Israel (Matt. 19:28).

Who are these additional saints who will reign with Christ? Dr. Henry M. Morris answered that question with these words:

They are the same saints, dressed in fine white . . . who comprised the armies accompanying Christ as He returned to earth (Revelation 19:8, 14, 19). All those who had been redeemed by His blood, resurrected from the grave, raptured into His presence, and evaluated for their rewards at His judgment seat will apparently be assigned individual thrones of authority and judgment. . . . This remarkable situation is promised in many scriptures, both directly and in parables. "Do ye not know that the saints shall judge the world?" (1 Corinthians 6:2)[4]

As I studied this, I was deeply impressed with 1 Thessalonians 3:13, which speaks of "the coming of our Lord Jesus Christ with all His saints." That seems to imply that when Jesus returns to earth, we'll be in His train, in His wake, accompanying Him as the delegation of His righteous ones. We will accompany Him back to earth and reign with Him here, serving in positions of authority and responsibility. If only we'd think about that a bit more, we'd find ourselves wanting to do nothing that would hinder our daily service for our King! The Lord told us these things to motivate us, to let us know that it will be worth it all when we see Jesus!

One group of people who will have special roles to play are those martyred for their faith during the Tribulation. Revelation 20 says this about the millennial period: "Then I saw the souls of those who had been beheaded for their witness to Jesus and for the word of God, who had not worshiped the beast or his image, and had not received his mark on their foreheads or on their hands. And they lived and reigned with Christ for a thousand years. . . . They shall be priests of God and of Christ, and shall reign with Him a thousand years" (vv. 4, 6).

The Lord will say to all His faithful, blood-bought servants: "Well done and just begun!" Yes, our primary motivation in this life is our love for Jesus and our burden for the souls for whom He died. But God wants us to keep our morale high with great expectations of the future.

Captain D. Michael Abrashoff was only thirty-six years old when he was selected to be the commander of the USS *Benfold*. He became the most junior commanding officer in the US Pacific fleet. When he arrived at his command, Abrashoff immediately perceived that morale was low. The ship had the highest turnover rate in the navy.

Within twelve months, the *Benfold* was ranked number one in performance.

Abrashoff later wrote, "I read some exit surveys . . . conducted by the military to find out why people [were] leaving. I assumed that low pay would be the first reason, but in fact it was fifth. The top reason was not being treated with respect or dignity; second was being prevented from making an impact on the organization; third, not being listened to; and fourth, not being rewarded with more responsibility."[5]

When He comes again, the Lord Jesus Christ—the King of grace and power—will treat His children with respect and dignity; He will bless our impact, listen to us, and reward us with more responsibility.

Your work for the Savior is never finished. It's just beginning!

CHAPTER 13

THE HIGHWAY OF HOLINESS

The Million Dollar Highway is one of the most beautiful drives in America—and one of the deadliest. It twists and turns for about twenty-five miles through the San Juan Mountains of Colorado at elevations reaching eleven thousand feet. The views are spectacular, but there are no railings. Falling rocks and ice sometimes hit cars, and there are occasional avalanches. One travel guide says, "The narrow two-lane road winds through the mountains like a drunk crazily stumbling, and there's no guardrail to protect cars attempting hairpin turns from hurtling into the jagged ravines that lie . . . hundreds of feet below."[1]

When the trail first opened in the late 1800s, wagons, cargo, horses, and humans tumbled over the sides in significant numbers, swept away by falls, snowslides, rockslides, and careless steps. Even today, an average of seven deaths occur each year when motorists run into trouble.

Why is it called the Million Dollar Highway? One local theory is that shortly after it was opened as a toll path, a traveler was so over-come by vertigo from the winding curves that he insisted he would never travel it again, even if he were paid a million dollars.

Well, the Bible talks about a highway that's more beautiful than any other on earth. It reaches heavenly altitudes, and it presents no dangers whatsoever for travelers. It's the Highway of Holiness that will lead travelers to Jerusalem during the coming Golden Age.

The prophet Isaiah included this highway in his description of the millennial kingdom: "They shall see the glory of the LORD, the excellency of our God. . . . Then the eyes of the blind shall be opened, and the ears of the deaf shall be unstopped. Then the lame shall leap like a deer, and the tongue of the dumb sing. For waters shall burst forth in the wilderness, and streams in the desert. . . . A highway shall be there, and a road, and it shall be called the Highway of Holiness" (35:2, 5–6, 8).

During the messianic kingdom, people will travel in a holy envi-ronment, for everything will be transformed by the King who is coming. It will be a holy kingdom.

HOLINESS: WHAT IS IT?

What does it mean to be holy? What does it mean for something, or even someone, to possess the attribute of holiness?

Let's start with a few misconceptions. Many people today, even in the church, make a connection between holiness and haughtiness. They've come to believe being holy means disliking or disdaining everything that is earthly, even other people. Such people often make a show of rejecting the material world in favor of the spiritual plane. That's not holiness. That's a holier-than-thou attitude, and it has caused great damage to the cause of Christ.

Others relate holiness to the somber symbolism of religious ritu-als. In this line of thinking, wearing a specific set of garments makes someone holy. Being washed in a certain way makes objects holy. Being used exclusively for sacred or spiritual purposes makes buildings holy. That's not holiness. That's religiosity. That's the type of external focus that caused Jesus to criticize the Pharisees for polishing the outside while failing to address what's inside—what's in the heart.

"For you are like whitewashed tombs," He told the Pharisees, "which indeed appear beautiful outwardly, but inside are full of dead men's bones and all uncleanness" (Matt. 23:27).

Last, some people assume there's a connection between holiness and the passing of time. In their minds, things become more holy the longer they are around, which is why buildings and objects that have endured for centuries or more take on the mystical label of "sacred." That's not holiness either. That's just oldness. Trust me, I've been around enough people to learn there's no automatic connection between growing older and growing more holy!

What is holiness, then? Simply this: being like God. Being connected with God. In many ways, God Himself is the definition of holiness. *Holiness* and *godliness* are synonyms. A holy person is a godly person, someone who fulfills the apostle Paul's precept: "Put on the new self, *created to be like God* in true righteousness and holiness" (Eph. 4:24 NIV).

Another way of putting it is Christlikeness. Ephesians 4:15 says we should be "growing in every way more and more *like Christ*" (NLT).

This concept is at the heart of the book of Leviticus in the Old Testament. We don't read through Leviticus as often as other books in the Bible, but if we read it carefully, we'd find that holiness is its major theme. For example, we read in Leviticus 11: "For I am the LORD your God. You shall therefore consecrate yourselves, and you shall be holy; for I am holy. Neither shall you defile yourselves with any creeping thing that creeps on the earth. For I am the LORD who brings you up out of the land of Egypt, to be your God. You shall therefore be holy, for I am holy" (vv. 44–45).

As children of God and citizens of His kingdom, we grow in holiness when we submit to Him and live in obedience to His will. True holiness means our hands, our hearts, and our heads belong to God, and our whole desire is to do His work by the power of His Spirit. In the process, we grow to be more like God, become more like Christ, and are set apart for the Lord.

According to J. C. Ryle, "Holiness is the habit of being of one mind with God, according as we find His mind described in Scripture. It is the habit of agreeing in God's judgment—hating what He hates—loving what He loves—and measuring everything in this world by the standard of His Word."[2]

This is the attitude and way of life that will permeate our planet during the coming Golden Age. Holiness will be a universal reality.

HOLINESS: WHO IS IT?

One of the reasons holiness will be so prevalent during the Golden Age is that only holy people will be present. That's because everyone who participates in the dawning of Christ's millennial kingdom will know the Lord.

Let's briefly review the timeline of what's to come on God's prophetic calendar. When Jesus appears at the Rapture, He will call to Himself the souls of all the saints who have passed away. Scripture says, "And the dead in Christ will rise first" (1 Thess. 4:16). In the next instant, Jesus will call to Himself every saint who is alive in that moment. We will "be caught up together with them in the clouds to meet the Lord in the air" (v. 17).

So, at the Rapture, every single believer in Jesus Christ (both living and dead) will be united with Him in the heavenly realm. There, we will avoid the terrors of the Tribulation.

During the Tribulation, however, more people on earth will become followers of Jesus. Many will repent of their rebellion, bow in submission, and confess with their mouths that Jesus Christ is Lord. The terrors of the Tribulation will drive people to Christ, especially under the preaching of the 144,000 evangelists mentioned in Revelation 7. John described these Tribulation converts as "a great multitude which no one could number" (v. 9). Many within that multitude will be martyred because of their faith, which means they will join the raptured saints in the heavenly realm.

Then, at the end of the Tribulation, Christ will return, riding His white horse and proclaiming Himself as the rightful King of kings. In that moment, He will judge and destroy all who have taken the mark of the beast and maintained their rebellion against God.

But Christ will not come alone. He will be joined by all the saints who were caught up together (the dead and the living) at the Rapture, *plus* all those who were martyred during the Tribulation. We will follow Jesus as "the armies in heaven, clothed in fine linen, white and clean" (Rev. 19:14).

When the millennial kingdom begins, then, everyone present on the earth will be saved. Most will possess glorified bodies, while those who confessed Christ during the Tribulation without being killed will still be clothed in their earthly bodies. As Jews and Gentiles, we will take up our place as rulers and servants in the kingdom of God.

Can you imagine a world in which every person in the populace has a saving knowledge of Jesus Christ? No more theological debates. No more religious persecution. No more strife born from directly conflicting worldviews. We will all be washed in the blood of Jesus, which means we will all be holy.

And don't forget—that old serpent, the devil, will be bound and imprisoned during this time, unable to deceive the nations any longer.

The Old Testament prophets foresaw the wonder of such a day. Habakkuk said, "For the earth will be filled with the knowledge of the glory of the LORD, as the waters cover the sea" (2:14).

HOLINESS: WHERE IS IT?

During the Millennium, that sentiment will extend to the entire planet. As we've seen, the earth at that time will be filled with holy people, but the city of Jerusalem will be the central hub of that holiness, and the nation of Israel will be what it has always been called—the Holy Land.

That's a biblical phrase. Zechariah 2:12 says, "And the LORD will take possession of Judah as His inheritance in *the Holy Land,* and will again choose Jerusalem."

In truth, the nation of Israel and its territories have been the scene of evil, wars, tumults, and one battle after another. But when Jesus comes, the land will finally live up to its name.

It will be the Holy Land, and Jerusalem will be the Holy City.

Isaiah wrote, "It shall come to pass that he who is left in Zion and remains in Jerusalem will be called holy—everyone who is recorded among the living in Jerusalem" (4:3).

It won't just be the people who are holy. The prophet Zechariah described how God's glory and holiness will permeate everything in His city, down to the smallest detail: "In that day 'HOLINESS TO THE LORD' shall be engraved on the bells of the horses. The pots in the LORD's house shall be like the bowls before the altar. Yes, every pot in Jerusalem and Judah shall be holiness to the LORD of hosts" (14:20–21).

In short, the millennial kingdom will be a holy kingdom. The King will be holy. The land will be holy. The city will be holy. The temple will be holy. All the subjects of the King will be holy. Holiness will be integrated into everything during the reign of King Jesus.

In a faraway land, a city on a hill was no longer shining. It was filled with violence, crime, immorality, graft, and greed. One day, a holy man walked down the highway and approached the city. The very aura of his presence radiated righteousness. As he entered town, he saw a gang terrorizing a victim. Suddenly the members of the gang dropped their heads, asked for forgiveness, and gave their victim money from their pockets.

The holy man walked down a street filled with trash. As he passed, shopkeepers came out of their stores with brooms, mops, and garbage bags and worked to make their sidewalk glisten. Walking past the hospital, the patients were instantly strengthened and healed. As the man passed by a home filled with fighting, the arguments ended in hugs.

This man's footsteps passed city hall, and within minutes politicians, officials, and judges were confessing their sins and asking one another for forgiveness. Gone was the filthy language. Even the rats in the basement ran out the back door and fled town.

The man continued his walk and passed a school. All the inappropriate material suddenly vanished from the library, and the teachers felt impressed to pray with their students. Next to the school was a vacant lot, and as the man passed by, it immediately turned into a garden of lovely flowers, shaded trees, and playground equipment for the children.

Everywhere this man went the power of his influence repelled the darkness and ushered in a cleanness, a cheerfulness, and a sense of holiness the city had never known. The city and its people would never be the same.

Wouldn't you like to live in a city or in a world where this man's dynamism radiated that kind of supernatural holiness?

This isn't a fairy tale or a parable. It's my way of helping us visualize something of what the world will be like when the Holy Son of God returns and sets up His kingdom.

During the messianic kingdom, people will breathe the pure air of a holy environment, for everything will be transformed by King Jesus.

But we must not forget that right now, at this very moment, we are God's holy children, washed in the blood of Christ and set apart for Him. The apostle Paul said, "He chose us in Him before the foundation of the world, that we should be holy and without blame before Him in love" (Eph. 1:4).

How important to act like it, empowered by the Holy Spirit.

Romans 12:1 says, "I beseech you therefore, brethren, by the mercies of God, that you present your bodies a living sacrifice, holy, acceptable to God."

The Bible says that God has "saved us and called us with a holy calling" (2 Tim. 1:9). One day the entire world will be holy; but for now the only examples of holiness the world can see are men and women who are growing more godly and more Christlike.

CHAPTER 14

OLD AGE IN THE GOLDEN AGE

They call her "Super Grandmother." At 117 years of age, she's the oldest living woman in the world. Maria Branyas was born in San Francisco in March 1907. When her father's health declined in 1915, her family moved back to their home region of Catalonia, Spain, where Maria has remained for more than a century.

Incredibly, Maria does not get sick. In her words, "I have not suffered from any illness or been through an operating room." She has no trace of cardiovascular disease commonly found in elderly people, nor has she suffered any memory loss or decline in cognitive function. In fact, she can vividly recount memories in great detail from when she was four years old. Aside from some slight hearing loss and mobility issues, she is in wonderful health even at 117 years old.

For Maria's part, she credits her longevity to a simple life and the daily consumption of natural yogurt. More specifically, she has benefited from "order, tranquility, good connection with family and friends, contact with nature, emotional stability, lots of positivity and [staying] away from toxic people."

As you might expect, many have taken notice of Maria's incredible combination of longevity and vitality. That includes world-renowned geneticist and researcher Dr. Manel Esteller, who is leading a study to analyze six billion segments of Maria's DNA, focusing on hundreds of genes connected with the aging process. His goal is to develop treatments that can address degenerative diseases in our neurological and cardiovascular systems that are currently associated with old age.[1]

I certainly hope Dr. Esteller and many other researchers are successful at improving the aging process for all people, myself included. But I'm afraid that's the best we can hope for in the near future—improvement. No matter who we study or what treatments we develop, our lives on this earth will continue to be measured in decades, not centuries.

What about the age to come? Is it reasonable for us to hope that lifespans will increase in Christ's millennial kingdom?

Yes! It's more than reasonable, and we can more than hope. We can believe in the historical testimony of God's Word, we can rely on the incredible authority demonstrated by Jesus during His earthly ministry, and we can accept in faith the inspiring promises God has already given us for that glorious Golden Age.

Remember, there will be two groups of people inhabiting the planet during the Millennium. One group will consist of Old Testament saints, raptured believers, and those martyred during the Tribulation. That group will possess heavenly bodies, which means our longevity will be everlasting. We'll dwell with Christ for a thousand years, then enter the new heaven and new earth with Him to dwell forever. No more death for us! Nor sickness or sin. No more pain or pining away.

The second group will include those who were saved and who survived to the end of the Tribulation, plus any children they produce during the Millennium. These people will still have earthly bodies, but they will experience the kind of longevity reminiscent of the early days of Genesis, which I'll discuss shortly.

THE REDUCTION OF LONGEVITY

When God created the human race, He had eternity in mind. Death had no part of the original creation. Death is the result of sin and disobedience. But God has put eternity in our hearts (Eccl. 3:11), and even after the fall—even after Adam and Eve sinned—humans lived for vast periods of time.

The oldest man in the Genesis record is Methuselah, who lived to the ripe old age of 969 years—almost a full millennium (5:27). But Methuselah wasn't the only example of extreme vitality recorded in God's Word. He wasn't even an outlier:

- Adam lived for 930 years (Gen. 5:5).
- Seth lived for 912 years (v. 8).
- Jared, Adam's great-great-great-grandson, lived to be 962 (v. 20).
- Lamech, the father of Noah, was 777 when he passed away (v. 31).
- Noah, who was 600 years old when God flooded the earth, lived for another 350 years after that flood. He died when he was 950 (9:29).

What are we to make of these numbers? Are they exaggerations intended to show the great stature of these great men? Are they the result of mishaps in translation? Are they intended to be symbolic in some way?

I don't think so. When it comes to Scripture, it has always been my firm belief that we should take God at His Word. Meaning, when the Bible speaks in plain language and offers a commonsense explanation for its claims, we should accept it. In this case, Genesis presents these extended ages as historical information, and we should understand them as such.

But Dr. Jeremiah, you might ask, *how would it be possible for human beings to live so long?*

We can't say for sure, but there are many possible explanations. Perhaps the climate of the earth was so different in those early days that it allowed for increased longevity. Some believe there was a vapor barrier or canopy around the earth that made our atmosphere more conducive to long life—something akin to the ozone layer. Maybe this canopy collapsed or dissipated during the flood. Maybe something completely different is responsible.

Perhaps the genetic pool was so young that people were more vigorous. Perhaps the grace of God was so fresh that His children lived for many centuries.

What the book of Genesis does make clear is that something changed after Noah's flood. Not only was the physical structure of our planet altered in major ways, but the span of human lives decreased significantly. Shem, one of Noah's sons, lived for 600 years (Gen. 11:10–11). But Shem's grandson, Salah, only lived 433 years (vv. 14–15). Terah, who was Abraham's father, only lived 205 years before he died in Haran (v. 32).

In Genesis 6:3, God adjusted the human lifespan from centuries to decades, writing, "My Spirit shall not strive with man forever, for he is indeed flesh; yet his days shall be one hundred and twenty years."

The cycles of human life continued to decline until Moses declared, "The days of our lives are seventy years; and if by reason of strength they are eighty years, yet their boast is only labor and sorrow; for it is soon cut off and we fly away" (Ps. 90:10).

Pastor and author John Piper wrote about this:

My suggestion is that God granted those long lives so that we, looking back, could see from which we have fallen. In other words, those long lives testify that death was not part of the perfect creation. God ordains as a lesson to us that the force of life be preserved for hundreds of years in very long lives in those early centuries to show that life, not death, was his design and our portion in creation at the beginning. So, the long lives of those first humans stand as a testimony of how utterly short our lives are and how God's design at the beginning and his design in the future is life—eternal life.[2]

I have one other thought about it. Perhaps it is the mercy and grace of God that reduces the amount of time we have to spend in this vale of tears we call the earth. Life is hard, and this world is a war zone for the soul. As Job said, "Yet man is born to trouble, as the sparks fly upward" (5:7).

Isaiah 57:1 is a fascinating verse: "Good people pass away; the godly often die before their time. But no one seems to care or wonder why. No one seems to understand that God is protecting them from the evil to come" (NLT).

THE RESTORATION OF LONGEVITY

Praise the Lord!—things will be different in the Millennium. The devil will be bound, the earth will again become the healthiest environment we could imagine for human life, and God will again extend the lifespans of the men and women who come out of the Tribulation and their children.

Christ will be the center of the millennial kingdom, ruling on the throne of His ancestor David in Jerusalem. His power and authority will radiate throughout that kingdom for the benefit of all its citizens. On a spiritual level, that means the Lamb of God will repair the effects of sin and Satan in our world. He will restore what was lost and reclaim the original intent of our Creator for His creation.

On a practical level, that means our physical bodies will no longer reflect the consequences of sin. We will no longer deal with the kinds of physical problems the world faces now.

Jesus gave us a preview of His power and authority during His life and public ministry more than two thousand years ago. There were many moments when His kingly nature broke through and He asserted His authority over sin and sickness and death.

Take a brief look at just one of those miracles: "It happened when He was in a certain city, that behold, a man who was full of leprosy saw Jesus; and he fell on his face and implored Him, saying, 'Lord, if You are willing, You can make me clean'" (Luke 5:12).

Leprosy was the most feared of all afflictions in ancient times. Not only was there no cure, but lepers died slowly from the continually escalating degradation of their bodies. Worse still, lepers were not allowed to be part of the community. They were cut off. Segregated. Isolated.

Can you hear the pain in this man's words when he begged Jesus for healing? "You can make me clean!" Jesus responded not as the sacrificial Lamb of God but as the Great Physician: "He put out His hand and touched him, saying, 'I am willing; be cleansed.' Immediately the leprosy left him" (v. 13).

In the Millennium, Christ will do for all what He did for the sick and handicapped in the Gospels. He will remove sickness, deformities, and disabilities. In the coming Golden Age, there will be no blindness, deafness, or muteness—no need for eyeglasses, hearing aids, speech therapy, wheelchairs, or crutches.

We have that promise from the Old Testament prophets:

- "In that day, the deaf shall hear the words of the book, and the eyes of the blind shall see out of obscurity and out of darkness" (Isa. 29:18).
- "Then the eyes of the blind shall be opened, and the ears of the deaf shall be unstopped. Then the lame shall leap like a deer, and the tongue of the dumb sing" (35:5–6).
- "I will restore health to you and heal you of your wounds" (Jer. 30:17).

During the thousand-year reign of Christ, sickness and death will not exist among the resurrected saints. Among the survivors of the Tribulation—those who still possess earthly bodies—it will be a rare occurrence.

THE REDEMPTION OF LONGEVITY

In 1900, the average life expectancy of a United States citizen was just forty-seven years. For more than a century, that number increased, reaching its peak around 2019, when the life expectancy for a US citizen was almost seventy-nine years. Quite an improvement! But that number dropped dramatically during and after the COVID-19 pandemic. As of 2021, the average life expectancy was only seventy-six years.[3]

Despite the best efforts of our medical experts, there is little chance any of us will become another Methuselah. But all of that will change during the Millennium. In that age, human longevity will return to pre-flood levels. Even better, the lives of the redeemed who rule this world with Christ will return to pre-fall levels. We will once again live forever!

It is as though history will come full circle. The quantity and quality of our years will once again reveal the goodness of our Creator and reflect His infallible design.

This is how Isaiah described life in the Millennium: "Never again will there be in it an infant who lives but a few days, or an old man who does not live out his years; the one who dies at a hundred will be thought a mere child; the one who fails to reach a hundred will be considered accursed" (65:20 NIV).

In the words of Alva J. McClain, "Disease will be abolished. . . . The crisis of death will be experienced only by those incorrigible individuals who rebel against the laws of the kingdom. The ordinary hazards of physical life will be under the direct control of One whose voice even the winds and the waves obey."[4]

Time magazine recently ran a profile called "The Man Who Thinks He Can Live Forever." That man is Bryan Johnson, a tech multimillionaire who has spent more than $4 million developing a life-extension system called Blueprint.

Johnson's goal is to claim victory over death—not only his own death but also the specter of death that haunts humanity. He believes death is a choice we accept rather than a reality we cannot avoid.

In order to prevent death, Johnson goes through a rigorous daily routine designed to de-age his organs. Prescribed by a team of doctors and run through an artificial-intelligence algorithm, that routine includes taking 111 pills every day, wearing a baseball cap that shoots red light into his scalp, collecting his own stool samples, ruthlessly monitoring his sleep, completely avoiding all unhealthy foods, applying eyedrops to prevent cataracts, daily workouts, and much more.

"I don't think there's been any time in history where Homo sapiens could say with a straight face that death may not be inevitable," says Johnson. "Until now."[5]

Of course, you and I know Bryan Johnson is both very wrong and very right. No human being alive today can prevent death through diet or exercise or supplements or any other routine. At the same time, Johnson's primary impulse—his vision that humans are meant to experience more than a few meager decades—is on the right track.

Sometimes I think old age is only an illusion for those with eternal life. How can we grow old when we're going to live forever? Believe me, I know about the aches, pains, and infirmities that come with time. Outwardly we are perishing, but inwardly we are being renewed day by day. Yet the suffering of this present age is nothing compared to the glory awaiting us.

The Millennium is where we will begin to experience our true destiny—our true design. Through the power of our Lord Jesus, and under the authority of His reign, our lives will stretch into the centuries with only the promise of paradise on the horizon.

CHAPTER 15

GLORY

"Phenomenal experience! . . . It's tough to describe how amazing it looks and feels."

"This was an absolutely mind-blowing experience."

"Attending this show was one of the greatest experiences of my life."

"Wow. Wow. Wow. . . . Mind blowing. Overwhelming. Hard to describe."

"This is almost for sure the best show in the history of the world."[1]

These are just a few selections from among the thousands of Google reviews celebrating the launch of what may be the most anticipated entertainment venue in history. I'm talking about the Sphere, which officially opened in Las Vegas near the end of 2023.

If you haven't seen it, the Sphere is exactly that: a huge technological globe that almost seems dropped into the Las Vegas desert from outer space. Actually, it's two spheres when you count the exterior and the interior. The outer sphere, called the Exosphere, is basically a 580,000-square-foot LED display that can produce more than 250 million colors.

But the interior of the Sphere is where the real magic happens. That screen encompasses 160,000 square feet of 16,000 x 16,000 resolution, making it the highest-resolution LED screen on the planet. (A normal HD TV offers 1,920 x 1,080 resolution, which means the Sphere is ten times sharper and clearer, but on a huge scale.) As a stadium, the Sphere is 366 feet tall by 516 feet wide, with a standing room capacity of about 20,000 people. It can host concerts, movies, sporting events, and more.[2]

In short, the Sphere may be the closest humanity has come to inventing something that can evoke the feeling of awe. Or wonder.

Or glory.

That's an interesting word: *glory*. In the Scriptures, that term is almost always connected with God. The Bible teaches that God Himself is glorious—it's part of His nature—and that His glory is communicated to us whenever He manifests Himself in our world. Importantly, God's glory is often expressed in visible ways. It is something tangible; something that can be seen, felt, and experienced.

As you might expect, glory will be a central pillar of the coming Golden Age. Christ will be physically present with us as King, and His glory will radiate throughout the world in ways humanity has never experienced.

I want to explore that future reality together, but let's start by gaining a little context from the past and the present.

ISRAEL: GOD'S GLORY REVEALED

What is God's glory? What do we mean when we talk about "the glory of the Lord"? More importantly, what does Scripture mean when it describes that glory? We can get an interesting answer to those questions by looking at a particular encounter between Moses and God after the Israelites were rescued from Egypt but before they entered the promised land.

Alone on Mount Sinai, standing in the presence of God, Moses made an audacious request: "Please, show me Your glory" (Ex. 33:18). Amazingly, incredibly, God said yes:

Now the LORD descended in the cloud and stood with him there, and proclaimed the name of the LORD. And the LORD passed before him and proclaimed, "The LORD, the LORD God, merciful and gracious, longsuffering, and abounding in goodness and truth, keeping mercy for thousands, forgiving iniquity and transgression and sin, by no means clearing the guilty, visiting the iniquity of the fathers upon the children and the children's children to the third and the fourth generation." (34:5–7)

Everything God declared to Moses in that moment is part of His glory. God's mercy and grace are glorious. His goodness and truth are glorious. His justice and power are glorious. Every aspect of God's nature and character radiates a magnificence and a splendor that combines together to form the essence of God's glory.

Remember when I said God's glory is physical and tangible? Well, look what happened to Moses after he became saturated in that glory: "Now it was so, when Moses came down from Mount Sinai (and the two tablets of the Testimony were in Moses' hand when he came down from the mountain), that Moses did not know that the skin of his face shone while he talked with Him. So when Aaron and all the children of Israel saw Moses, behold, the skin of his face shone, and they were afraid to come near him" (vv. 29–30).

Moses was transformed by his exposure to God's glory. It changed him in a profound way.

That's what was supposed to happen with the nation of Israel as a whole. The Jewish people were chosen by God for the express purpose of revealing God to the nations. They were supposed to soak up God's glory by means of their special connection with Him—including the revelation of God's law—and then convey that glory to the rest of the world through their lives, through their worship, and through the culture they established as children of God.

As we know from reading the Old Testament, Israel failed in her mission. Even so, God continued to reveal His glory in different ways and to different groups throughout the centuries:

- When Moses completed construction of the tabernacle: "Then the cloud covered the tabernacle of meeting, and the glory of the LORD filled the tabernacle. And Moses was not able to enter the tabernacle of meeting, because the cloud rested above it, and the glory of the LORD filled the tabernacle" (Ex. 40:34–35).
- When Solomon dedicated the first temple: "And it came to pass, when the priests came out of the holy place, that the cloud filled the house of the LORD, so that the priests could not continue ministering because of the cloud; for the glory of the LORD filled the house of the LORD" (1 Kings 8:10–11).
- When God called Ezekiel to serve as a prophet: "And above the firmament over their heads was the likeness of a throne, in appearance like a sapphire stone; on the likeness of the throne was a likeness with the appearance of a man high above it. Also from the appearance of His waist and upward I saw, as it were, the color of amber with the appearance of fire all around within it; and from the appearance of His waist and downward I saw, as it were, the appearance of fire with brightness all around. Like the appearance of a rainbow in a cloud on a rainy day, so was the appearance of the brightness all around it. This was the appearance of the likeness of the glory of the LORD" (Ezek. 1:26–28).

Over and over, God revealed His glory to the children of Israel. Over and over, they failed to accept or acknowledge the gravity of that revelation.

Thankfully, that's not the end of the story.

THE CHURCH: GOD'S GLORY REFLECTED

God's glory was first revealed to Israel, but they are not the only group privileged to encounter that glory or to extend it. Ever since the death and resurrection of Jesus Christ, those who place their faith in Him—namely, all who are part of the church—have been called to reflect His glory to the world.

In 2 Corinthians 3, Paul used Moses' encounter with God's glory to illustrate the way Christians are called to reflect God's glory: "But if the ministry of death, written and engraved on stones, was glorious, so that the children of Israel could not look steadily at the face of Moses because of the glory of his countenance, which glory was passing away, how will the ministry of the Spirit not be more glorious?" (vv. 7–8).

The "ministry of death" refers to the Old Testament law, which Moses received "on stones." The "ministry of the Spirit" is the gospel of salvation through faith in Jesus Christ—the message all Christians are called to carry into the world.

Moving into the next section of the chapter, Paul noted the way Moses "put a veil over his face" (v. 13) because of the Israelites' fear. The glory of God was veiled when communicated through the Law, which leads to death. But that glory has been unveiled through the death and resurrection of Jesus Christ, which leads us to life.

In Paul's words, "But we all, with unveiled face, beholding as in a mirror the glory of the Lord, are being transformed into the same image from glory to glory, just as by the Spirit of the Lord" (v. 18).

Remember, exposure to God's glory is transformative. It changes us. As Christians, we have received God's glory through the indwelling of the Holy Spirit in our hearts. We have become little tabernacles, or little temples (1 Cor. 3:16), in which God's glory is manifest. Through that same Spirit, then, we can reflect that glory where it is needed within our families, our communities, and our nations.

This is how we fulfill the words of Jesus: "You are the light of the world. A city that is set on a hill cannot be hidden. Nor do they light a lamp and put it under a basket, but on a lampstand, and it gives light to all who are in the house. Let your light so shine before men, that they may see your good works and glorify your Father in heaven" (Matt. 5:14–16).

Those of us who make up the church are like the citizens of Rjukan, Norway. For several months a year, Rjukan does not receive direct sunlight. The sun rises each day, but it does not elevate above the mountains that surround the town—which means its residents lived in a shadowy gloom for much of the winter season.

I wrote "lived" there because something has changed. In 2013, the town council sponsored the construction of three mirrors, each about seventeen square meters, near the top of the mountain above the town. Those mirrors function as a solar-powered heliostat. Meaning, they track with the path of the sun each day and reflect its rays down into the town.[3]

After centuries of darkness, the people of Rjukan received the gift of light!

In a similar way, we as the church are called to reflect the warmth and power of God's glory into the darkness of our world.

THE MILLENNIUM: GOD'S GLORY RADIANT

You may be wondering, *What do Israel and the church have to do with the coming Golden Age?* The answer is that the same glory revealed to Israel in the past and reflected by the church today will become radiant in the future millennial kingdom.

The difference between those times and this future time will be the dramatic increase in God's direct, physical presence in our world. In the ancient world, the manifestations of God's glory were largely localized with the nation of Israel and specifically within the tabernacle and the temple; that's where His name dwelled. In the church age, God's glory has been dispersed and reflected throughout the world through the presence of the Holy Spirit. But during the coming Golden Age, our planet will be suffused by the incarnate glory of God through the continuing physical presence of Christ our King.

Jesus will be the central pillar of the millennial kingdom, and that pillar will shine like the sun at the center of our solar system.

The prophet Isaiah wrote about this future manifestation of glory more than any other biblical author. "Then the moon will be disgraced and the sun ashamed," he prophesied, "for the LORD of hosts will reign on Mount Zion and in Jerusalem and before His elders, gloriously" (24:23).

The same prophet later declared, "Arise, shine; for your light has come! And the glory of the LORD is risen upon you. For behold, the darkness shall cover the earth, and deep darkness the people; but the LORD will arise over you, and His glory will be seen upon you. . . . Then you shall see and become radiant, and your heart shall swell with joy" (60:1–2, 5).

As mentioned earlier, a great portion of God's visible glory will be concentrated in the remade city of Jerusalem, which will be raised up as a high mountain at the second coming. Christ will inhabit that city, filling it with His glory. The temple will be present in that city, again manifesting the glory of God's presence and the greatness of His name.

But God's glory will not be limited to Jerusalem. It will saturate our world and radiate outward through the lives of every citizen in Christ's earthly kingdom. In the words of Habakkuk, "The earth will be filled with the knowledge of the glory of the LORD, as the waters cover the sea" (2:14).

You and I will experience that glory. There will no longer be such a thing as a "normal day." Instead, our entire world will be saturated with the glory of God.

Even now, in Christ we are enveloped in an atmosphere of glory. Don't take that for granted! The psalmist referred to God as "My glory and the One who lifts up my head" (Ps. 3:3). The apostle Paul said, "He who glories, let him glory in the LORD" (1 Cor. 1:31). Whether we eat or drink, or whatever we do, we're to do it for the glory of God (10:31).

We rejoice in the glory of God. But even more so, we will revel in the golden glory of the Millennium even as we carry out the most mundane of tasks—from folding laundry to pruning our garden to taking an afternoon stroll. Everything we encounter will be suffused by the light of God's radiant glory.

Speaking of radiance, I can't think of many natural occurrences in our world today more visually spectacular than a sunrise. And I think it's interesting that a very select group of individuals have experienced that phenomenon in a way different from everyone else in human history.

Back in 1943, the Royal Australian Air Force began operating a weekly flight between Perth, Australia, and Ceylon—the island nation now known as Sri Lanka—in the Indian Ocean, which was a heavily fortified British colony at that time. These flights were part of a larger effort to reconnect London with Australia via the airways after Japanese forces captured Singapore during World War II.

What's most interesting about these weekly flights is that they typically lasted between twenty-seven and thirty-three hours of direct flight time. Specialized "Catalina" airplanes took off from Australia in the dark hours before dawn and landed more than a full day later. For that reason, those flights were named the "Double Sunrise" operation—because those on board the aircraft had the privilege of witnessing two glorious sunrises over the ocean horizon.

Not many people enjoyed that privilege. Each flight could only carry up to three passengers because of the massive fuel requirements, and there were very few pilots qualified to endure such long spans of airtime. There are only a few dozen individuals in human history who have remained airborne for more than twenty-four hours—and almost all of them were on "Double Sunrise" flights. Therefore, every person who took part in those flights was given a special certificate and inaugurated as a member of the "Secret Order of the Double Sunrise."[4]

What a title! In many ways, those of us in the church make up our own secret order. We've experienced the glory and wonder of salvation through Jesus Christ as individuals, which is an incredible blessing. But we also look forward to that future moment when we will experience that glory and that wonder on a global setting—the setting of the coming Golden Age.

Let's never forget our privileged status as we live and work and minister during this current age. And let's never stop looking forward to that future sunrise when Christ returns and reasserts His rightful place as King!

CHAPTER 16

JUSTICE

On the last night of his life, Senior Airman Roger Fortson was alone in his apartment near Fort Walton Beach, Florida. He was on the phone with a friend when he heard a knock on his apartment door. It was late. Fortson wasn't expecting visitors. He put down the phone and picked up his weapon.

Outside the door was an officer from the Okaloosa County Sheriff's Department. Someone in the apartment complex had called the police to report a domestic disturbance, and the officer had arrived at Fortson's apartment to investigate.

According to bodycam footage, the officer knocked on the door, then paused. He knocked again more loudly, announcing, "Sheriff's Department." Still no answer. The officer shifted to the other side of the door and knocked more loudly still, once again saying, "Sheriff's Department, open the door."

That's when Roger Fortson did open the door. He was holding his weapon pointed down at the floor. He did not get a chance to speak.

Seeing the gun, the officer cried, "Step back!" In the same moment, he fired his weapon at Fortson several times.

Only after Airman Fortson hit the ground did the officer shout, "Drop the gun!"

The medical examiner later reported that Fortson was shot six times. The young soldier was pronounced dead at the local hospital.

He was twenty-three years old.[1]

What can we say about such a tragedy? Such a waste of a young and valuable life? Our first reaction typically is to assign blame, which forces us to grapple with difficult questions. On the one hand, should Airman Fortson have carried his weapon to the door? Did he hear the officer announce himself? On the other hand, shouldn't a citizen— especially a member of the US Air Force—have the right to bear arms in his own home? Shouldn't the officer have given this young man the chance to drop his weapon before opening fire?

These questions demand the kind of answers that are difficult to find. Worse, it's not really answers we are looking for in such moments because answers don't solve anything. Answers don't relieve our pain or return what we've lost.

What we're really looking for is justice. We want the wrongs we're carrying to be made right. We want our hardships to be resolved so that we can let go of our heavy load of grief and move forward.

Sometimes it seems like there's nothing we can do about injustice— which may be correct. There's often very little we can do. Thankfully, there is always something God can do. He is the standard of justice in our world today—although that standard is often circumvented by sinful choices.

When we reach the coming Golden Age, however, our King will set all things right. He will establish perfect justice for a thousand years.

THE SOURCE OF MILLENNIAL JUSTICE

Justice is one of the attributes that make up God's nature and character. In the same way that God is loving, merciful, and gracious,

He is also just. For that reason, justice is a key theme in Scripture. Specifically, justice is part of the foundation God established for the nation of Israel.

"You shall appoint judges and officers in all your gates, which the LORD your God gives you, according to your tribes, and they shall judge the people with just judgment," God declared through His servant Moses. "You shall not pervert justice; you shall not show partiality, nor take a bribe, for a bribe blinds the eyes of the wise and twists the words of the righteous. You shall follow what is altogether just, that you may live and inherit the land which the LORD your God is giving you" (Deut. 16:18–20).

This was the expectation for God's chosen people. They were commanded to be purveyors of justice within their own community and also in all their dealings with the outside world.

Yet the Israelites failed to administer justice according to God's command. The kings, priests, and other leaders chose to oppress the people rather than work on their behalf. As a result, the community of Israel became a place of idolatry, corruption, and injustice of all kinds.

God sent prophets and other messengers to call His people back toward justice, including the prophet Zechariah, who wrote, "Thus says the LORD of hosts: 'Execute true justice, show mercy and compassion everyone to his brother. Do not oppress the widow or the fatherless, the alien or the poor. Let none of you plan evil in his heart against his brother'" (7:9–10). Those warnings failed, resulting in the conquest of Israel and Judah.

The issue was that sinful human beings were responsible for the administration of justice. They failed, despite God's continual warnings and instructions in Scripture.

What will be different about the coming Golden Age? Simply that human beings will no longer be primarily responsible for the administration of justice during God's millennial kingdom. Jesus Christ will establish justice on earth—and He will maintain that justice from His throne for a thousand years.

Here is how the prophet Jeremiah framed that promise: "'Behold, the days are coming,' says the LORD, 'that I will raise to David a Branch of righteousness; a King shall reign and prosper, and execute judgment and righteousness in the earth'" (23:5).

Jesus Himself will cement and sustain a system of justice in our world. He will be our sole source of justice for a thousand years.

THE SINCERITY OF MILLENNIAL JUSTICE

When Adele Andaloro's parents passed away, she inherited their house in the town of Flushing, New York. Because of the location, the home was valued at over a million dollars, and Andaloro decided to sell.

In the middle of that process, however, she encountered a group of strangers living in the home she had inherited. They were squatters, and they claimed to have signed a lease giving them access to the property, although they were unable to produce any documentation supporting that claim. Despite Ms. Andaloro's protests, the squatters refused to leave. They even went so far as to replace the door on the home and change the locks.

Fed up, Ms. Andaloro called the police, who successfully escorted two of the squatters off the property. Then she called a locksmith—which ended up being a mistake.

A man named Brian Rodriguez forced his way into the home while Ms. Andaloro and her daughter were still inside. The police were called once more, but this time the result was different. Apparently, it is illegal in New York state for landlords to cut utilities, change locks, or remove the property of someone who claims to be a tenant. By making such a claim after Ms. Andaloro changed the locks, Rodriguez accused her of unlawful eviction.

Incredibly, Adele Andaloro was arrested. She was taken into custody for occupying the home she owned and changing the locks so that invaders could no longer access her property. Even more incredibly, she's not the only one! The phenomenon known as "squatter's rights" has become a major problem in New York, California, and several other states where the process of evicting even an illegal tenant can now take up to twenty months.

"It's not fair that I, as the homeowner, have to be going through this," Adele Andaloro said. "I'm really fearful that these people are going to get away with stealing my home."[2]

There are not many examples of injustice more flagrant than a homeowner being arrested for trying to prevent vagrants and thieves from stealing her property. But such is the world we live in. We have police forces in every community. We have courts and lawyers and legal think tanks. We have an entire Department of Justice that should be focused entirely on seeing justice be done!

Yet justice escapes us.

Not so in the Millennium. When Christ the King is enthroned in Jerusalem, He will ensure that justice is extended to every member of His kingdom. Every single person will have access to true, practical, genuine justice.

"They shall build houses and inhabit them," wrote Isaiah about the coming Golden Age. "They shall plant vineyards and eat their fruit. They shall not build and another inhabit; they shall not plant and another eat; for as the days of a tree, so shall be the days of My people, and My elect shall long enjoy the work of their hands. They shall not labor in vain, nor bring forth children for trouble; for they shall be the descendants of the blessed of the LORD, and their offspring with them" (65:21–23).

Justice will no longer be an exclusive privilege for the privileged. All will be treated fairly. All will receive the blessings of their own work and the sincerity of a system that works on their behalf.

Take a moment to imagine living in a world where heavenly justice is the standard, not the exception. Imagine knowing for certain that your government is treating you fairly and equitably. No questionable taxes. No political policies that prop up the "haves" and push down the "have-nots." No more mortgaging future generations in order to prop up ridiculous programs.

This is the world that awaits us in Christ's millennial kingdom. A world of perfect peace because it is founded on perfect justice.

THE SWORD OF MILLENNIAL JUSTICE

The coming Golden Age will be a thousand-year period marked by the character of Jesus Christ—including His justice. Our Lord will be both the Source and Sustainer of that justice. Therefore, the Millennium will be a time of genuine justice for all people in all places.

In order for our King to achieve that kind of justice, it seems logical that He will need to employ quite a lot of force. After all, that's the way our best attempts at justice have been established throughout human history. Kingships, empires, and governments have wielded the sword in order to maintain law and order.

Yet that will not be the case during the Millennium. When describing the coming Golden Age in another prophecy, Isaiah indicated that King Jesus will not secure His rule with thunder or threats. Instead, He will maintain justice as a gentle ruler:

Behold! My Servant whom I uphold, My Elect One in whom My soul delights! I have put My Spirit upon Him; He will bring forth justice to the Gentiles. He will not cry out, nor raise His voice, nor cause His voice to be heard in the street. A bruised reed He will not break, and smoking flax He will not quench; He will bring forth justice for truth. He will not fail nor be discouraged, till He has established justice in the earth; and the coastlands shall wait for His law. (42:1–4)

How could Jesus establish true justice during the Millennium without a strong show of force? I think there are three solid explanations.

First, remember that only followers of Jesus will be present on earth at the beginning of the thousand-year reign of Christ. The Tribulation will wipe out much of our human population, and Jesus' judgment against evil at His second coming will remove all who maintained their rebellion against Him throughout the Tribulation. Therefore, the Millennium will begin with a full complement of kingdom citizens who have been transformed by the grace and blood of Jesus.

Second, not only will unbelievers be removed from our world, but so will Satan and all his demons. They will be locked away in the abyss for a thousand years. Consequently, people will not be forced to deal with the temptation, corruption, and chaos of the Enemy. People will still make mistakes and even sin, yet the manifest presence of the Holy Spirit will steer all parties toward resolution and restitution.

Third, Jesus will not have to be heavy-handed during the Millennium because the next stage in human history—the stage that will take place after the Millennium—will bring about a final judgment for all who reject God's love. That phase is called the great white throne judgment, and we will explore it more deeply in a later chapter. But the crux of the matter is that all who refuse God's plan (including their own salvation) will experience the consequences of that rejection with finality. Therefore, our King can be patient during the Golden Age.

Leonard Mack has a special understanding of that kind of patience. Back in 1976, Mack was accused of raping a young woman in the town of Greenburgh, New York. Police pulled him over while he was driving through the neighborhood. Despite a lack of evidence—Mack was wearing a completely different outfit than what the girls described and had an alibi for his whereabouts at the time of the attack—he was arrested. Then convicted. Then jailed.

Leonard Mack served a full term in prison for that crime, then attempted to restart his life in South Carolina.

His breakthrough finally came in 2023, which was forty-seven years after his conviction. Lawyers convinced the Justice Department to perform a review of Mack's cause using new DNA technology. Those tests proved Mack's innocence. They also identified the true perpetrator, who had a long and sordid criminal record.

"I never lost hope that one day that I would be proven innocent," Mack told reporters after the hearing. "Now the truth has come to light and I can finally breathe. I am finally free."[3]

Nobody should have to wait forty-seven years to receive justice. Not victims, and certainly not those wrongfully accused and unjustly convicted. We have a long way to go in our society to achieve a more workable system of justice. But followers of Jesus can be comforted with the knowledge that our experience in the coming Golden Age will include a thousand years of perfect justice through the perfect rule of our Lord and Savior Jesus Christ!

We can also be comforted by something else. Even now, if you've been the object of injustice, if you've been abused or exploited in some way, remember that Jesus is even now reigning as Judge. When we can't make things right on our own, we can refer the case to Him. Romans 12:19 has this advice for anyone who has been taken advantage of: "Beloved, do not avenge yourselves, but rather give place to wrath; for it is written, 'Vengeance is Mine, I will repay,' says the Lord."

CHAPTER 17

THE END OF WAR

Vladimir Putin called it a "special military operation." The rest of the world called it the largest ground invasion in Europe since World War II.

In the early hours of February 24, 2022, explosions erupted across Ukraine, including in the cities of Odessa, Kharkiv, Mariupol, and Kyiv. Russian airborne forces descended by the thousands, quickly amassing at the Hostomel Airport outside the capital. Ground forces also poured into Ukraine by the hundreds of thousands from Russia and Belarus.

Speaking on Russian national television, Putin offered many justifications for his "operation," and he warned other nations that interfering with his plans would lead to "consequences you have never seen."[1]

The first eighteen months of full-scale war between Russia and Ukraine resulted in nearly five hundred thousand soldiers wounded or killed on both sides.[2] According to the United Nations Refugee Agency, more than three million civilians have been displaced in Ukraine, with more than six million more refugees forced to flee into neighboring nations across Europe and the globe. Almost fifteen million Ukrainians require humanitarian assistance, including those without proper access to food.[3]

Russian civilians have also fared poorly during the war. Many husbands and fathers have been lost. International sanctions have negatively impacted the Russian economy, making life difficult for families. Fear and anxiety are rampant.

These are the consequences of the terrible reality we call war.

Will we ever be able to escape that reality? Is it possible for our world to experience an extended period of peace?

So far, the odds have not been in our favor. Scholars estimate that over the last 3,400 years, there have been only 268 years of peace. Meaning, for more than 92 percent of human history, we have been forced to endure the specter of war.[4]

In more recent history, things have become even worse! Even a "peaceful" nation such as the United States has endured two world wars, a Cold War, the Korean War, the Vietnam War, two wars involving Iraq, the war in Afghanistan, the war on terror, and more.

The Bible explains why war is so prevalent in our world, but the reason is not encouraging: "Where do wars and fights come from among you? Do they not come from your desires for pleasure that war in your members? You lust and do not have. You murder and covet and cannot obtain. You fight and war" (James 4:1–2).

The fallen heart of humanity explains why we fail at peace. But will that always be true?

A WORLD OF WAR

During World War I, C. S. Lewis was sent to the front lines of France late in 1917. After a few weeks, he was hospitalized with a bout of trench fever. When he was discharged from the hospital, he immediately returned to the front lines, where two months later he was wounded in three places by an exploding shell that killed the sergeant standing next to him.

Not surprisingly, Lewis carried those experiences with him for the rest of his life. When World War II arrived, he wrote:

> My memories of the last war haunted my dreams for years. Military service, to be plain, includes the threat of every temporal evil: pain and death which is what we fear from sickness: isolation from those we love which is what we fear from exile: toil under arbitrary masters, injustice and humiliation, which is what we fear from slavery: hunger, thirst, and exposure which is what we fear from poverty. I'm not a pacifist. If it's got to be, it's got to be. But the flesh is weak and selfish and I think death would be much better than to live through another war.[5]

Most of us feel the same way. Is war always harmful? Yes. Is war always destructive? Yes. Does war always involve a cost that feels too heavy to bear? It certainly seems so, yes.

But is war always wrong? No.

I will never forget the first time I read the following statement: "War is an ugly thing, but not the ugliest of things. The decayed state of moral and patriotic feeling, which thinks nothing is worth a war, is worse. A man who has nothing which he cares more about than his own personal safety is a miserable creature, and has no chance of being free unless he is made free and kept so by the exertions of better men than himself."[6]

Even a cursory glance through history reveals several seasons when war was necessary. What's more, in a world corrupted and poisoned by the reality of evil, there are times when war becomes something noble—even a force for good.

For example, there are many cases in the Bible when God commanded His people to go to war—and even commended them for actively participating in violent conflict.

Moses obeyed God's command to attack pagan kings and leaders, including in the land of Bashan: "So the LORD our God also delivered into our hands Og king of Bashan, with all his people, and we attacked him until he had no survivors remaining. And we took all his cities at that time; there was not a city which we did not take from them" (Deut. 3:3–4).

Throughout the book of Joshua, God commanded the Israelites to make war against those occupying the promised land. "Now the LORD said to Joshua: 'Do not be afraid, nor be dismayed; take all the people of war with you, and arise, go up to Ai. See, I have given into your hand the king of Ai, his people, his city, and his land. And you shall do to Ai and its king as you did to Jericho and its king'" (8:1–2).

The book of Revelation describes the moment at the end of the Tribulation when Jesus Himself will lead the armies of heaven in a brutal war against all who defy God's rightful reign: "And I saw the beast, the kings of the earth, and their armies, gathered together to make war against Him who sat on the horse and against His army. . . . And the rest were killed with the sword which proceeded from the mouth of Him who sat on the horse. And all the birds were filled with their flesh" (19:19, 21).

None of these passages describes war as a necessary evil. Instead, they simply describe war as necessary.

Thankfully, that won't be the case forever.

A KINGDOM OF PEACE

Someone has observed that Washington, DC, contains a large assortment of peace monuments. That's not because Americans value peace, but because we build a new monument after each war.

Think back through the great leaders of history, and you'll quickly make the connection that most of them became textbook-worthy because of their participation in war.

The pharaohs of Egypt were masters of war, including the pyramid-building Ramses. Cyrus and Darius of Persia built an empire through conquest. Alexander the Great wept because he had no more worlds left to conquer. The caesars of Rome were men of war. Cleopatra and Joan of Arc were women of war. Charlemagne, William the Conqueror, Genghis Khan, the conquistadors, Napoleon, George Washington, Abraham Lincoln, Winston Churchill—all of them used war as a tool to accomplish their aims. Each of them used weapons to manage and maintain their respective kingdoms.

But not Jesus. Once the Millennium is established, the kingdom of Christ will be a kingdom of peace.

PEACE BETWEEN PEOPLE

As we've seen, the absence of Satan will be a major reason for the absence of war during the Millennium. The "prince of the power of the air" (Eph. 2:2) will be locked away, his influence removed. Instead, the Spirit of Christ will pervade our world like incense in a closed room.

The psalmist described the Lord as the One who "makes wars cease to the end of the earth; He breaks the bow and cuts the spear in two; He burns the chariot in the fire. . . . In His days the righteous shall flourish, and abundance of peace, until the moon is no more" (46:9; 72:7).

Writing of this time, Isaiah said, "The work of righteousness will be peace, and the effect of righteousness, quietness and assurance forever. My people will dwell in a peaceful habitation, in secure dwellings, and in quiet resting places" (32:17–18).

The prophet Zechariah added, "I will cut off the chariot from Ephraim and the horse from Jerusalem; the battle bow shall be cut off. He shall speak peace to the nations; His dominion shall be 'from sea to sea, and from the River to the ends of the earth'" (9:10).

PEACE BETWEEN NATIONS

The prophet Micah was especially vivid in portraying the unprecedented peace of Jesus' rule. He began by describing Jesus' seat of power on Zion, which—as we've seen—will fulfill the prophecy of the Messiah sitting on David's throne: "Many nations shall come and say, 'Come, and let us go up to the mountain of the LORD, to the house of the God of Jacob; He will teach us His ways, and we shall walk in His paths.' For out of Zion the law shall go forth, and the word of the LORD from Jerusalem" (4:2).

Then Micah described the consequences of Jesus' reign. In doing so, he wrote what has become one of the most famous prophecies about the Millennium in Scripture: "He shall judge between many peoples, and rebuke strong nations afar off; they shall beat their swords into plowshares, and their spears into pruning hooks; nation shall not lift up sword against nation, neither shall they learn war anymore" (v. 3).

If you visit the gardens of the United Nations in New York City, you may see the bronze sculpture by Soviet artist Evgeniy Vuchetich depicting a figure of a man holding a hammer aloft in one hand and beating a sword into a plow. It's called *Let Us Beat Our Swords into Ploughshares*. The sculpture suggests that one of the missions of the United Nations is converting implements of war into implements of peace and productivity.

Of course, the United Nations has utterly failed in that mission. All human efforts for true, lasting peace will not come to fruition until Christ returns to set up His kingdom.

Dr. M. R. DeHaan helps us grapple with the practical applications of this powerful truth:

> The Bible is replete with prophecies of a coming age of peace and
> prosperity. It will be a time when war will be utterly unknown. Not
> a single armament plant will be operating, not a soldier or sailor
> will be in uniform, no military camps will exist, and not one cent
> will be spent for armaments of war, not a single penny will be used
> for defense, much less for offensive warfare. Can you imagine such
> an age, when all nations shall be at perfect peace, all the resources

available for enjoyment, all industry engaged in the articles of a peaceful luxury?[7]

Is that really possible? Not here; not now. Only when Jesus returns.

PEACE BETWEEN ENEMIES

Let's try to add another layer to this promise of peace for a thousand years. During my lifetime, no earthly conflict has been more caustic and contentious than the ongoing strife in the Middle East.

First and foremost, of course, is the naked hatred that most of the Arab world feels for the nation of Israel. Throughout the decades since 1948, the leaders of Iran, Egypt, Syria, Jordan, Iraq, and many others have expressed their unfiltered desire and active intention to destroy Israel as a nation and all Jewish people as individuals—literally to wipe them off the face of the earth.

The attacks of October 7, 2023, were one more bitter eruption in that unceasing volcano of rage.

Yet even within the larger Muslim world of the Middle East, there has been constant aggression and strife. Sunni Muslims dislike and distrust Shia Muslims. Shia Muslims dislike and distrust Sunni Muslims. The divide is palpable.

Given that background, look with wonder at these amazing words from the book of Isaiah: "In that day there will be a highway from Egypt to Assyria, and the Assyrian will come into Egypt and the Egyptian into Assyria, and the Egyptians will serve with the Assyrians. In that day Israel will be one of three with Egypt and Assyria—a blessing in the midst of the land, whom the LORD of hosts shall bless, saying, 'Blessed is Egypt My people, and Assyria the work of My hands, and Israel My inheritance'" (19:23–25).

God's Word, which is divine truth and cannot deceive, tells us that a day will come in which Israel will be considered a blessing to Egypt and Assyria, which represent the descendants of Ishmael in our modern world.

This is a shocking notion, as W. A. Criswell reminds us:

Can you imagine a thing like that? Think of the bitterness among the Palestinian people. Think of the years of hatred ever since Ishmael and Isaac grew to despise one another. From that day until this has there ever not been war between Israel and the Arabs? But there is coming a time, says the Lord, when the Lord of hosts will bless them all, saying, 'Blessed be Egypt my people, and blessed be Assyria the work of my hands, and blessed be Israel mine inheritance.' All of us, saved Jews, and saved Gentiles, are to be together in the glorious and ultimate kingdom of our Lord.[8]

During the Millennium, all war will cease. All religious extremism will cease. All fascism will cease. All nationalist aggression will cease. All socialist destruction will cease.

There will be peace.

Hollis Godfrey wrote a science fiction novel called *The Man Who Ended War*. Published originally in 1908, the story follows a mad scientist of sorts who discovers a type of radiation that can dissolve metal in moments. As the only person possessing that technology, this scientist demands that all world governments unilaterally disarm and dismantle all of their weapons of war.

Here's the letter the mad scientist sent to the leaders of every nation:

To the United States of America and to all other
nations—Greeting!

Whereas war has too long devastated the earth and the time has now come for peace, I, the man destined to stop all war, hereby declare unto you that you shall, each and all, disarm; that your troops shall be disbanded, your navies sunk or turned to peaceful ends, your fortifications dismantled. One year from this date will I

THE END OF WAR

allow for disarmament and no more. At the end of that time, if no
heed has been paid to my injunction, I will destroy, in rapid succes-
sion, every battleship in the world. By the happenings of the next
two months you shall know that my words are the words of truth.

Given under my hand and seal this first of June, 19—
Signed—
The man who will stop all war.[9]

As novels go, Mr. Godfrey's story is interesting and inventive,
if perhaps a little far-fetched. But it points us forward to an important truth. Namely, there *is* a Man who will stop all war. More than a
man—our King. Our Savior. Our God.

That man's name is Jesus. And He is your source of peace today!

CHAPTER 18

WEALTH AND PROSPERITY

"A chicken in every pot and a car in every garage."

During the 1928 presidential campaign, Herbert Hoover sought to win the hearts and votes of Americans with a slogan that was both practical and inspirational. Who wouldn't be interested in daily food and the luxurious freedom offered by a reliable automobile?

The conditions of America at the time made such a promise seem believable—even inevitable. After the carnage of World War I, many families prospered during the 1920s. Advances in technology spurred new industries and accelerated growth. People were optimistic about the future.

In one of his final speeches before the 1928 election, Hoover even promised that his forthcoming term in the White House would bring "a final triumph over poverty."[1]

Less than a year after Hoover's inauguration, however, America endured the shock of Black Tuesday—the stock market crash of

THE COMING GOLDEN AGE

1929, which led into the 1930s and the grinding misery of the Great Depression.

Herbert Hoover is far from the only politician to make promises of economic abundance during a campaign. Franklin D. Roosevelt defeated Hoover in 1932 in part because of his promise of a "New Deal" for the American people. Dwight D. Eisenhower pointed voters to "Peace and Prosperity" in 1956. Bill Clinton reminded his supporters in 1992 that he was "Putting People First." And Donald Trump rose to the presidency in 2016 by vowing to "Make America Great Again."[2]

Hopefully, we've learned by now that no human leader can establish an economic system that produces prosperity for all people. Greed and injustice are all too prevalent in the human condition for that to occur.

Yet a day will come when we will no longer rely solely on human leaders. A day will come when Christ Himself will set His steady hand to the wheel of the world's economic fortunes—and produce blessings unimaginable in our day.

A TIME OF ABUNDANT PRODUCTIVITY

As we've already seen, the Millennium will be a thousand-year period of glorious grace and heavenly harmony. Satan will be completely removed from society, his influence entirely withdrawn. There will be no more war. No more destruction. No more injustice.

Because we will no longer invest our time and energy fighting with or attempting to manage the consequences of sin, everyone present in the millennial kingdom will have an abundance of time and energy at their disposal.

That begs the question: What will we do with all that time? How will we spend it?

Scripture does not directly answer that question, but it seems reasonable to me that much of our time during the Millennium will be spent working. Yes, working! And that work will be productive!

The prophet Amos was looking forward to the millennial kingdom when he wrote, "Behold, the days are coming," says the LORD, "when the plowman shall overtake the reaper, and the treader of grapes him who sows seed; the mountains shall drip with sweet wine, and all the hills shall flow with it" (9:13).

Amos was telling us that the earth will be so fertile during the Golden Age that there will be no barren "dead space" of winter between harvesting and planting. Of course, Amos was using terms that fit the day in which he wrote. As I imagine his words coming to fulfillment in the upcoming Millennium, I see a farmer at work in the fields, surrounded by vast fields of green crops. The sound of a new Case IH combine harvester fills the air as it collects a bountiful harvest. Just behind it, a John Deere 8R tractor pulls a twenty-four-row tiller/planter, eagerly preparing the soil for the next season's crop.

A few years ago on a *CBS Evening News* segment called "The American Spirit," correspondent Richard Schlesinger reported on the philanthropy of Doris Buffett, the sister of Warren Buffett. Her brother's management of her inherited wealth had made her extremely rich, but making more money was not her goal. Doris was striving to "give away the money she has left in the time she has left."

For most of us, that would not take too much effort. But after giving away more than $80 million, Doris Buffett told Schlesinger, "We'd give away money during the month and then the bank statement would come and I'd have more money than I started out the month with, so it seemed like we were on a treadmill after a while."[3]

The woman was literally making more money than she could give away. Most of us would like to know where you get one of those treadmills!

My point is this: Doris Buffett's experience may well depict what is prophesied for us during the Millennium. It will be a time of more abundance than we can imagine in our present world of struggle and scarcity.

Ezekiel said it this way: "I will call for the grain and multiply it, and bring no famine upon you. And I will multiply the fruit of your trees and the increase of your fields" (36:29–30).

A TIME OF ABUNDANT PURPOSE

Back to Amos 9:13. Notice that there are four jobs listed in that verse: plowman, reaper, treader of grapes, and sower of seed. Remember, the millennial kingdom will not be established as a spiritual existence on a heavenly cloud somewhere in the sky. No, we will live here on earth. We will have glorified bodies, yes, but they will be physical bodies. They will still require food and clothing and shelter. For that reason, there will still be farmers and tailors and builders.

There will still be work.

"But Dr. Jeremiah," you say, *"I thought the Millennium would be a time of happiness and joy! How can that be if I have to work?"*

My answer is that all of us were created to work. Adam and Eve, in their perfection, were created to contribute. To build. To serve. Look at Genesis 1: "Then God said, 'Let Us make man in Our image, according to Our likeness; let them have dominion over the fish of the sea, over the birds of the air, and over the cattle, over all the earth and over every creeping thing that creeps on the earth'" (v. 26).

Look at Genesis 2: "Then the LORD God took the man and put him in the garden of Eden to tend and keep it" (v. 15).

You and I were always intended to enjoy the blessing of work. The wonderful difference between now and the millennial kingdom is that God's original plan for work will be restored. There will be no drudgery in the Millennium. No humiliating assignments. No oppressive organizations.

Instead, each person will have the opportunity to explore and engage their passions through the blessing of meaningful work. We won't just understand our purpose—we will pursue it. And achieve it. And fulfill our dreams by producing what is right and good and helpful.

Those gifted with the ability to build will turn their eyes and arms to incredible structures without worrying about budget constraints or red tape. Those gifted to teach will impart knowledge and wisdom without the hassle of disruptive or rebellious students. Artists will enjoy unlimited creative capacity. Innovators will enjoy unlimited opportunity.

In short, the millennial kingdom will offer the perfect labor situation: meaningful work that is genuinely productive, genuinely helpful for society, and genuinely fulfilling.

A TIME OF ABUNDANT PROSPERITY

As you would expect, the perfect labor situation will produce amazing results on an incredible scale. The kingdom age will be a thousand-year season of unparalleled prosperity.

Several of the Old Testament prophets looked forward to this future age with joy. Whenever they did so, they highlighted the abundant provision of the Lord. Joel, for example, wrote, "Be glad then, you children of Zion, and rejoice in the LORD your God; for He has given you the former rain faithfully, and He will cause the rain to come down for you—the former rain, and the latter rain in the first month. The threshing floors shall be full of wheat, and the vats shall overflow with new wine and oil" (2:23–24).

In Joel's day, Israel had a few rivers but relied mostly on rain and water storage, like cisterns and wells, to sustain the land. The first rain was crucial for preparing the soil for planting, while the latter rain was vital for the growth of crops. A successful harvest depended on both rains. In the Millennium, Joel said, both will be provided like clockwork by the Lord.

Isaiah added, "I will open rivers in desolate heights, and fountains in the midst of the valleys; I will make the wilderness a pool of water, and the dry land springs of water" (41:18).

The primary result of this ecological restoration is that food will be present in abundant supply. Harvests will be plentiful. Pantries will be packed. Nobody will be habitually hungry or daily deprived under the rule and reign of Jesus Christ.

According to Mark Hitchcock, "The millennial kingdom will have no need for rescue missions, welfare programs, food stamps, or relief agencies. The world will flourish under the hand of the King of heaven."[4]

Importantly, this abundance will go beyond our bellies and reach into our hearts. We will be satisfied in every way that matters. The Lord will shower us with blessings of every kind.

A TIME OF ABUNDANT PLEASURE

Picture a world where God's perfect provision endures for one thousand years. A world where people thrive and fulfill their divine purpose and where there is no such thing as scarcity. The result? Joy!

Look again at this description from the prophet Isaiah: "They shall build houses and inhabit them; they shall plant vineyards and eat their fruit. They shall not build and another inhabit; they shall not plant and another eat; for as the days of a tree, so shall be the days of My people, and My elect shall long enjoy the work of their hands. They shall not labor in vain" (65:21–23).

One of the curses for breaking God's law in the Old Testament was that a person would not get to enjoy the results of their work. The disobedient person would work hard to build a house only for someone else to move in. They would plant vineyards only for a stranger to eat the fruit. What a picture of the frustration and futility of sin!

But in the coming Golden Age, this will all change. God's people will want to obey their God and they will follow His ways. As a result they will experience fulfillment and satisfaction, not frustration. They will have stable and long-lasting lives like trees planted near a stream. Unlike withered grass or fallen trees, they will bear fruit consistently and have time to enjoy their blessings fully.

The prophet Jeremiah wrote, "Therefore they shall come and sing in the height of Zion, streaming to the goodness of the LORD . . . their souls shall be like a well-watered garden, and they shall sorrow no more at all" (31:12).

"Their souls shall be like a well-watered garden." Isn't that a wonderful promise?

A well-watered garden is a *productive place*. Imagine the green grass and tall, towering trees. Imagine the flowers bursting with color and the branches laden with fruit. When all the material needs are provided for, there's no limit to what can grow.

A well-watered garden is also a *peaceful place*. The kind of spot you would take your spouse for a picnic or your little girl to see her dance and twirl—or even visit alone to read a book or take a nap. Such a garden radiates safety and security and the chance for rest.

Finally, a well-watered garden is a *pleasing place*. Can you hear the laughter and cries of joy? Can you hear the shouts of children as they discover a new flower or a new creature? Can you see the smiles on their faces as they splash in the streams and pools?

That will be you during the Millennium. A garden watered all the way down to your soul. Filled with the abundance of productivity and peace and pleasure. I like how one author describes the type of people we will be: "You will have a rich supply of gifts to share with others; you will be a source of delight and encouragement. You will not be like the thornbush in the desert, all of whose energy is consumed in the grim business of survival, but will have fruits and flowers to give from the overflow of your abundance."[5]

Thanks to Lauren Schroeder, many people in and around Dixon, Iowa, have experienced a taste of that abundance. At fourteen, Lauren was volunteering at a local food nonprofit when she noticed something missing from the bags of groceries she packed for local families: vegetables. Those bags were filled with cans and cardboard but lacked anything green—anything fresh.

"I thought it would be great to change that," says Lauren, who is now seventeen. "I wanted people to get the nutrition they needed from fresh vegetables." So she asked her parents to borrow a little space for a garden on their 150-acre soybean and corn farm.

Her first crops were lettuce, carrots, tomatoes, and zucchini. Her initial harvest was forty pounds, which she distributed to eight "local groups, including food banks, a soup kitchen, a nursing home and several social service nonprofits." It was hard work. Lauren spent several hours each day hand-watering her crops, and she learned that harvesting requires a lot of bending. But she kept going.

Lauren planted fifteen varieties of vegetables during her second spring, adding carrots, cauliflower, cucumber, squash, herbs, and more. Incredibly, in her first two years, she donated more than seven thousand pounds of fresh, nutritious food right to her community. Her goal is to donate twenty thousand pounds before she leaves home for college.

"I'm learning a lot as I go, and I love giving back," she says. "I'm happy to do it. Everyone deserves to have something healthy to eat."[6]

Such donations will be unnecessary during the Millennium, but that's the kind of spirit that will permeate our world under the rule and reign of Jesus Christ. His kingdom will be a place of generosity, goodness, and abundance for all.

CHAPTER 19

HEALTH AND HEALING

Was it cancer?

Dr. Thomas P. Trezona studied the image of his own CT scan, dreading the possibility of pancreatic cancer—the same disease that had killed his mother. That was the most likely explanation of the symptoms that had overtaken his life. Trezona, seventy-two, a retired surgical oncologist, knew what he was looking for.

But he didn't see it. To his relief, there was no sign of cancer.

What, then, was causing the severe pain in his abdomen, leading to weight loss? It came in waves. Sometimes the pain was severe enough to drive him writhing to the floor. Was it an infectious disease caused by a parasite? An unusual allergy? Something in his diet? One by one, Trezona and his medical team eliminated those possibilities, even as his pain, bloating, and nausea worsened. Could it be one of those stomach diseases that use every letter in the alphabet in its name?

Finally, a radiologist spotted a small bit of metal in Trezona's left upper abdomen. A further test showed the bit of metal was magnetic. It was shifting position, and whenever it entered his gallbladder, it triggered a new episode of pain and severe, nonstop vomiting. That's when doctors finally determined the cause of the illness.

At some point, Trezona had eaten a steak containing a small piece of wire broken off from the brush used to clean the barbecue grill. Doctors removed his gallbladder and showed him the small wire, still coated with burned barbecue sauce.

Dr. Trezona is doing well now, but he still remembers the fear and helplessness he felt during his illness. "I remember thinking, 'I'm dying from this thing, and no one can figure out what it is.'"[1]

The thought of dying is never pleasant, but for followers of Jesus Christ, the sting of death is gone. The Bible says, "The gift of God is eternal life in Christ Jesus our Lord" (Rom. 6:23). That's why the apostle Paul was convinced that going to be with the Lord is "far better" than remaining too long on this sinful globe (Phil. 1:23).

Still, imagine living in a world where sickness is virtually non-existent and death is very rare. Think of a place where hospitals are no longer needed and pharmacies are converted to farmers' markets. Could such a paradise ever come to pass on this side of heaven?

Yes! In this chapter I want to show you a great prediction, a great prescription, and a great Physician.

A GREAT PREDICTION

Welcome to the Golden Age! The reigning King is also the Great Physician, and there is no charge for His services. The prophet Isaiah said about this era: "Your eyes will see the King in His beauty. . . . And the inhabitants will not say, 'I am sick'" (33:17, 24).

In other words, the Millennium will be a season of unprecedented health and wellness in our world. People will live for hundreds of years without worrying about their bodies breaking down.

Of course, one reason there will be so few sicknesses during the coming Golden Age is that so many residents of earth will possess a new type of physical body. Christians who died before the Rapture or were caught up to heaven during the Rapture will receive their heavenly bodies in paradise—and those heavenly bodies will be incompatible with illness of any kind.

The Bible says, "Our earthly bodies are planted in the ground when we die, but they will be raised to live forever. Our bodies are buried in brokenness, but they will be raised in glory. They are buried in weakness, but they will be raised in strength.... For our dying bodies must be transformed into bodies that will never die" (1 Cor. 15:42–43, 53 NLT).

Things will be slightly different for those who accepted God's gift of salvation during the Tribulation. Those believers will enter the Millennium still clothed in their earthly bodies, which means they will not possess the invulnerability of someone with a glorified body. Even so, the Lord's promises from Scripture will apply to all the inhabitants of this Golden Age.

Scripture says, "I will restore health to you and heal you of your wounds" (Jer. 30:17).

Remember, the millennial reign of Christ is a transition toward the new heaven and new earth, where "there shall be no more pain" (Rev. 21:4). In eternity, we'll have no sickness, pain, sorrow, suffering, or death in any capacity. Those things are rampant in this present age, but during the thousand-year reign of Christ they will be very rare, even among those with earthly bodies.

What will be the source of our collective wellness? Here is the kind of healthcare we'll have during the Millennium.

A PURE ATMOSPHERE

If you want to talk about climate change, let me tell you what the Bible says about the Golden Age: "It will come to pass in that day that the mountains shall drip with new wine, the hills shall flow with milk, and all the brooks of Judah shall be flooded with water; a fountain shall flow from the house of the LORD and water the Valley of Acacias" (Joel 3:18).

We have no idea how many of our illnesses today are caused by impurities in the air and water and food—though it seems like scientists are uncovering new links every day between our atmosphere and our health. During the Millennium, the Lord will rid the world of carcinogens the way a Jewish housewife swept every speck of yeast out of her home during the Passover.

A WHOLESOME DIET

Our diets will also improve during the Golden Age. Even now we're told to load up on fresh, organic grains, fruits, and vegetables. You'll have a feast of those every day for a thousand years.

Isaiah 4:2 says, "In that day the Branch of the LORD shall be beautiful and glorious; and the fruit of the earth shall be excellent and appealing."

The nation of Israel will be the breadbasket of the world, for "Israel shall blossom and bud, and fill the face of the world with fruit" (27:6).

Ezekiel described the transformation of the desert lands south of Jerusalem, which will be irrigated by water flowing from unleashed underground rivers beneath the temple. He said, "Along the bank of the river, on this side and that, will grow all kinds of trees used for food; their leaves will not wither, and their fruit will not fail. They will bear fruit every month. . . . Their fruit will be for food, and their leaves for medicine" (47:12).

I have a feeling all these fruits, grains, and vegetables will be organic, pesticide-free, and grown without hormones or human engineering. And talk about the taste! And nutrition! Imagine if every apple contained all the nutrients found in a vitamin pill.

A BANISHED ADVERSARY

In the Golden Age, we won't have the devil to make us sick. Remember how Satan afflicted the patriarch Job with a skin disease that drove the poor man to sit in the dump and scrape his sores with the edges of broken pottery?

The apostle Paul also suffered some kind of affliction, which he called his "thorn in the flesh." He called his illness "a messenger of Satan to buffet me" (2 Cor. 12:7).

Jesus once met a woman who had suffered eighteen years from a spirit of infirmity. Jesus said she had been bound by Satan (Luke 13:16).

Now the tables will be turned, and Satan will be bound. For a thousand years!

Similarly, people will be much less likely to become sick from their own sins. We'll be free from addictions and self-destructive tendencies. And few, if any, will become sick as a judgment for sin, like those in Corinth who so abused the Lord's Supper that, according to Paul, "many are weak and sick among you" (1 Cor. 11:30).

Even now, I submit to you that a godly lifestyle is the healthiest.

A QUIET AND WORRY-FREE LIFESTYLE

We know how anxiety and disorder can affect our health. We need quiet and worry-free souls to be truly healthy. In the Golden Age, "My people will dwell in a peaceful habitation, in secure dwellings, and in quiet resting places. . . . Sorrow and sighing shall flee away" (Isa. 32:18; 35:10).

The peace and tranquility of the world and our individual homes and communities will make every day a wholesome joy. Gone will be the stress and anxiety that plague our bodies and minds now. Our lives will be defined by rhythms of meaningful work and restful refreshment.

A GREAT PRESCRIPTION

All this is a prediction for tomorrow, but we can glean from it a prescription for today. As Christians, we are stewards of our own bodies. The Bible says, "Do you not know that your body is the temple of the Holy Spirit who is in you, whom you have from God, and you are not your own?" (1 Cor. 6:19).

We can't avoid illness and sickness in this current age—as I well know from sad experience, and so, likely, do you. But we can do our part to stay as healthy as possible. Specifically, we can do our best to replicate some of the millennial features that promote a healthy life.

For example, we can try to avoid anything that sullies the atmosphere around us. I'm talking about the literal climate in the places we live. Smoke is bad for the lungs. There are lots of substances we can put in our bodies that may bring a moment of pleasure, but they are dangerous contaminants that pollute us from within.

Along these lines, we should check our houses for deadly emissions. I know of a great Bible teacher who developed lung cancer in his fifties. He never smoked, and he worked out every day with a personal trainer. In tears he asked, "Why did I get lung cancer?" After his death, a friend tested his house for radon, and the levels were off the charts.

Then there's the matter of a wholesome diet. We may not have millennial fruits and vegetables yet, but most of us could be tending to the nutritional needs of our bodies better than we are.

I'll tell you what else will preserve your health: a quiet lifestyle. Remember what Isaiah said: "My people will dwell in a peaceful habitation, in secure dwellings, and in quiet resting places" (32:18). There's a sense in which we can do that now as we trust in God and let Him handle the issues that tie our nerves in knots.

Proverbs 17:22 says, "A merry heart does good, like medicine." The Golden Age will be filled with merry hearts and with unbounded joy. But we don't have to wait till then. The Lord wants us to live in happiness right now—and that's the best medicine of all.

A GREAT PHYSICIAN

During His remarkable three years of ministry, Jesus went about healing the sick, giving sight to the blind, restoring the hearing of the deaf, cleansing the lepers, and even raising the dead.

Our Lord didn't cure everyone on earth—only a few. But that ministry was simply a preview of the healing ministry He will exercise in the Golden Age to come.

The Bible says, "In that day the deaf shall hear the words of the book, and the eyes of the blind shall see out of obscurity and out of darkness" (Isa. 29:18). Also, in that day He will strengthen weak hands and feeble knees. "The lame shall leap like a deer, and the tongue of the dumb sing" (35:6).

For every miracle Christ performed in the Gospels, He will multiply that exponentially and globally during the time to come. Yet even now He touches our lives as our personal Great Physician.

Jesus is the one who gave Himself that title. After the tax collector Matthew, who later wrote the first Gospel, came to Jesus for salvation, he threw a great feast for the Lord. Some of Christ's critics scolded Him for associating with the assembled collection of sinners who attended the feast. But Jesus said, "Those who are well have no need of a physician, but those who are sick" (Matt. 9:12).

Jesus was referring to the sickness of sin, and He offered Himself as a Great Physician, fulfilling Isaiah's poignant prophecy: "And by His stripes we are healed" (Isa. 53:5).

More than sixty million people die every year. What causes death? The leading global cause of death is heart disease, followed by strokes, lung disease, and neonatal conditions.[2] According to the Centers for Disease Control and Prevention, the leading causes of death for Americans are heart disease, cancer, accidents, COVID-19, and strokes.[3]

But the real cause of death is sin. The Bible says, "The soul who sins shall die" (Ezek.18:20). And "the wages of sin is death" (Rom. 6:23). And "sin, when it is full-grown, brings forth death" (James 1:15).

Only the Great Physician can give us everlasting, eternal healing of body, mind, and soul.

Many years ago, a doctor was sitting in front of the fireplace when he picked up a Bible and began to read it. His granddaughter, watching, asked, "Is that your Bible, Grandfather?"

"Yes, it goes with me everywhere I go," said the doctor, "and when I have a few minutes I read a bit from it."

"Why?" asked the child.

The grandfather replied, "Long ago, when I first began my practice, I was often not too sure of myself. I found that reading about the Great Physician helped me to see where my help came from. That it was not me, but God working through me that did the healing. I am sure it made me a better doctor."[4]

The Great Physician can make you a better person, a healthier person. He can touch you more deeply than you can imagine. He can even transform your soul and give you a joy that will last a thousand years—and for eternity.

CHAPTER 20

JOY

Did you know there is an International Day of Happiness? It's a day designed to encourage everyone in every nation on earth to be happy, and it occurs on March 20. Every year! This annual day of joy is promoted by the United Nations General Assembly and coincides with the UN's annual *World Happiness Report*. Those involved in the project affirm that "our success as countries should be judged by the happiness of our people."[1]

Researchers believe three factors determine a person's happiness:

1. genetics, which accounts for about a third of our level of emotional happiness in life,
2. our unique environment—the people and events close to us, which accounts for half of our quality of life, and
3. our shared environment, or the nation in which we live. This environment contributes about 20 percent of our sense of well-being.

The happiest nations in which to live, according to the most recent report, are Finland and Norway. The government of Norway has even started developing a "national quality of life strategy" to measure the nation's sense of happiness.[2]

If the *World Happiness Report* is still around during the Millennium, the numbers will fly off the charts. According to the Bible, the Millennium will be an exhilarating era of happiness, contentment, and joy. It will be the answer to many ancient and anguished prayers from all those who have struggled to find joy in this fallen world of pain and tragedy.

We can catch a preview of this joy by studying a different "golden age" described in Scripture: Solomon's rule over Israel.

JOY IN THE KINGDOM OF SOLOMON

Starting with the days of Abraham, God patiently built the nation of Israel until it reached its Old Testament zenith under the rule of Solomon. That zenith was itself a type of golden age for the Jews of that day.

Now, to make sure there is no misunderstanding, Solomon's glorious period pales in comparison to the coming earthly kingdom of Jesus, who is "greater than Solomon" (Matt. 12:42). Yet in some ways Solomon's reign provides a biblical sneak peek of what's to come for you, me, and every other person saved by the blood of Christ.

In Solomon's best years, he sat upon his throne as gold poured into his coffers and his people streamed to Jerusalem to hear his wisdom and his teaching. That kingdom became a marvel to the entire world.

The news spread all the way to the region of Sheba (modern-day Yemen), and the queen of Sheba traveled to Jerusalem to make a state visit so she could see for herself what was happening. She came "with a very great retinue, with camels that bore spices, very much gold, and precious stones" (1 Kings 10:2). She had a lot of questions, and Solomon answered them all with explanations that satisfied her mind and heart.

In awe, the queen surveyed Solomon's palace, his temple, the gleaming city of Jerusalem, the food that filled the city, the elegance of his state dinners, the clothing worn by the citizens, and the expressions on their faces. She exclaimed, "How happy your people must be! How happy your officials, who continually stand before you and hear your wisdom! Praise be to the LORD your God, who has delighted in you and placed you on the throne of Israel" (vv. 8–9 NIV).

The queen of Sheba returned home impressed with Israel's God and with the peaceful, prosperous, happy kingdom of Solomon. But alas! Solomon's heart turned away from the Lord, his kingdom encountered problems, and his golden age tarnished like rusted iron. The happiness that filled the homes and streets of Jerusalem slowly died like a fire reduced to dying embers.

Thankfully, the same will not be true of the greater kingdom that is coming through the rule and reign of Christ.

JOY IN THE KINGDOM OF CHRIST

In the golden age of Solomon, we have just a foretaste of the joy that will fill the land of Israel and spread throughout the world during the thousand-year reign of the One greater than Solomon—the King of kings, Jesus Christ.

In the biblical descriptions of this future era, it's the prophet Isaiah who most richly described the euphoria and the sense of well-being that will cover the land at that time. In his prophecies about the Millennium, Isaiah said, "You have multiplied the nation and increased its joy; they rejoice before You according to the joy of harvest, as men rejoice when they divide the spoil" (9:3).

In chapter 12, Isaiah spoke of how people will draw water with joy from the wells of salvation (v. 3). Two chapters later, he wrote, "The whole earth is at rest and quiet; they break forth into singing"

(14:7). He went on to say, "And the LORD GOD will wipe away tears from all faces. . . . You shall have a song as in the night when a holy festival is kept, and gladness of heart as when one goes with a flute. . . . For you shall go out with joy, and be led out with peace; the mountains and the hills shall break forth into singing before you, and all the trees of the field shall clap their hands" (25:8; 30:29; 55:12).

In chapter 65, Isaiah preached, "But be glad and rejoice forever in what I create, for I will create Jerusalem to be a delight and its people a joy. I will rejoice over Jerusalem and take delight in my people; the sound of weeping and of crying will be heard in it no more" (vv. 18–19 NIV).

In other words, the world will be happy because Jerusalem is happy, and Jerusalem will be happy because her King is happy. There's a lesson there for us. Our joy is derived from the joyful nature of God's personality. We can be joyful because we serve a joyful King.

If Isaiah makes the Millennium seem like a thousand-year celebration, it's because that's essentially what it will be. Every day will bring a Christmas-like elation of peace, well-being, and goodwill. Joyful feelings that currently come to us only at certain seasons and in our best moments will be a permanent feature of the Millennium. Isaiah 35:10 says, "Those the LORD has rescued will return. They will enter Zion with singing; everlasting joy will crown their heads. Gladness and joy will overtake them, and sorrow and sighing will flee away" (NIV).

That's one of the greatest verses of well-being in the whole Bible! Have you ever noticed it before? It's a visual verse, so try to picture it: people who were endangered by the Antichrist and his vicious forces at Armageddon will enter the millennial Jerusalem with throngs of others, all singing as they stream into the city. Can you see it? Gladness and joy will chase after them and overtake them and overwhelm them. And among these multitudes—not a sorrow, not a sigh.

Remember, this is what Isaac Watts had in mind when he wrote "Joy to the World" in his 1719 hymnbook, in which he selected some favorite psalms and turned them into songs having messianic value. He had studied Psalm 98, which says, "Shout joyfully to the LORD, all the earth; break forth in song, rejoice, and sing praises. . . . For He is coming to judge the earth. With righteousness He shall judge the world" (vv. 4, 9).

Watts realized that psalm was about the second coming of Christ and His millennial reign, so he adapted it into his famous hymn. At Christmas, we sing that hymn in celebration of our Lord's first coming, which did indeed bring joy to the world. But consider how much joy the world will experience when Jesus comes again in the glory of His kingdom.

Let's review these words:

> Joy to the world!
> The Lord is come;
> Let earth receive her King.
> Let every heart prepare Him room,
> And heaven and nature sing,
> And heaven and nature sing,
> And heaven, and heaven and nature sing.
> Joy to the world! The Savior reigns;
> Let men their songs employ,
> While fields and floods, rocks, hills and plains
> Repeat the sounding joy,
> Repeat the sounding joy,
> Repeat, repeat the sounding joy.
> No more let sin and sorrow grow,
> Nor thorns infest the ground.
> He comes to make His blessings flow
> Far as the curse is found,
> Far as the curse is found,

Far as, far as the curse is found.
He rules the world with truth and grace
And makes the nations prove
The glories of His righteousness
And wonders of His love,
And wonders of His love,
And wonders, wonders of His love.

Did these things happen when Jesus came the first time to be wrapped in swaddling clothes and placed in a manger? Did earth receive her King at that time? Was nature transformed—its fields and floods, rocks, hills, and plains? Did thorns stop infesting the ground? Was the curse lifted? Did sin and sorrow cease, and does Christ currently rule the world with grace and truth? Do the nations of the world acknowledge His righteousness and the wonders of His love?

No. Not yet. These statements reflect biblical promises, but they're not about the first coming of Christ. They reference His second coming and the glorious Millennium that will occur when He returns.

I don't intend to stop singing "Joy to the World" at Christmas. But as I sing the words, I'll be looking forward to Christ's return and the era of peace He will establish on earth. I'm eager for the day when the earth will receive her King, when every heart will prepare Him room, when thorns stop infesting the ground, and when Christ will rule the world with truth and grace. That is what will happen during the thousand-year reign of Christ, which will come after His second coming.

The prophet Joel also spoke of the millennial happiness that will fill the earth, saying, "Surely the LORD has done great things! Do not be afraid, you wild animals, for the pastures in the wilderness are becoming green. The trees are bearing their fruit; the fig tree and the vine yield their riches. Be glad, people of Zion, rejoice in the LORD your God . . . because he is faithful" (2:21–23 NIV).

JOY IN YOUR LIFE NOW

We may be as little as seven years away from this joyful kingdom, but we aren't there yet. Does that mean we're a minimum of seven years away from joy? Are we doomed to trudge in sadness until that moment arrives?

No. The One who will bring joy to the whole world at His return can bring joy to your heart right now. God has endless reserves of joy. He can fill our lives with rejoicing without endangering or diminishing the reserves He needs for the future.

Wherever the King of kings reigns, there is joy. As I said earlier, our joy is drawn from the personality of our King, who is joyous by nature. He has nothing that worries or troubles Him, and there is nothing He cannot do. He knows how to meet the needs of His children, and He knows how the story of our world will end. He also knows that after the Millennium, He will have the pleasure of saying to His children, "Enter into the joy of your lord" (Matt. 25:23).

Despite the efforts of human governments and agencies, there's little joy in the world today. When you go to an amusement park, look at the faces of the people. They're in the middle of an adrenaline rush on a ride with most of their faces unsmiling, tired, and even stressed. People everywhere are seeking amusement because they experience so little joy.

Is the joy of the Lord filling your heart today?

Perhaps the happiest command in the Bible is the one Jesus issued on the day of His resurrection. According to Matthew 28, a group of women rose early in the morning to walk through the streets of Jerusalem, making their way to the garden tomb to tend to the corpse of Jesus of Nazareth. Arriving at the tomb, the stone was rolled away from its entrance, and they were met by angels who told them the Lord had risen from the dead. The women ran back into the city to take the news to the disciples. But they were stopped in their tracks when a man suddenly appeared in front of them with a one-word command.

Matthew 28:9 says, "And as they went to tell His disciples, behold, Jesus met them, saying, 'Rejoice!'"

That simple decree has reverberated through the ages, and it echoes down to you and me. No matter what we're going through or facing, Jesus is alive. He who died for us has risen from the dead and is alive forevermore to care for us, to keep His promises for us, and to infuse us with His joy.

I've come to believe biblical words like *happiness* and *joy* and *gladness* and *cheer* are synonyms. God wants us to be happy right now. A. W. Tozer said, "The people of God ought to be the happiest people in all the wide world! People should be coming to us constantly and asking the source of our joy and delight."[3]

C. S. Lewis said, "It is a Christian duty . . . for everyone to be as happy as he can."[4]

Too many of us somehow feel guilty when we find ourselves happy. It helped me a great deal when I read how Randy Alcorn countered that attitude in his book on happiness, writing,

> Until Christ completely cures us and this world, our happiness will be punctuated by times of great sorrow. But that doesn't mean we can't be predominately happy in Christ. . . . God is clear that seeking happiness—or joy, gladness, delight, or pleasure—through sin is wrong and fruitless. But seeking happiness in him is good and right. . . . When we find in him all the reasons that we should be the happiest people in the world, the world will notice, God will rejoice, and we, his privileged children, will begin the celebration that will never end.[5]

We may only be seven years away from worldwide joy the likes of which the earth has never seen, but don't wait until then. Choose to enjoy the happiness of the Lord right now. Live today with constant deliberate obedience to the resurrection command of your risen Savior:

"Rejoice!"

CHAPTER 21

THE ANIMAL KINGDOM RESTORED

The couple's names were never given in the news, but their story made national headlines. This husband and wife rented a cabin in the Rocky Mountains for a much-needed vacation. It was March; snow and ice covered the ground. The cabin came with a hot tub several yards away from the main building, and the relaxing steam rose into the air like a hand beckoning them forward. Making their way through the snow by flashlight, the couple sank into the warm waters and felt their pressures melt away.

But not for long.

Out of the corner of his eye, the man saw something lunge at his head. He felt pain. He tried to swat away whatever had touched him while his wife, now screaming and splashing, turned the flashlight beam in his direction. They both saw the attacker at the same time—a snarling mountain lion!

Thankfully, the brilliant beam of the flashlight along with the couple's continued screams scared off the animal. The man suffered no more than a few deep scratches across his scalp. But the episode did ruin their enjoyment of the hot tub that week.[1]

As human beings, it's sometimes easy to forget that we're not the only beings created by God to occupy our world. The animal kingdom is part of God's creation for a reason. And I, for one, am grateful.

From childhood, we're intrigued by animals. We teach our toddlers to make animal noises—"What does the cow say?"—as soon as they can form the sounds. We read them books like *Peter Rabbit, The Ugly Duckling, The Three Little Pigs, Paddington Bear,* and *The Very Hungry Caterpillar.* Children of all ages are delighted with the talking animals in the Chronicles of Narnia and the vast array of creatures we find in zoos and safari parks. Arguably the first zoo was established when Solomon, during his own golden age, collected exotic animals like apes and monkeys from remote regions (1 Kings 10:22).

We bring animals into our homes as pets. Usually, cats and dogs. Sometimes hamsters, goldfish, or parakeets. But not mountain lions! As we all know, some animals are truly dangerous—with an instinct to strike, sting, bite, or kill.

Have you ever wondered why that's the case?

THE ANIMAL KINGDOM: RUINED

In biblical times, people in Israel were terrified of encountering lions as they traveled from village to village. We don't usually associate lions with Israel, but even in the time of Christ, Asiatic lions inhabited the Holy Land. Samson killed one with his bare hands (Judg. 14:5–6), and David fought off both a lion and a bear while guarding his flock of sheep (1 Sam. 17:34–35). The prophet Amos told of a man who fled from a lion only to meet a bear, and when he finally escaped to his house and leaned his hand against the wall, he was bitten by a viper (Amos 5:19).

That's a bad day!

Most theologians believe the original animals that populated the garden of Eden were not hostile, dangerous, or predatory. The book of Genesis says, "Out of the ground the LORD God formed every beast of the field and every bird of the air, and brought them to Adam to see what he would call them. And whatever Adam called each living creature, that was its name. So Adam gave names to all cattle, to the birds of the air, and to every beast of the field" (2:19–20).

There's no suggestion any of the animals were dangerous or that Adam was afraid of them. But after Adam and Eve sinned, a curse fell over the earth that affected the totality of creation. The Bible says, "Creation was subjected to frustration" (Rom. 8:19–20 NIV). The curse spread among the animals like a plague, upsetting the tranquility of nature.

THE ANIMAL KINGDOM: RESTORED

When Jesus sets up His Golden Age, the world of animals will be transformed. The prophet Isaiah made this unmistakably clear in his glorious description of the millennial reign of Christ in chapter 11. This passage begins by introducing Jesus Christ as the "Rod from the stem of Jesse" and as the "Branch" (v. 1). We're told the Spirit of the Lord will rest upon Him and He will strike the earth with the rod of His mouth. "Righteousness shall be the belt of His loins, and faithfulness the belt of His waist" (v. 5).

The next paragraph offers a beautiful picture of the natural world during the Millennium. Isaiah painted incredible scenes of animal life, beginning with a prediction that "the wolf also shall dwell with the lamb" (v. 6).

Lambs are the most helpless of all animals. They have no means of self-defense. They cannot run; they cannot bite; they cannot scratch; they cannot climb; they cannot hide. Their tender flesh is fresh meat for wolves. A hungry wolf can kill dozens of sheep in a single night.

But not during our Lord's reign. We'll see wolves and lambs romping together in playful fun.

Isaiah next says, "The leopard shall lie down with the young goat" (v. 6). If you've ever seen leopards in a zoo, you know they're beautiful with their golden fur dotted with black rosettes. They're also attack machines—slender and muscular and equipped with saber teeth and razor claws. But when Christ reigns on earth, you'll be able to have a goat and a leopard curled up at your feet by the fireplace.

That's not all. "The calf and the young lion and the fatling [shall dwell] together; and a little child shall lead them" (v. 6). You'll smile when you look out the window of your millennial-period home and see a little child leading a lion, a young calf, and a yearling out to pasture. These scenes are not symbolic but a glimpse of what life will truly be like for a thousand years.

Isaiah went on to say, "The cow and the bear shall graze; their young ones shall lie down together; and the lion shall eat straw like the ox" (v. 7). This indicates predatory animals will no longer be carnivores. They won't hunt other animals for food.

If you're like me, you don't like to watch nature shows in which animals kill and eat one another. Somehow that seems savage to us, and it is. Yes, the food chain is part of life under the curse. But during Christ's reign, all the wild animals will become herbivores, eating grass and leaves and plants. When you drive through the countryside, you'll see lions and bears and cattle all grazing contentedly in the pastures.

The most shocking picture Isaiah paints is in verse 8: "The nursing child shall play by the cobra's hole, and the weaned child shall put his hand in the viper's den." Children were weaned later in biblical times than they are now, so picture toddlers playing with cobras and vipers the way they'd play with a puppy or a set of building blocks. That's hard to imagine, but Isaiah was using vivid images to make a point. Nature will be different. Animals will be kind. The curse will be lifted. During the Millennium, you'll be able to enjoy most any animal on earth as a pet without fear.

Why? The concluding verse of this paragraph says, "They shall not hurt nor destroy in all My holy mountain, for the earth shall be full of the knowledge of the LORD as the waters cover the sea" (v. 9). Meaning, all of creation will be tinged with the golden hue of Christ's reign.

This isn't the only passage on this subject in Scripture. Near the end of his book, Isaiah again brings up the theme of how King Jesus will revolutionize the temperament of animals, returning them to their former state in the garden of Eden. He wrote, "'The wolf and the lamb shall feed together, the lion shall eat straw like the ox, and dust shall be the serpent's food. They shall not hurt nor destroy in all My holy mountain,' says the LORD" (65:25).

The prophet Ezekiel adds a word about this from the Lord: "I will make a covenant of peace with them, and cause wild beasts to cease from the land; and they will dwell safely in the wilderness and sleep in the woods" (34:25).

Hosea 2:18 says, "In that day I will make a covenant for them with the beasts of the field, with the birds of the air, and with the creeping things of the ground."

According to one commentary writer, "The curse will be lifted, peace and harmony will be present, and wild animals will again be tame and harmless to domesticated animals and humans."[2]

All this is keeping with the overall redemption of nature that Christ will accomplish when He returns and sets up His kingdom. As Paul made clear, "The creation itself will be liberated from its bondage to decay and brought into the freedom and glory of the children of God" (Rom. 8:21 NIV).

Oh, think of this wonderful new world! The creation liberated from bondage! Even the animals will feel the warmth of the power of Jesus Christ, and they will lose their savage ways and become as gentle as lambs in His world. I can hope that even mosquitos will no longer bite, nor will flies disrupt our picnics.

John Wesley said, "The whole brute creation will then undoubtedly be restored, not only to the vigour, strength, and swiftness, which they had at their creation, but to a far higher degree of each than they ever enjoyed."[3]

THE ANIMAL KINGDOM: REJOICING

Not only will animals continue to exist during the Millennium, but they will also continue to perform their created purpose—namely, worshiping God.

Even now, there's a sense that animals live to praise God. Psalm 148 says, "Praise the LORD from the earth, you great sea creatures and all the depths . . . beasts and all cattle; creeping things and flying fowl. . . . Let them praise the name of the LORD" (vv. 7, 10, 13).

Can we not feel the way nature's beauty and incredible diversity seems to join in praise of its Creator? If the world of nature sings God's praises now, imagine how loudly that voice will ring during the coming Golden Age.

Now let's take this a step further. If God loves animals so much that He created them with all their diverse beauty (Gen. 1:20–25), if He saved them from the flood (6:19), if He was so concerned for the cattle of Nineveh that He withheld judgment (Jonah 4:11), if He showed Job His glory by taking him on a zoological tour of the world (Job 39:1–30), if He cares for the sparrows and knows when even one of them falls to the ground (Matt. 10:29)—if He so delights in animals on earth, don't you think there will be lots of animals, not just during the Millennium but in the new heaven and new earth?

I think so too.

God intends for us to see His attributes reflected in the animal kingdom. After all, God the Father is compared to an eagle (Isa. 40:31), the Holy Spirit to a dove (Matt. 3:16), and the Lord Jesus to a hen who gathers her chicks under her wings (23:37). Think of the loyalty of dogs, the majesty of lions, the innocence of lambs, the strength of horses, the industriousness of ants and honeybees, the surefootedness of gazelles.

Animals have always been part of God's living creation. Yes, they are lower than the angels and lower than humans, but they are still living creatures that have personalities and beauty and purpose. Even now they fill an indispensable role in our world.

Michelle Caulder, a volunteer for the Make-A-Wish Foundation, heard about Emily, a little girl diagnosed with "PCDH19 epilepsy, a rare form of epilepsy causing regular seizures and requiring five medicines per day." Emily longed for a puppy, and Michelle granted that wish with a beautiful Bernedoodle named Ryder. The girl and dog bonded in a single moment.

"It was pure magic," said Michelle.

Ryder, the pup, provides much-needed therapy. He's better than medicine. "Ryder helps to slow Emily down and bring her back when she is having a tough time. When she is upset, Ryder calms her. . . . When Ryder is around, Emily can go from upset and frustrated to laughing and giggling, whether this is through snuggling, playing, or taking him everywhere."[4]

There's no doubt that animal interactions in our current state are a mixed bag. Some are tender while others are terrifying. But imagine a world in which every animal was joyous and could be a joy. I have a feeling the Millennium will make animal lovers out of us all!

That's what it will be like in the coming Golden Age.

CHAPTER 22

EZEKIEL'S TEMPLE

It is perhaps the most controversial rock in the entire world. Called the Foundation Stone or the Noble Rock, it can be found at the center of the Dome of the Rock in Jerusalem.

According to Jewish tradition, that particular chunk of Mount Moriah's bedrock was the place from which God began the creation of the world. Jews also identify the Foundation Stone as the location where Abraham bound Isaac as a sacrifice (until God provided a replacement ram) and as the site within the holy of holies on which the ark of the covenant rested.

Talk about a significant stone!

Of course, if you have paid any attention to the politics of Jerusalem in recent decades, you are aware that the Dome of the Rock is not a Jewish construction. It is a Muslim shrine and the third holiest site according to the Islamic religion. Muslims claim the prophet Muhammad was standing on that rock when he was transported to Mecca during an encounter with Allah.

The Dome of the Rock is part of a larger area called the Temple Mount, which has great historical importance in the past and the present—and, as we'll see in this chapter, will be a place of great significance during the Millennium.

Before we explore the future role of the Temple Mount in Jerusalem, however, let's make sure we're on the same page when it comes to the concept of the temple itself. Most Christians are familiar with that term, but we don't always realize the different buildings (and more) to which it can be applied.

In fact, there are five temples mentioned in the Bible, and all five play an important role in biblical history.

The first temple was built by Solomon around 950 BC. Construction of this temple was a massive undertaking of many years, resulting in one of the most impressive structures of the ancient world. Measuring 180 feet long, 90 feet wide, and up to 207 feet high, Solomon's temple was a glorious exhibition of white stone, polished cedar, and gleaming gold.

The second temple was a much different affair. Built by the exiles who returned to Jerusalem from Babylon around 515 BC, this version of the temple was far less grand. Indeed, Scripture says those who had seen the glory of the first temple "wept with a loud voice when the foundation of this temple was laid before their eyes" (Ezra 3:12).

The third version of the temple was a revision or restoration of that second temple led by the unlikely patronage of Herod the Great— the same Herod who attempted to murder baby Jesus! Herod's temple was visually impressive, with a sprawling courtyard and huge, interlocking stones. The disciples even marveled at its splendor, telling Jesus, "Teacher, see what manner of stones and what buildings are here!" (Mark 13:1). But Herod's creation lasted only a few decades. The Romans pulled down every stone during the destruction of Jerusalem in AD 70.

The fourth temple is quite different from the first three, because it is the church! Every individual Christian is indwelled by the Holy Spirit, which means we are walking temples containing the very presence of God. As Paul wrote, "Or do you not know that your body is the temple of the Holy Spirit who is in you, whom you have from God, and you are not your own?" (1 Cor. 6:19).

It would be natural to believe that this fourth temple is the final version of God's "house" on earth. Moving from a single, physical structure to the massive network of believers known as the church universal seems like a final step in God's plan for the place in which His name dwells.

But not so fast! The Bible mentions a fifth temple that will be built in the future. Specifically, this temple will become manifest during the Millennium and will play a major role in the thousand-year reign of Christ from Jerusalem. Let's take a closer look at that temple's size, structure, and splendor.

THE TEMPLE'S SIZE

As we've seen throughout these pages, many of the Old Testament prophets received visions of what life will be like during the coming Golden Age. The prophet Ezekiel was blessed with an experience that was deeper and more detailed than most. Through the power of the Holy Spirit, Ezekiel was introduced to an angel who gave him an extended tour of a magnificent temple located on the outskirts of Jerusalem.

The result is a detailed record of everything the millennial temple will encompass:

> In the visions of God He took me into the land of Israel and set me
> on a very high mountain; on it toward the south was something like
> the structure of a city. He took me there, and behold, there was a
> man whose appearance was like the appearance of bronze. He had
> a line of flax and a measuring rod in his hand, and he stood in the
> gateway. And the man said to me, "Son of man, look with your eyes
> and hear with your ears, and fix your mind on everything I show

you; for you were brought here so that I might show them to you. Declare to the house of Israel everything you see." (Ezek. 40:2–4)

You might be wondering, *Isn't it possible that Ezekiel saw a vision of one of the other four temples? Maybe Solomon's temple or the one built by Herod?*

Actually, no. The details and measurements included in Ezekiel's prophecy are quite precise, and they are far different from the instructions given to Solomon or the records kept by Josephus and others regarding Herod's temple. Therefore, we can say with certainty that Ezekiel was shown a vision of a future temple—one that has yet to be constructed but *will be* constructed during the Millennium.

As you read through Ezekiel's descriptions of that temple in chapters 40–48 of his prophecy, the first thing that stands out is the enormous size connected with the temple complex and the land around it. Ezekiel 45:1 describes a "district for the Lord, a holy section of the land" set apart within the future nation of Israel. Once again, Ezekiel's measurements of this district are precise: "The entire district shall be twenty-five thousand cubits by twenty-five thousand cubits, foursquare. You shall set apart the holy district with the property of the city" (48:20).

When you do the math, this "district for the Lord" will be an incredible square of fifty miles long by fifty miles wide—a staggering twenty-five hundred square miles of space!

You might think, *Dr. Jeremiah, there isn't enough room in Jerusalem for such a large area.* That's true—today. But remember, tremendous geological changes will take place at the second coming of Christ. Our Savior's return will coincide with an incredible earthquake that will crumble mountains and totally reshape the landscape visible in present-day Israel. The result will be an elevated plain upon which the citizens of the coming Golden Age will build this amazing district.

The millennial temple will not occupy the entirety of this twenty-five-hundred-square-mile plateau. Part of the district will include a remade city of Jerusalem that will comprise a hundred square miles all by itself. Other parts will be zoned for growing food, housing for priests, property for Prince David, and more. So, the millennial temple will be a smaller part of this huge area.

Yet the temple will be incredibly impressive in its own right. In Ezekiel 40, great pains were taken to measure the various courts and structures included in the temple complex. Here's how Dr. Arnold G. Fruchtenbaum summarizes those measurements: "From all these various measurements, it is obvious that this particular temple will be larger than all previous temples, measuring about one mile square. The area of the present temple compound is not large enough to hold the temple described by Ezekiel and will require some major geographical changes. That is why the new mountain of Jehovah's house will be necessary."[1]

In 2020, Elon Musk made headlines by starting construction on a "giga factory" in Austin, Texas, that was almost a mile long, making it the second largest building in the world by volume.[2] Imagine the glory and splendor of the millennial temple that will stretch a full mile on every side!

THE TEMPLE'S STRUCTURE

Ezekiel's vision of the millennial temple also includes many details about its physical structure. Chapter 40 describes a wall surrounding the temple complex that will be about ten feet high and ten feet thick (v. 5). The temple will include a large outer courtyard with gates facing north, east, and south. The outer edges of this courtyard will house various storage rooms, kitchens for preparing sacrifices, and chambers for the priests.

There will also be an inner court with similar proportions to Solomon's temple that will contain the altar, the Holy Place, and the Most Holy Place (also called the holy of holies). This inner court will also have three gates facing north, east, and south, and will be accessed by ascending or descending seven steps.

Like Solomon's temple, the millennial temple will emphasize beauty and visual appeal. Describing the gates of the outer courtyard, Ezekiel wrote, "There were beveled window frames in the gate chambers and in their intervening archways on the inside of the gateway all around, and likewise in the vestibules. There were windows all around on the inside. And on each gatepost were palm trees" (40:16).

Likewise, when describing the galleries along the outside of the temple area, Ezekiel noted they were "made with cherubim and palm trees, a palm tree between cherub and cherub. Each cherub had two faces, so that the face of a man was toward a palm tree on one side, and the face of a young lion toward a palm tree on the other side; thus it was made throughout the temple all around. From the floor to the space above the door, and on the wall of the sanctuary, cherubim and palm trees were carved" (41:18–20).

In terms of its physical structure, the millennial temple will be a place of light and beauty. A place of intricate art and meticulous design. It will be a loving reflection of the loveliness of God.

THE TEMPLE'S SPLENDOR

Do you remember what happened when Solomon dedicated the first temple in Jerusalem? He brought the ark of the covenant into the holy of holies, and then God responded with a visible expression of His presence and power: "And it came to pass, when the priests came out of the holy place, that the cloud filled the house of the LORD, so that the priests could not continue ministering because of the cloud; for the glory of the LORD filled the house of the LORD" (1 Kings 8:10–11).

The glory that filled Solomon's temple in the form of a cloud was a sign of God's approval and acceptance. The Creator of the universe manifested Himself in that temple through the appearance of a cloud, just as He had previously manifested Himself to the Israelites in the wilderness through a pillar of fire and a pillar of smoke.

I bring that up because there are two important moments in Ezekiel's prophecy that are worth exploring as we consider the future splendor of the millennial temple. The first concerns the removal of God's glory from Solomon's temple. Ezekiel was granted a vision of angelic cherubim interacting with the temple, culminating in a tragic moment for the Jewish people: "Then the glory of the LORD departed from the threshold of the temple and stood over the cherubim. And the cherubim lifted their wings and mounted up from the earth in my sight" (10:18–19).

This vision represented God removing His presence from Solomon's temple before it was destroyed. It also symbolized God removing His presence from His people because of their continued idolatry and rebellion.

The second moment occurs in Ezekiel 43 during the prophet's vision of the millennial temple. Look what he saw and see if it sounds familiar:

> Afterward he brought me to the gate, the gate that faces toward the east. And behold, the glory of the God of Israel came from the way of the east. His voice was like the sound of many waters; and the earth shone with His glory. . . . And the glory of the LORD came into the temple by way of the gate which faces toward the east. The Spirit lifted me up and brought me into the inner court; and behold, the glory of the LORD filled the temple. (vv. 1–2, 4–5)

During the coming Golden Age, the glory of God will once again fill His temple. The splendor and majesty of God will be manifest in our world not only in the Person of Christ our King but also in the place where His name dwells.

Don't forget: you and I will be able to visit this millennial temple. We will walk along the outer wall and hear the river flowing from west to east. We will pass through one of the three primary gates, marveling at the beautiful architecture. We will join the crowds passing through the outer court and into the interior where we'll see the altar and the holy of holies.

There will be no curtain in that new inner court. No separation between divinity and humanity. We will walk in that sacred space where Aaron walked millennia before, carrying out the offices of high priest. Unlike those priests, however, we will bask in the presence of God with no fear of condemnation.

Imagine the wonder of that future day!

I remember back in 1990 when violence erupted at the Temple Mount in Jerusalem. A group of extremist Jews calling themselves the Temple Mount Faithful announced plans to lay a foundation for a rebuilt temple that would replace the Dome of the Rock and the Al-Aqsa Mosque, despite a court order prohibiting them from approaching the site.

When the festival of Sukkot arrived—the day of the planned foundation laying—thousands of Muslims and Jews gathered in counterdemonstrations. Shouts and slogans turned into hurling rocks and physical attacks. The police were called as the violence escalated.

In the end, more than a dozen were killed and as many as 150 were wounded. It was a tragic day. A day that highlighted once again the high tensions connected with that sacred site and that significant city.

Today, I often have people ask me how it could be possible for anyone to rebuild the temple in Jerusalem given the explosive atmosphere of the region. "How could any organization or government remove those Muslim holy sites without sparking war across the world?"

The answer is simple: no organization can achieve such a thing. No government will achieve it. Instead, God will accomplish what He has promised in His Word.

May I end on a personal note? Whenever I've taught about the temples of the Bible, I've tried to remind myself that I am God's temple today. The apostle Paul said, "Or do you not know that your body is the temple of the Holy Spirit who is in you, whom you have from God, and you are not your own?" (1 Cor. 6:19). It's also true that when we gather physically to worship Him, the living church is His temple. Speaking in the plural, Paul also said, "Don't you realize that all of you together are the temple of God and that the Spirit of God lives in you?" (1 Cor. 3:16 NLT).

Oh, how wonderful! We are walking temples. God dwells within us by His Spirit. I'm not sure that even the golden temple of the Millennium could be greater than knowing that God's glory dwells within us right now, every day, for all the world to see!

CHAPTER 23

ANIMAL SACRIFICE RENEWED

Five red cows graze serenely in Israel near the ancient ruins of Shiloh, not far from the site of the ancient tabernacle. They don't realize they're under constant surveillance and carefully guarded behind thick fences. These animals, originally from Texas, have never worked, given birth, or been milked. They're the result of decades of effort by the Temple Institute of Jerusalem to prepare a perfect red heifer.

Many Jewish leaders believe the sacrifice of a red heifer is needed to purify the Temple Mount in Jerusalem in preparation for building what they call the Third Temple. If this happens, it would be the first example of Jewish animal sacrifice since Rome destroyed Herod's temple in AD 70.

The Muslims who now worship in the Al-Aqsa Mosque on Jerusalem's Temple Mount fret about those in Israel who reportedly want to raze the mosque and cleanse the area through the ashes of a sacrificed red heifer, combined with red yarn, cedar wood, and hyssop (Num. 19:1–10).[1] In fact, Hamas spokesman Abu Ubaida partially justified the massacre of October 7, 2023, in Israel by accusing Jews of "'bringing red cows' to the Holy Land."[2]

Whether these cows will fulfill their destiny, I don't know. But I do know from biblical prophecies that animal sacrifices will once again take place at a Jewish temple in Jerusalem. As we've seen, the latter chapters of the book of Ezekiel describe the vast and glorious temple Christ will build and occupy during the Millennium. The temple furnishings will include an altar on which sacrifices will be offered (43:13–17).

This may seem surprising, given that Jesus has already fulfilled the significance of the Old Testament sacrifices by offering Himself on the cross. Hebrews 9, discussing the nature of Old Testament sacrifices, says,

> He [Jesus] did not enter by means of the blood of goats and calves; but he entered the Most Holy Place once for all by his own blood, thus obtaining eternal redemption. The blood of goats and bulls and the ashes of a heifer sprinkled on those who are ceremonially unclean sanctify them so that they are outwardly clean. How much more, then, will the blood of Christ, who through the eternal Spirit offered himself unblemished to God, cleanse our consciences from acts that lead to death, so that we may serve the living God! (vv. 12–14 NIV)

The book of Hebrews tells us that Christ put an end to all sacrifices for sin. This is actually one of the major objections to belief in a literal millennial reign of Christ among some branches of the church. They believe the mention of animal sacrifices in prophetic passages must mean millennial prophecies aren't pointing toward our future.

Yet when I turn to the prophet Ezekiel, I can't deny what I see. To my amazement, I find Levitical rituals of animal sacrifice once again being implemented during the thousand-year reign of Christ.

Let's tackle this mystery together.

THE RESUMPTION OF THE SACRIFICES

Remember, Ezekiel wasn't just a prophet. He was a priest. He was vitally interested in the temple routines and the sacrificial systems of Judaism. In his description of the millennial temple, he talked about a door leading into a room "where the meat for sacrifices was washed. On each side of this entry room were two tables, where the sacrificial animals were slaughtered for the burnt offerings, sin offerings, and guilt offerings" (40:38–39 NLT). Nearby were other rooms and tables where the sacrifices were cut into pieces. Even the butchering knives were mentioned (v. 42).

Two chapters later, we're told about the rooms in the temple complex where the sacred offerings will be stored—the grain offerings, sin offerings, and guilt offerings (42:13). The next chapter includes a detailed plan for the altar and the kinds of sacrifices that will be offered there.

Ezekiel 45 tells us that holy days such as the Passover and the Feast of Tabernacles will be celebrated by the offering of animal sacrifices (vv. 21–25). Chapter 46 gives more details, saying, "You shall daily make a burnt offering to the LORD of a lamb of the first year without blemish; you shall prepare it every morning" (v. 13). The last part of the chapter describes the temple kitchens where the sacrifices will be roasted or boiled on cooking hearths.

Ezekiel isn't the only prophet who predicts animal sacrifices during the Millennium. Isaiah 56:7 says, "Even them I will bring to My holy mountain, and make them joyful in My house of prayer. Their burnt offerings and their sacrifices will be accepted on My altar; for My house shall be called a house of prayer for all nations."

Jeremiah describes the coming Golden Age as a time when "Judah will be saved, and Jerusalem will dwell safely," and when there will never be a lack of priests or Levites to offer burnt offerings before the Lord (33:16–18).

Zechariah indicates the same thing (14:20–21), and the final Old

Testament prophet, Malachi, said that in those days "the offering of Judah and Jerusalem will be pleasant to the LORD, as in the days of old, as in former years" (3:4).

THE REASON FOR THE SACRIFICES

Dr. Dwight Pentecost explained the reason for the resumption of this sacrificial system, writing, "The sacrifices will be memorial in character."[3] In other words, animal sacrifices will be a teaching tool to show the people of Israel the vital importance of what Jesus did in shedding His blood for them on the cross.

The popular Methodist minister Arno Gaebelein wrote, "While the sacrifices Israel brought once had a prospective meaning, the sacrifices brought in the millennial temple have a retrospective meaning."[4]

Most of the scholars I've read hold a memorial view about the millennial sacrifices. Dr. John Walvoord wrote, "First of all, it should be observed that the sacrifices in the Old Testament did not take away sin. They were prophetic, looking forward to the death of Christ which was the final sacrifice. In the Millennium, apparently, sacrifices will also be offered, though somewhat different than those required under the Mosaic Law, but this time the sacrifices will be memorial."[5]

Dr. Thomas Ice said, "The presence and purpose of millennial sacrifices neither diminish the finished work of Christ, nor violates the literal interpretation of these prophetic passages. Nothing in Ezekiel 40–48 conflicts with the death of Christ or New Testament teaching at any point. . . . The millennial Temple and its ritual will serve as a daily reminder of fallen man's need before a Holy God and lessons about how this same God lovingly works to remove the obstacle of human sin for those who trust Him."[6]

The idea of Old Testament animal sacrifices goes all the way back to the garden of Eden, when God clothed Adam and Eve's shame with the skin of an animal (Gen. 3:21), and to righteous Abel bringing the firstborn of his flock as an offering to the Lord (4:4). In Exodus 12, all the families of Israel coated the doorposts of their houses with the blood of a lamb (vv. 21–24). Later at Mount Sinai, the Lord instituted a system of sacrificial rituals.

Over the centuries, thousands of gallons of blood flowed from the altars of Israel, but not one drop actually had the power to forgive sin. It was all pointing toward the Lord Jesus, the Lamb of God who would take away the sins of the world (John 1:29).

Every offering in the Old Testament was prefiguring Jesus Christ. The apostle Peter wrote, "You were not redeemed with corruptible things . . . but with the precious blood of Christ, as of a lamb without blemish and without spot" (1 Peter 1:18–19).

In a similar way, the future offerings on the altar of millennial Israel will look backward at what Jesus did during the days of His first coming. These offerings will be a vivid, crimson reminder of the cross.

Dr. Charles Lee Feinberg, who wrote one of the finest commentaries on Ezekiel, was often asked about the necessity of such offerings with the Lord dwelling in the midst of His people. His reply: "Remember that during the earthly ministry of Christ sacrifices were offered, and He was present then. And there were sacrifices still offered at the time of the Lord's forty-day resurrection ministry."

Feinberg emphasized, "Again it must be reiterated . . . the sacrifices are never intended to be propitiatory, but commemorative and retrospective."[7]

The offering of these memorial sacrifices will also be instructional. Dr. Thomas Ice wrote, "The Millennium will return history to a time when Israel will be God's mediatory people but will also continue to be a time in which sin is present upon the earth. Thus, God will include a new Temple, a new priesthood, a new Law, etc., at this future time because He will be present in Israel and still desires to teach that holiness is required to approach Him."[8]

As the Jewish people watch these sacrifices being offered, they will learn the importance of holiness and the cost Christ paid to clothe us in His righteous grace.

THE RELEVANCE OF SACRIFICES

What does this mean for us now?

Perhaps you've already made the connection I'm about to mention. For Israel past and future, the commemoration of the atonement of Jesus Christ, which He accomplished by the shedding of His blood, is bound up with the Levitical sacrificial system.

For the church, it is symbolized by the Lord's Supper! Our regular observances of Communion are memorials for us, reminding us of our Lord's broken body and shed blood. The apostle Paul told us, "For as often as you eat this bread and drink this cup, you proclaim the Lord's death till He comes" (1 Cor. 11:26).

That verse suggests that after the second coming, we'll no longer observe the Lord's Supper. The redeemed nation of Israel will return to its own customs. The temple sacrifices will serve the same purpose as the Lord's Supper to us—a remembrance of what He has done for us in the offering of His body and the shedding of His blood.

The Lord ordained the symbol of sacrifices for Israel, past and future, just as He ordained the symbol of bread and wine for the church here and now.

As a pastor who believes deeply in the Lord's Supper, I'm glad the Lord didn't give me the responsibility of killing a lamb every week or every month in front of my congregation. Instead, during this age of grace, He has kindly lifted that requirement and replaced it with the simple ceremony of the Lord's Supper. That is our memorial. That's how we regularly remember what Jesus has done for us and the tremendous price He paid for our redemption.

For two thousand years, Christians in every land have cherished the Lord's Supper during times of plenty and times of famine, during seasons of revival and moments of grief, amid scenes of peace and the horrors of war. We must treat it with the utmost reverence.

That's what one chaplain did during the Second World War.

In 1943, General Douglas MacArthur captured the Indonesian island of Biak. A few months later, Chaplain Leon Maltby arrived on the island to minister to the Allied troops. His chapel was primitive, covered by material from a yellow parachute. He enlisted carpenters who built pews, a platform, and an altar table. He made candlesticks and a makeshift cross from .40 mm shells. But what about Communion cups? Chaplain Maltby had nothing in which to serve the wine of Communion.

An unusual idea came to him. He found some unused .50 caliber bullets. They had to be new and unused because he didn't want to use any shells that might have killed someone. He carefully pulled out the lead and gunpowder and set off the firing caps. Then he pressed the shells into the right shape. Each bullet took about two hours to mold into a Communion cup, and he made eighty of them—enough for two trays.

Later, Chaplain Maltby became the first Protestant chaplain to enter Japan. He took his unusual Communion set with him and served the Lord's Supper alongside a Japanese pastor as an incredible token of unity. Today, the set is on display at the Veteran's Museum in Daytona Beach. A sign sums up the significance: "The pastor clearly understood the significance of 'instruments of death becoming a symbol of eternal life.'"[9]

The Bible teaches that the blood of Jesus is the only substance that can turn death into life by atoning for our sins. How that transformation is represented—by sacrificial offerings or by the communal bread and cup—well, those are simply memorials. They are significant tokens and regular reminders that there is wonder-working power in the precious blood of the Lamb.

Have you experienced the power of the blood of Jesus Christ? If not, why not do so now. In the words of that great hymn of invitation, you can pray:

> Just as I am, without one plea
> But that Thy blood was shed for me,
> And that Thou bidd'st me come to Thee,
> O Lamb of God, I come! I come![10]

CHAPTER 24

WORSHIP IN THE MILLENNIUM

I read of a missionary—his name is withheld for security reasons—who traveled to a nation where the gospel is outlawed. This country was "the most unsafe place I've been in my life," he said. This man was on a hazardous ten-day mission trip to teach theology to local Christians. On the first day of the training, he walked two miles from the city into the desert. He followed the directions to a hole in the sand. Church leaders had dug through the sand to a threshold of rock, then carved tunnels under the desert floor.

There the missionary worshiped literally underground with local Christians. The worship and training went on for five days, the maximum amount of time believers can be away from their jobs without raising suspicion. Even so, the missionary later learned that two attendees were killed and several others severely beaten.[1]

Millions of believers gather secretly every week to worship, and in some cases they have to whisper their songs, sermons, and prayers. It's a sign of demonic evil when the simple songs and genuine worship rendered toward the Prince of Peace are outlawed. But that's the way it is in one country after another.

It won't be that way forever! When Jesus Christ returns and establishes His Golden Age, the whole world will erupt in worship. The underground church will rise to the surface, and our songs of praise will fill the air. We will worship together for a thousand years, and that's just a prelude to the eternal joy of being with the Lord and praising Him for who He is and what He does forever and ever.

Our worship experience during that time will be different from anything we have encountered so far, even at the very best of our weekend services. For a thousand years, our worship will be of millennial grade.

OUR WORSHIP WILL BE UNCORRUPTED

During the Golden Age, our worship will be utterly authentic, genuine, Christ-centered, and uncorrupted. We'll truly fulfill our Lord's words in John 4: "But the hour is coming . . . when the true worshipers will worship the Father in spirit and truth; for the Father is seeking such to worship Him. God is Spirit, and those who worship Him must worship in spirit and truth" (vv. 23–24).

When we worship the Lord now, we strive to do so with all our hearts. That striving is great preparation for millennial worship!

For a thousand years, the purity of our worship will be greater and more genuine than at any point in history since the garden of Eden. Our worship will be authentic. It will be bright and natural. It will be offered in Spirit and truth.

Isn't it interesting there are no worship services mentioned in Genesis 1 or 2? We don't read about Adam and Eve praying to God or singing songs of praise. Our first parents didn't rely on those types of spiritual disciplines to connect with God and worship Him because their fellowship with Him was constant and unbroken. They knew

God, they were known by God, and their worship thrived in the midst of that face-to-face relationship.

Genesis 3 says Adam and Eve "heard the sound of the LORD God walking in the garden in the cool of the day" (v. 8). They enjoyed perfect intimacy with the Father.

That intimacy was broken by the fall. By sin. A separation took place. Our ability to worship God has been hampered ever since by our loss of fellowship with Him. But our Lord instantly began a process to reverse the separation and to restore the fellowship we crave with Him. His plan began with the covenant He made with Abraham and with the nation that descended from Him. From that nation came our Savior—the Lord Jesus Christ.

The key player in Old Testament days was the nation of Israel. The Lord told Moses, "For I will look on you favorably and make you fruitful, multiply you and confirm My covenant with you. You shall eat the old harvest, and clear out the old because of the new. I will set My tabernacle among you, and My soul shall not abhor you. I will walk among you and be your God, and you shall be My people" (Lev. 26:9–12).

Do you see the glimpses of Eden in those promises? The Lord longs to be among His people so we can know Him, praise Him, and enjoy His fellowship.

When Jesus came to earth through His Jewish lineage, He took the next step in restoring fellowship between God and humanity by offering Himself on the cross to pay the penalty for our sins. Because of that sacrifice, the church has greater intimacy with God and a greater opportunity for worship.

As Paul wrote, "Now, therefore, you are no longer strangers and foreigners, but fellow citizens with the saints and members of the household of God, having been built on the foundation of the apostles and prophets, Jesus Christ Himself being the chief cornerstone, in whom the whole building, being fitted together, grows into a holy temple in the Lord, in whom you also are being built together for a dwelling place of God in the Spirit" (Eph. 2:19–22).

We are the temple of God! Jesus followers are a house dedicated to His worship, and our experiences in praise will only intensify during the Millennium.

Why? For two reasons.

First, because Satan—the serpent who deceived Adam and Eve in the garden—will be locked away in the abyss. His influence will be removed from our world and from our worship.

Second, because God Himself will once again walk among His people. He will once again be physically part of our world as Christ takes up David's throne in Jerusalem.

OUR WORSHIP WILL BE UNDIVIDED

Not only will our worship be uncorrupted for a thousand years, but it will be undivided. According to the Guinness World Records organization, the largest simultaneous singalong occurred at 2:45 P.M. on December 9, 2005. At 1,616 locations across the United Kingdom, a grand total of 293,978 people joined together to sing "Lean on Me" at the same time. The goal was not only to set a world record but also to raise money for charity.[2]

Wouldn't it be interesting if churches around the world could coordinate a simultaneous sing-along of a hymn or a praise song? We could shatter that record by millions!

But even that would pale in comparison to what we'll experience in the Millennium. Why? Because in the Golden Age, the entire planet will be unified in our worship of the one true God. Isaiah once again foresaw the wonder of that reality, writing, "'And it shall come to pass that from one New Moon to another, and from one Sabbath to another, all flesh shall come to worship before Me,' says the LORD" (66:23).

I'm often asked why, if the church is supposed to be unified, there are so many denominations and factions of Christians. Much of the answer is historical. In the centuries after Christ, the Roman Empire divided into the Western Empire based in Rome and the Eastern (or Byzantine) Empire based in Constantinople (modern Istanbul). This geographical split created two different churches—the western Catholic Church and the eastern Orthodox Church.

When the western church became highly corrupted, the Protestant Reformation created another branch of Christian history. As the Reformation passed through different nations, various denominations began to form—the German Lutherans, the Scottish Presbyterians, the English Anglicans. None of this is necessarily bad. But over time it has created many different "families" within the church.

One day the walls dividing those families will collapse, and we'll truly be one.

Furthermore, we'll worship with undivided hearts. Throughout human history, idolatry has degraded our attempts to worship God and praise His name. Because of the corrupting influence of sin, all people have been distracted in their worship. Their praise, which should be reserved for God alone, has been refracted between a number of idols—false religions, the worship of self, the worship of money, the worship of pleasure, the worship of popularity, and much more.

A. W. Tozer put it this way: "Among the sins to which the human heart is prone, hardly any other is more hateful to God than idolatry, for idolatry is at bottom a libel on His character. The idolatrous heart assumes that God is other than He is—in itself a monstrous sin—and substitutes for the true God one made after its own likeness."[3]

The Millennium will be an age not of religious diversity but of spiritual unity. All people will worship one God—the only God. All people will direct their praise to Him and no other.

What Paul wrote in Ephesians 4:4–6 will become a reality: "There is one body and one Spirit, just as you were called in one hope of your calling; one Lord, one faith, one baptism; one God and Father of all, who is above all, and through all, and in you all."

This worldwide unity will be a blessing for the Jewish people.

After centuries of antisemitism, God's chosen people will be given an exalted and respected place in the millennial culture.

The prophet Zechariah gave us a variety of descriptions of this era, including this one: "'Yes, many peoples and strong nations shall come to seek the LORD of hosts in Jerusalem, and to pray before the LORD.' Thus says the LORD of hosts, 'In those days ten men from every language of the nations shall grasp the sleeve of a Jewish man, saying, "Let us go with you, for we have heard that God is with you"'" (8:22–23).

OUR WORSHIP WILL BE UNENDING

During the Golden Age to come, our practice of worship will be more pure and powerful than at any point since the fall. We'll once again enjoy genuine, face-to-face fellowship with God. Moreover, our experience of worship will be boosted by worldwide unity in our focus on Jesus Christ. No more division, religious strife, or idolatry.

But there's something more! The practice of worship during the Millennium will be constant. Our worship will never end. It will be a regular, repeating, self-replicating foundation of our everyday lives. Isaiah 60:11 says: "Your gates shall be open continually; they shall not be shut day or night, that men may bring to you the wealth of the Gentiles, and their kings in procession."

As we've seen, Jerusalem will be the center of the millennial world—including its spiritual center. Christ will be there, reigning on the throne of David. A new and glorious temple will be there. And the doors of that temple, just like the gates of that city, will never be closed.

What a wonderful picture! What an amazing promise! The city of God will be open to all comers at all times.

This is a picture presented several times throughout Scripture. In Revelation 4, for example, John described the throne room of heaven as a place of unending praise. In verses 8–11, specially assigned angels circle around the throne day and night, saying:

"Holy, holy, holy, Lord God Almighty, who was and is and is to come!" Whenever the living creatures give glory and honor and thanks to Him who sits on the throne, who lives forever and ever, the twenty-four elders fall down before Him who sits on the throne and worship Him who lives forever and ever, and cast their crowns before the throne, saying: "You are worthy, O Lord, to receive glory and honor and power; for You created all things, and by Your will they exist and were created."

During that Golden Age, we'll be able to carry out the biblical command to "Rejoice always, pray without ceasing, in everything give thanks; for this is the will of God in Christ Jesus for you" (1 Thess. 5:16–18). Because our fellowship with the Savior will be unbroken, our worship will be unceasing. Every act of our lives will be an offering of praise.

How can our worship be unending if it lasts only a thousand years? Because the Millennium is the transition between time and eternity. After the end of the Millennium, we'll simply carry on our worship with even greater joy in the new heaven and new earth and New Jerusalem.

For twenty years now, Keith Getty has been one of the key leaders of the church in the realm of worship. Along with his wife, Kristyn, and his lyrical partner, Stuart Townend, Keith has written dozens of modern hymns that have helped transform modern worship, including the classic hymn "In Christ Alone."

Keith has won numerous awards, including recognition from Queen Elizabeth II as an Officer of the Order of the British Empire for his contributions to music and hymnody. The Gettys have also launched a network of songwriters to transform worship in the church, and the Getty Music Foundation, which is a nonprofit entity, educates and supports hymn writers around the globe.

Keith and Kristyn Getty are just getting warmed up for the Golden Age! They are preparing themselves and the church to worship in spirit and in truth.

According to Keith, "What we sing becomes the grammar of what we believe."[4]

In the millennial kingdom of Jesus Christ, that grammar will be uncorrupted, undivided, and unending. We'll be singing "O for a Thousand Tongues" for a thousand years!

Praise God from whom all blessings flow!

CHAPTER 25

SIN IN THE MILLENNIUM

On a particular evening in 2011, a man named Roger Dean, age thirty-seven, snuck into the bedroom of two residents at a nursing home in Sydney, Australia, and started a small fire. Dean was a nurse at the facility, and he apparently feared he was suspected of stealing more than two hundred prescription pills from the in-house pharmacy.

Dean's fire quickly spread throughout the nursing home. Two years later, he was convicted by a jury on eleven counts of murder.

The terror wrought that night is hard to comprehend. Helpless elderly people in bed or in wheelchairs could not escape the smoke and flames. During the trial, a psychiatrist said there was no indication Dean was confused or delusional.

So why did he do it?

This was Dean's explanation: "You won't believe it, but it was like Satan saying to me that it's the right thing to do. I love the residents very much and I have a really good rapport with them. So I feel extremely bad and I just feel evil, that I'm just corrupted with evil thoughts that made me do that."[1]

This arsonist didn't realize he had just given a sound theological answer for his crimes. Why is there so much violence in the world? Why do we do things that are self-destructive and destructive to others?

It's because we are corrupted with evil thoughts and spurred on by Satan. We are extremely bad. The Bible says, "The heart is deceitful above all things, and desperately wicked; who can know it?" (Jer. 17:9). The apostle Paul wrote, "For all have sinned and fall short of the glory of God" (Rom. 3:23). The apostle John said, "If we say that we have no sin, we deceive ourselves, and the truth is not in us" (1 John 1:8).

That's why each day brings more news of wars, shootings, road rage, domestic violence, racial injustice, and runaway materialism. That also explains why all of us individually struggle every single day with temptations to do things we know are wrong.

Galatians 5:17 puts it in terms we can understand from our own experience: "For the flesh desires what is contrary to the Spirit, and the Spirit what is contrary to the flesh. They are in conflict with each other, so that you are not to do whatever you want" (NIV).

There is a single solution for this problem. God became human in the person of Jesus Christ so He could offer Himself in our place, taking our punishment upon Himself. The blood that ran down the cross and watered the ground is the atoning sacrifice that allows us to be forgiven and cleansed in God's sight.

At the moment of rapture and resurrection, we'll be set totally free from our sinful flesh, and temptation will be a thing of the past. By God's grace and power, we'll be sinless forever with nothing between us and the Savior throughout eternity. During the Millennium, the raptured and resurrected residents—you and me!—will be free from the taint of sin.

But what about the mortals who survive the Tribulation and enter the Golden Age? What about those who followed the Lamb despite the threats and thundering of the Antichrist? And what about the children they bear and the generations of mortals who will populate the Golden Age?

Will they, too, be sinless? Will there be no wrongdoing at all for a thousand years?

THE ENEMY IS BANISHED

The short answer is that sin will still be a reality during the millennial reign of Christ. But there is one important mercy to consider: Satan will be bound. I've devoted an earlier chapter to this truth, but I want to reemphasize its importance in terms of human sin.

The arsonist at the top of the chapter blamed his crime, in part, on Satan. While the devil cannot make us sin, he does everything possible to motivate us and tempt us. He's had a lot of experience, starting in the garden of Eden when he deceived Eve and Adam. He's been at it ever since. The Bible teaches, "He who sins is of the devil, for the devil has sinned from the beginning" (1 John 3:8).

Satan attacked the patriarch Job with every available tool, trying to get him to renounce his faith in God (Job 1:9–12). In Old Testament days, "Satan rose up against Israel and incited David to take a census of Israel" (1 Chron. 21:1 NIV). The devil wanted David to take excessive human pride in the number of people over whom he reigned.

Can you believe that Satan even tried to lure the holy Son of God into temptation at the beginning of our Lord's ministry (Matt. 4:1–10)?

Later Jesus told a group of His critics, "You belong to your father, the devil, and you want to carry out your father's desires. He was a murderer from the beginning, not holding to the truth, for there is no truth in him. When he lies, he speaks his native language (John 8:44 NIV).

In the early days of the church, a man named Ananias lied to the church in Jerusalem and to the apostles. Peter confronted him, saying, "Ananias, why has Satan filled your heart to lie to the Holy Spirit?" (Acts 5:3).

The apostle Paul encouraged intimacy in marriage "so that Satan does not tempt you because of your lack of self-control" (1 Cor. 7:5).

None of those experiences will be replicated during the Golden Age. Satan and his influence will be completely removed from our world.

Just imagine the relief of knowing our Enemy is in prison! He can no longer tempt, accuse, attack, or incite us to evil. For a thousand years, we'll be free from that old serpent. No mortal who sins during the Golden Age can say, like the arsonist, "It was like Satan saying to me ..."

THE EARTH IS BETTER

Nevertheless, the binding of Satan doesn't mean the earth will be perfectly holy. Just as a sinless Christ walked among sinful people during His natural life on earth, so those who are raptured and resurrected will dwell among people on the millennial earth who still struggle with the weakness of the flesh. The earth will be far better with Satan bound and Christ enthroned, but it will not be perfect.

As mentioned earlier, trouble on earth comes from three sources: the world, the flesh, and the devil. The devil will be removed from the playing board, and evil in the world will be tempered by the rule of Christ. But mortals on the earth will still struggle with the flesh. Even during the Golden Age, sin will not be totally absent from mortal hearts or headlines.

The book of James says, "But each one is tempted when he is drawn away by his own desires and enticed. Then, when desire has conceived, it gives birth to sin; and sin, when it is full-grown, brings forth death" (1:14–15).

Again, death will be rare during the Millennium, and people will live for centuries rather than for decades. But death—the result of sin—will still occur.

According to Psalm 72, which is a millennial psalm, the Messiah will rule from sea to sea (v. 8). All kings will bow down to Him and all nations will serve Him (v. 11). He will "take pity on the weak and the needy and save the needy from death. He will rescue them from oppression and violence" (vv. 13–14 NIV).

Oppression and violence? During the Golden Age? Yes, because the mortals born during this time will still possess the fallen nature of Adam.

The prophet Zechariah has an interesting prophecy about this:

> Then the survivors from all the nations that have attacked Jerusalem will go up year after year to worship the King, the LORD Almighty, and to celebrate the Festival of Tabernacles. If any of the peoples of the earth do not go up to Jerusalem to worship the King, the LORD Almighty, they will have no rain. If the Egyptian people do not go up and take part, they will have no rain. The LORD will bring on them the plague he inflicts on the nations that do not go up to celebrate the Festival of Tabernacles. This will be the punishment of Egypt and the punishment of all the nations that do not go up to celebrate the Festival of Tabernacles. (14:16–19 NIV)

In other words, some peoples and nations will be lukewarm or resistant to worshiping the Lamb. Their rejection of Christ the King will in some cases lead to serious consequences.

THE END IS BITTER

All this will culminate with a bitter end to the Golden Age—another war against the rule and reign of Jesus Christ. Revelation 20 says,

When the thousand years are over, Satan will be released from his prison and will go out to deceive the nations in the four corners of the earth—Gog and Magog—and to gather them for battle. In number they are like the sand on the seashore. They marched across the breadth of the earth and surrounded the camp of God's people, the city he loves. But fire came down from heaven and devoured them. And the devil, who deceived them, was thrown into the lake of burning sulfur, where the beast and the false prophet had been thrown. (vv. 7–10 NIV)

After a thousand years, the human race—multitudes of people like the grains of sand—will rise up in a final, short-lived rebellion against Jesus Christ.

George Eldon Ladd wrote, "After a thousand years in an almost perfect environment, it will become clear that sin—rebellion against God—is not due to an evil society or a bad environment. It is due to the sinfulness of the hearts of men."[2]

Dr. Dwight Pentecost makes the same point, writing, "The millennial age is designed by God to be the final test of fallen humanity under the most ideal circumstances, surrounded by every enablement to obey the rule of the king, from whom the outward sources of temptation have been removed, so that man may be found and proved to be a failure in even this last testing of fallen humanity."[3]

To sum up, everybody who goes into the Millennium will be righteous. But during this thousand-year period, there will be marriages among the mortals who come out of the Tribulation. Children will be born, and some of those children will rebel against the things of God. Just like today, every person born during the millennial age will make a personal decision for or against Jesus Christ.

Only the new heaven and new earth and New Jerusalem—our eternal home—will be pure, sinless, and forever holy. That's why the apostle Peter said, "But in keeping with his promise we are looking forward to a new heaven and a new earth, where righteousness dwells" (2 Peter 3:13 NIV).

Pastor Tim Chaddick said that when he was fourteen he got into an argument with a classmate. The other youngster, frustrated with Tim's teenage ego, yelled at him, "You're conceited."

Tim roared back, "No I'm not!"

Tim had no idea what the word *conceited* meant, so he went home and looked it up in a dictionary. That's one of the first times he was forced to examine himself regarding his failures.[4]

Since then, Tim has come to understand the importance of occasional times of prayerful, personal evaluations. We may not have to look up *conceited* in a dictionary, but we do have to look up our attitudes and actions in another Book—the Word of God.

Tim suggests taking a paper and prayerfully making two lists: your strengths and your weaknesses. He did this following a planned sabbatical, and he said, "To be honest, I was a bit surprised when the list was completed. Most of my strengths were connected to my gifts—abilities that God has given me to help other people, to teach, and so on. But my weaknesses, I noticed, were mostly character issues—bad attitudes and behaviors that remained unaddressed. While the big temptations had always been on my radar, I realized I was giving in to smaller ones."

Next, Tim did something few of us would have the courage to do. He showed the list to his spouse and said, "You know me better than anyone. Are these observations true?"

She studied the list and said, kindly but truthfully, "Yes, yes they are."

Tim said he walked away sulking. But he began working on the list, asking for God's help and looking to Jesus. He said, "The gospel transforms us so that even moments of temptation become the training ground for a life of abundance, as our hearts are radically reshaped and reordered by the love of Jesus. Because ultimately, the key to facing temptation is not a principle; it's a Person."[5]

For you and me, the main question isn't really, "Will there be sin in the Millennium?" It's, "Lord, is there sin in me right now? Is there a wicked pattern I need to correct? How can I grow in my daily walk of holiness, becoming more like Jesus Christ?"

Our Lord Jesus gives us insight and victory. The psalmist prayed, "Search me, O God, and know my heart; try me, and know my anxieties; and see if there is any wicked way in me, and lead me in the way everlasting" (139:23–24).

Why not ask the Lord to be preparing you now for millennial life and for eternal living by "beholding as in a mirror the glory of the Lord" and "being transformed into the same image from glory to glory, just as by the Spirit of the Lord" (2 Cor. 3:18)?

"For sin shall not have dominion over you, for you are not under the law but under grace" (Rom. 6:14). And for that, we'll be eternally thanking our wonderful King—the Lord Jesus!

CHAPTER 26

SALVATION IN THE MILLENNIUM

My friend Robert Morgan has a friend named Esther Edwards whose father, Edward Le Beau, served in the Marines during World War II. One evening while stationed at Guantanamo Bay in Cuba, Edward saw something floating in the water near a Navy ship. Grabbing a palm branch he fished it out of the bay. It was a copy of the Gospel of John. Apparently, a sailor had tossed it overboard.

Edward cleaned it off and put it under his bunk to dry. Shortly afterward, he began reading it. When he came to page 21, he read John 5:39: "Search the Scriptures; for in them ye think ye have eternal life: and they are they which testify of Me."

"It stood out to me, practically as neon lights," Edward later wrote.

He read through the booklet several times. When Edward's ship docked in Puerto Rico, he went into San Juan and found a copy of the whole English Bible in a drug store. Soon he had read through the entire New Testament. Its message gripped his heart, and, kneeling on the dusty coral floor of his tent, he confessed his sins and received Jesus Christ as his Savior.

"He gave me peace that is steadfast and sure," said the Marine. "Since these many years His Word has been my source and anchor of my soul."[1]

Imagine! A discarded, waterlogged booklet floating among US Navy ships in Guantanamo Bay changed a man's life! Salvation is a miracle that happens every day in our world. Every hour, people from Salvation is a miracle that happens every day in our world. Every hour, people from every tribe and tongue hear the truth of the gospel and believe. Those who were spiritually blind can suddenly see. Those who are lost become found within the worldwide family of the church. Those who were dead become alive through the power of Jesus' blood shed for them.

Which raises an interesting question: Will that process continue throughout the coming Golden Age? Will people need to be saved during the Millennium—and will they choose to be washed in the blood of Christ?

The answer may surprise you!

THE OPPORTUNITY FOR SALVATION

As we've seen, every person who is present at the beginning of Christ's millennial kingdom will be saved. Everyone will be a Christian at the start of the Golden Age, although there will be some major divisions or categories that define the population.

First, the millennial population will include those with *glorified* bodies and those with *earthly* bodies. Those who receive glorified bodies will come from three distinct groups:

- Saints from the Old Testament who followed God before the arrival of the Messiah. Examples include Abraham, Moses,

Deborah, Ruth, David, the prophets (including John the Baptist), and all the Israelites who trusted God for salvation.

- Raptured believers and every member of the church who died (or will die) prior to the Rapture—those whose souls are now with Jesus in paradise. That includes Jesus' original disciples, Augustine, Martin Luther, Billy Graham, and every person who trusted through faith in the death and resurrection of Jesus Christ.

- Those who are saved during the Tribulation and are then martyred for their faith. Revelation 20:4 says, "Then I saw the souls of those who had been beheaded for their witness to Jesus and for the word of God, who had not worshiped the beast or his image, and had not received his mark on their foreheads or on their hands. And they lived and reigned with Christ for a thousand years."

Every person from these three groups will enter the Millennium with glorified bodies, which means they will endure forever. They will live in perfect health for the entirety of Christ's thousand-year reign, and then they will transition into the new heaven and new earth when the Golden Age comes to a close.

What about salvation, then? Does that mean there will be no opportunities for people to receive Christ during the coming Golden Age?

Not so fast. Remember, there will be millions of people who enter the Millennium with earthly bodies. They will cling to Christ during the Tribulation, refusing the mark of the beast or any association with the Antichrist, and they will survive through great hardship until the second coming of our Lord.

Immediately after His second coming, Jesus will separate the godly survivors of the Tribulation from the ungodly, as described in Matthew 25:

When the Son of Man comes in His glory, and all the holy angels with Him, then He will sit on the throne of His glory. All the nations will be gathered before Him, and He will separate them one from another, as a shepherd divides his sheep from the goats. And He will set the sheep on His right hand, but the goats on the left. Then the King will say to those on His right hand, "Come, you blessed of My Father, inherit the kingdom prepared for you from the foundation of the world. . . ." Then He will also say to those on the left hand, "Depart from Me, you cursed, into the everlasting fire prepared for the devil and his angels." (vv. 31–34, 41)

You might be wondering, *Those who enter the Millennium with earthly bodies will already be saved as well. So again, is there no opportunity for salvation during the Golden Age?*

The answer is that millennial Christians with earthly bodies will have children. In fact, in a world that is completely prosperous and peaceful, chances are good that the residents of the Golden Age will have many, many children! As with Noah's family after the flood, they will be charged with repopulating the earth.

Here's where it gets interesting. Every child born during the Millennium will come into the world like you and me. They will be born with a sin nature, which means they will need to experience salvation in order for their names to be written in the Lamb's Book of Life. Just like you and me, they will need to believe in the gospel in order to gain eternal life.

So yes, there will be a need for salvation during the coming Golden Age. Each new generation will present a critical opportunity for evangelism—for training up children in the way they should go. As the population booms, there will be countless new souls ready to join the ranks of the faithful.

THE OPERATION OF SALVATION

One of the truths we've established in these pages is that the world of the Millennium will be quite different from the world of today.

Satan and his demons will be stripped of their authority, bound, and thrown into the abyss. Jesus will be fully and physically present as King. Humanity will flourish in a society with no war, no corruption, and seemingly limitless prosperity.

Given those vast changes, it's logical to wonder how the process of salvation will be carried out during the coming Golden Age. What will need to happen in order for individuals to see their names written in the Lamb's Book of Life?

Let's answer that question about the future by taking a quick detour to the past.

It's a common misconception that salvation operated differently in the Old Testament era than it does now. For example, many people assume the ancient Jews were saved by obeying the law—by following the different commandments listed in Scripture, observing the festivals and holy days laid out by Moses, and offering animal sacrifices as a way of purchasing forgiveness for sin.

This is not correct. Believers in the Old Testament were not saved by works, including sacrifices, circumcision, or observing the law. Instead, believers in the Old Testament were saved in the same way as you and me: by faith.

Paul explained the mechanism of salvation in the Old Testament by using Abraham as an example: "What then shall we say that Abraham our father has found according to the flesh? For if Abraham was justified by works, he has something to boast about, but not before God. For what does the Scripture say? 'Abraham believed God, and it was accounted to him for righteousness'" (Rom. 4:1–3).

The saints of the Old Testament believed God would send the Messiah, the Savior, to defeat evil and establish God's kingdom on earth. They placed their faith in that future event, looking forward to what would come. We place our faith in the same event—the sacrifice of Jesus on the cross—except that we are looking backward to what has already occurred.

Those who are saved during the Millennium will follow the

same path. Looking into history, they will exercise faith by believing in the death and resurrection of Jesus. They will follow the pattern established in Ephesians 2:8–9, which says, "For by grace you have been saved through faith, and that not of yourselves; it is the gift of God, not of works, lest anyone should boast."

It bears repeating: just like today, every individual in the Golden Age will make a personal decision for or against Christ.

Of course, millennial converts will have the advantage of living in an era free from the influence of Satan and filled with the tangible, visible figure of Christ. What an opportunity for evangelism!

THE OUTLOOK OF SALVATION

Can we assume, then, that salvation will be a given during the coming Golden Age? As people live under the protection of their King and witness the wonders of His kingdom, surely they will believe in their hearts and confess with their mouths that Jesus Christ is Lord. Right?

Sadly, even tragically, there is evidence in Scripture that many people will drift away from Christ during the later generations of the coming Golden Age—even to the point of rejecting salvation and rebelling against the King.

For example, we've already examined Isaiah 65:20 as evidence that lifespans will be dramatically increased during the Millennium. But take another look at that verse, in the New Living Translation: "No longer will babies die when only a few days old. No longer will adults die before they have lived a full life. No longer will people be considered old at one hundred! Only the cursed will die that young!"

The concept of "the cursed" does imply that people's longevity could still be influenced by sin during the Golden Age, and that those who give themselves to sin instead of to God will suffer the consequences of that choice—namely, death. Perhaps even eternal death.

Several times throughout the Bible, Jesus is described as ruling over the nations with a "rod of iron" (Ps. 2:9; Rev. 12:5; 19:15). This is likely the rod of a shepherd, which fits with Jesus' role as our protector. But it also points to the possibility of punishment and judgment against those who require it.

Most sobering of all is John's vision of humanity's final rebellion at the end of the Millennium: "Now when the thousand years have expired, Satan will be released from his prison and will go out to deceive the nations which are in the four corners of the earth, Gog and Magog, to gather them together to battle, whose number is as the sand of the sea. They went up on the breadth of the earth and surrounded the camp of the saints and the beloved city. And fire came down from God out of heaven and devoured them" (Rev. 20:7–9).

As the growing population of the millennial kingdom expands chronologically through time and geographically throughout the world, the seed of rebellion will be sown. It will flourish and flower into humanity's final war. John's phrasing of the opposing armies as "the sand of the sea" indicates a large amount of people who will ultimately reject God's free gift of salvation—and instead choose an eternity of separation from God.

What a shame. What a waste!

At the beginning of 2024, an art project created a digital portal between Dublin, Ireland, and New York City. Two large screens were installed in those cities as part of a frame in the rounded shape of a door or porthole. Those screens allowed residents of each city to catch a glimpse of what was happening halfway around the world.

If you've done much observing of human nature in recent years, you can probably guess what happened next. Less than a week after its launch, the portal was taken offline because one too many bad apples had ruined the bunch.

"There's been a .1% interaction that includes some hateful messages, some nudity, and that ruins it for everyone," said James Mettham, president of the company operating the portal. "The vast majority are really enjoying the fact that they can peer into the city like this."[2]

I would be remiss if I didn't end this chapter with a direct and personal question: When Jesus returns and establishes His glorious millennial kingdom, will you be part of it? Will you be a welcome guest of the King in a remade and refashioned Jerusalem—or will you spend eternity longing for some magic portal to grant you access to those blissful streets?

If there is any chance that you are not intimately connected with Jesus as your Lord and Savior—that you have not experienced salvation in *this* age, in *this* moment—then don't let another second go by without securing your eternal destiny!

Jesus died on the cross to pay the penalty for your sin. He offered Himself to death so that He might offer you life. Not just life, but life abundant. Life eternal. Life as you were always meant to experience it.

Say yes to that gift. Say yes to that Savior. And say it today.

CHAPTER 27

NO MORE EXCUSES

In 1979, a man named Albert Flick murdered his wife, Sandra. He stabbed her to death while her young daughter was nearby. Convicted by a jury of his peers, Flick spent twenty-five years in a federal penitentiary.

He was released in 2004 but was later accused of assaulting two more women in 2010, this time in Maine. Once again, the evidence against him was strong; Flick was convicted and sentenced to jail for a second time. The prosecutors in that case petitioned the judge to make sure Mr. Flick stayed behind bars for a long sentence—not only as punishment for his previous crimes but also to prevent any opportunities for new assaults. Or worse.

The judge disagreed. "At some point, Mr. Flick is going to age out of his capacity to engage in this conduct," he declared, "and incarcerating him beyond the time that he ages out doesn't seem to me to make good sense from a criminological or fiscal perspective."

In short, the judge believed Flick was too old to kill again.

After only four years in prison, Flick was released once more in 2014. He moved to the town of Lewiston, Maine. There he became infatuated with Kimberly Dobbie—a woman in her forties with two young children.

Tragically, terribly—but also predictably—Albert Flick murdered Kimberly Dobbie in 2018. He stabbed her while her twin sons were watching. The murderer released from incarceration because he was deemed too old to keep committing murder abused his freedom in the most horrible way imaginable, and innocent victims paid the price.[1]

I'm sure reading that story produces many emotions for you, as it does for me: anger, frustration, confusion, sorrow, and more. We feel sick that someone so obviously dangerous could be allowed to cause such harm once again.

There are four verses in the book of Revelation that will likely produce similar emotions. They tell us how the coming Golden Age will come to an end. Frankly, they express one of the most unexpected and shocking realities in Scripture. As is always the case, it's best to confront those realities with openness and honesty, which is what I'd like to do in this chapter.

Let's explore the story of those four verses as told in four separate acts.

SATAN RELEASED

Here's the first of our four verses: "Now when the thousand years have expired, Satan will be released from his prison" (Rev. 20:7).

The word *released* brings to mind the image of a prisoner being granted parole. Importantly, Satan will not escape the abyss after a thousand years. It will be God's decision to free him.

But why? Why would God choose to do this after all the pain and suffering Satan has caused? Dr. J. Vernon McGee offered an explanation:

When the late Dr. Chafer (founder of Dallas Theological Seminary) was once asked why God loosed Satan after he once had him bound, he replied, "If you will tell me why God let him loose in the first place, I will tell you why God lets him loose the second time." Apparently Satan is released at the end of the Millennium to reveal that the ideal conditions of the Kingdom, under the personal reign of Christ, do not change the human heart. This reveals the enormity of the enmity of man against God. Scripture is accurate when it describes the heart as "desperately wicked" and incurably so. Man is totally depraved. The loosing of Satan at the end of the 1,000 years proves it.[2]

In other words, Satan's release will produce a second chance for humanity—a second chance to rebuff the serpent's lies from the garden of Eden.

When Satan is released from his prison cell, he will go right back to what he does best—deceiving people, just as he did with Adam and Eve. Satan will "go out to deceive the nations which are in the four corners of the earth, Gog and Magog, to gather them together to battle, whose number is as the sand of the sea" (Rev. 20:8).

The mention of "Gog and Magog" does not necessarily connect to the battle described in Ezekiel 38–39, as the invading army in that passage comes from the North while the one in Revelation comes from all directions. One commentator describes Gog and Magog this way:

This is a general term in the Bible for the enemies of God spread throughout the remotest parts of the earth (Ezek. 38–9; Rev. 20:8). Those enlisting in Satan's army will likely be *geographically remote*, from among those cities and regions farthest from the center of the Messiah's kingdom in Jerusalem. They will also be *generationally removed* from their original ancestors who had survived the onslaught of the Beast, the memory of which will sound to these distant descendants like mere fables. Finally, the rebels will be *spiritually distant*, perhaps conforming to the outward expectations of worship and civil duty, but inwardly harboring cynicism, selfishness, and rebellion.[3]

Even after a thousand years of living in Christ's millennial kingdom, humanity will fail the test of the garden of Eden once more. Many people will listen to Satan's deception and will reject God. Why? Because even at our best, we are not able to save ourselves. We will always rely on Christ for redemption.

According to Warren W. Wiersbe:

In one sense, the millennial kingdom will "sum up" all that God has said about the heart of man during the various periods of history. It will be a reign of law, and yet law will not change man's sinful heart. Man will still revolt against God. The Millennium will be a period of peace and perfect environment, a time when disobedience will be judged swiftly and with justice; and yet in the end the subjects of the King will follow Satan and rebel against the Lord. A perfect environment cannot produce a perfect heart.[4]

JERUSALEM SURROUNDED

The next verse tells us exactly where Satan will lead his army: "They went up on the breadth of the earth and surrounded the camp of the saints and the beloved city" (Rev. 20:9).

Following the strategy of ancient warfare, the army of darkness will completely encircle and besiege God's people in Jerusalem, known as "the beloved city." This title holds great significance in the Bible. It is a reminder that Jerusalem is the city cherished by God, and He will protect her.

"The LORD loves the gates of Zion more than all the dwellings of Jacob" (Ps. 87:2).

"In that day it shall be said to Jerusalem: 'Do not fear; Zion, let not your hands be weak. The LORD your God in your midst, the Mighty One, will save; He will rejoice over you with gladness, He will quiet you with His love, He will rejoice over you with singing'" (Zeph. 3:16–17).

Notice what the faithful followers of Jesus will do at the end of the Millennium. Rather than engaging in physical combat, they will gather before the presence of the Lord and place their unwavering trust in Him. There is a lesson in this for us today. When we are surrounded by our enemies, will we do the same? Will we draw close to the Lord and trust in Him to deliver us?

In his commentary on the book of Revelation, New Testament scholar Craig S. Keener writes, "We can stand firm against evil even when the battle appears futile; victory belongs to the Lord! As the entire Bible and our Christian experience reminds us, however, we cannot triumph against this world's odds apart from his help."[5]

THE SAINTS SAVED

The Enemy unleashed. A rebellion began. An army mustered. You might expect this saga of rebellion to end in a long and terrible battle. It won't. Instead, God will deal with this revolt quickly and powerfully. Here is the third of our four verses: "And fire came down from God out of heaven and devoured them" (Rev. 20:9).

Imagine the powerful and awe-inspiring sight this will be! God will swiftly decimate Satan's army with fire from heaven. This is a common form of judgment in the Bible for those who oppose God.

- "The LORD rained brimstone and fire on Sodom and Gomorrah, from the LORD out of the heavens" (Gen. 19:24).
- "Then Nadab and Abihu, the sons of Aaron, each took his censer and put fire in it, put incense on it, and offered profane fire before the LORD, which He had not commanded them. So fire went out from the LORD and devoured them, and they died before the LORD" (Lev. 10:1–2).
- "So Elijah answered and said to the captain of fifty, 'If I am a man of God, then let fire come down from heaven and consume

you and your fifty men.' And fire came down from heaven and consumed him and his fifty" (2 Kings 1:10).

Earth's final battle will serve as a powerful reminder that no evil can overpower God. Whether it be a person, angel, demon, or any other force, there is no match for God Almighty's power.

THE DEVIL TORMENTED

In one of the most satisfying verses in the Bible, we learn how the coming Golden Age will end: "The devil, who deceived them, was cast into the lake of fire and brimstone where the beast and the false prophet are. And they will be tormented day and night forever and ever" (Rev. 20:10).

This is the end of the devil! At the close of the Millennium, Satan will share the same fate that the Antichrist and the False Prophet experienced one thousand years before. The devil will join them in the lake of fire, where they will be tormented forever and ever.

Jesus spoke about this future moment in Matthew's gospel (25:41), which means that moment *will* come to pass. It's a guarantee. Why is that important? Because it reminds us that Satan's punishment has always been part of God's design. That truth should bring us great encouragement and hope. Even today, our Enemy's days are numbered. God knows it. You and I know it. Even the devil knows it.

Let me close with a question you've probably never before considered. If you were an actor, would you ever agree to play the role of Satan in a movie? Neal McDonough did. While he has frequently played villains and bad guys, he took on the role of Satan for the first time in the faith-based film *The Shift*.

McDonough's sinister character didn't appear to be a monster but a subtle fellow full of tricks and lies who created "concrete temptations that most of us can relate to." In the process of creating the role,

McDonough said, "I got to learn so much about myself, about how blessed I am to have [God's] backing in everything that I do. . . . We all at times have a very mean person in us, all of us; we're human. There was only one person who was perfect."[6]

McDonough, a Christian who refuses questionable scenes, said he wanted "the audience to really understand and hate the devil. And hopefully by doing this, will make people think, 'You know maybe I should try a little bit harder to be a better husband, a better dad, a better worker, a better child of God.'"[7]

"You have to be careful," McDonough said, "because [the devil] is out there every day to take anything he can away from all of us if we don't start to believe wholehearted that God loves us so much."[8]

Yes, Satan is out there every day to take everything from us. But one day, he will be consigned to the lake of fire with no possibility of parole and no hope of escape. Until then, let's believe wholeheartedly that our Lord loves us so much. And with His help, let's be better children of God as we await the impending return of our victorious Lord Jesus Christ.

CHAPTER 28

THE FINAL JUDGMENT

In 2005, former governor of Alabama Don Siegelman was indicted. The following year, he was convicted of bribery and obstruction of justice. He spent six years in prison amid lots of opinions about whether his conviction was fair. Whatever the case, I was gripped by his description of the moment he stood before the judge for sentencing.

As Siegelman entered the courtroom, his brother, Les, told him he would be sentenced and immediately taken into custody. Siegelman disagreed, believing that, if convicted, he'd have time to get his affairs in order before entering prison.

"Trust me, they'll take you away as soon as you're sentenced," said Les. "They don't want you talking to the press. Give me your car keys and wallet." With growing apprehension, Siegelman did so. The tension increased exponentially when the judge entered and took his seat above the crowd and ordered the defendant to stand to hear his punishment.

Siegelman said, "I felt weak, helpless, and nauseous as I stood to hear my sentence: 'Eighty-eight months.'"

The judge then said, "Marshals, take him away."

Siegelman said, "I looked around for my wife, brother, and friends but all I could see were marshals. They hustled me out the aisle and to the side door. 'Face the wall,' they said. 'Put your hands over your head.' My new life had begun."[1]

For most of us, courtrooms aren't pleasant places. The prospect of standing before a robed judge, being convicted, sentenced, and led away in chains is the stuff of nightmares. Yet where would the world be without justice?

There is right and wrong in this world. There is good and evil, righteousness and wickedness. Someone has to enforce the laws. On earth, justice is fallible and subject to error and distortion. But one day, justice in our world will be leveled through infallible righteousness. Evil will be judged, wrongs will be righted, suffering will be abolished, sin will be ended, and truth and goodness will prevail.

One day, the Judge of all the earth will do what is right (Gen. 18:25).

Most Christians understand that everyone on earth will face a final judgment. As the Bible says, "It is appointed for men to die once, but after this the judgment" (Heb. 9:27). But there will be two separate judgments that take place—one at the beginning of the Tribulation and one at the conclusion of the Millennium. These two judgments will occur more than a thousand years apart and in two totally different courtrooms.

The first is called the judgment seat of Christ; the second is the great white throne judgment.

All authentic Christians will be judged in the first courtroom, which will immediately follow the Rapture. The apostle Paul said, "We must all appear before the judgment seat of Christ, that each one may receive the things done in the body, according to what he has done, whether good or bad" (2 Cor. 5:10).

Paul wrote those words to the church in Corinth, and he included himself in the "we." So, when he said, "We must all appear," he was clearly referring to Christ followers throughout the eras of Christian history—including you and me. This will be a "judgment" in the same sense as the Olympics uses judges. Meaning, the judgment seat of Christ will be an event where our works are evaluated to determine how we should be rewarded. There is no condemnation in this scene, only rewards.

The second judgment will be vastly different. This judgment is called the great white throne judgment. There will be a Judge but no jury, a prosecutor but no defender, a sentence but no appeal.

This is the final judgment of the world, and the verses that describe it comprise one of the most sobering passages in Scripture. All unbelievers will be judged at the great white throne judgment. They will not be evaluated by cultural opinions of right and wrong. They will be judged by the unbending standard of God's truth.

Here is a simple way to keep these two judgments separate: no unbelievers will appear before the judgment seat of Christ; no believers will appear before the great white throne judgment.

Let's look at the four elements that will dominate the great white throne judgment as described in Revelation 20:11–15.

THE JUDGE

The passage begins, "Then I saw a great white throne and Him who sat on it, from whose face the earth and the heaven fled away" (Rev. 20:11).

Who is this Judge? Jesus said, "The Father judges no one, but has committed all judgment to the Son. . . . And has given Him authority to execute judgment also, because He is the Son of Man" (John 5:22, 27).

Christ will be the Judge at the great white throne judgment. Think of it! The One who came and died for the sins of the world is now enthroned as the Judge of those who refused His free offer of eternal life.

THE JUDGED

Though this is the last place anyone would ever want to be, billions of people will find themselves standing in the dock, and every one of them will feel utterly alone. Revelation 20:12–13 says, "I saw the dead, small and great, standing before God. . . . The sea gave up the dead who were in it, and Death and Hades delivered up the dead who were in them."

In John's vision, he saw the bodies and souls of unbelievers of all ages called up from "Death and Hades" to stand before this blinding throne. This vast throng will include both the "small and great," meaning all classes and all ranks and all races of people. Many of them thought of themselves as religious during their lifetimes, yet here they are, naked before God.

Whether rich, poor, famous, obscure, beautiful, plain, powerful, weak, intelligent, dull, religious, or agnostic, all who stand before the great white throne judgment will share one common attribute: they will be utterly without hope because they died without truly knowing Christ.

THE JUDGING

Every verse in this passage grows more intense. We next read, "And another book was opened, which is the Book of Life. And the dead were judged according to their works, by the things which were written in the books" (Rev. 20:12).

When the unsaved dead stand before God, the books will be opened. This simply means their past deeds will be exposed. One of the books is identified as the Book of Life. The names of the others are not mentioned here, but various Scriptures indicate their identity and purpose in this final judgment.

THE BOOK OF LAW

The apostle Paul said, "By the deeds of the law no flesh will be justified in His sight. . . . For all have sinned and fall short of the glory of God" (Rom. 3:20, 23). In other words, if the law is the standard, then obedience to the law must be perfect in order to attain salvation. But perfect obedience is impossible for fallen humans.

Those who claim justification by the law sign their own death warrant, for the law itself will condemn those who fail to obey it perfectly.

THE BOOK OF WORKS

John saw the unregenerate dead "judged, each one according to his works" (Rev. 20:13). Earlier, the apostle Paul had written about those "whose end will be according to their works" (2 Cor. 11:15). Even earlier, Jesus had said, "The Son of Man will come in the glory of His Father with His angels, and then He will reward each according to his works" (Matt. 16:27).

God possesses a detailed record of every act ever committed by every person on earth. For the unbelievers who stand before the great white throne, every sordid sin will be revealed. For those who stood on the claim, "I deserve to go to heaven because I'm a good person," that claim will crumble into dust.

THE BOOK OF SECRETS

Jesus warned, "Nothing is secret that will not be revealed, nor anything hidden that will not be known and come to light" (Luke 8:17).

Paul added, "God will judge the secrets of men by Jesus Christ" (Rom. 2:16).

Solomon wrote, "God will bring every work into judgment, including every secret thing, whether good or evil" (Eccl. 12:14).

You may think your sins are hidden, but if they aren't covered over by the blood of Christ, they'll reappear before your very eyes on that terrible day of reckoning.

THE BOOK OF WORDS

Every word ever spoken will be available as evidence against the unsaved at the great white throne judgment. Our Lord Jesus said, "For every idle word men may speak, they will give account of it in the day of judgment. For by your words you will be justified, and by your words you will be condemned" (Matt. 12:36–37).

THE BOOK OF CONSCIENCE

Imagine the book of conscience. Paul wrote that people's consciences will bear witness to their thoughts: "Accusing or else defending them, on the day when . . . God will judge the secrets of mankind through Christ Jesus" (Rom. 2:15–16 NASB).

Conscience is our built-in, God-given guide to right and wrong. But the conscience is not infallible because it can be manipulated, ignored, retrained, or stifled.

Those standing before Christ at that judgment will be confronted with every time they ignored what they knew to be right and chose what they knew to be wrong.

THE BOOK OF LIFE

But to the praise of the Lord Jesus, there is another book. The Bible contains several references to a certain "Book of Life." (If you want to trace this out for yourself, study Ex. 32:32–33; Ps. 69:28; Dan. 12:1; Phil. 4:3; Rev. 3:5; 13:8; 17:8; 21:27; 22:19.)

Those whose names are in the Book of Life are the redeemed of all the ages. They will not be standing before this throne of final judgment. But those who *are* standing there awaiting their judgment will desperately cry out, "Surely, surely, my name is there! Look again! It must be there!"

Who can imagine the terror of that moment!

THE JUDGMENT

Last comes the instant of final judgment. Revelation 20:14–15 says, "Then Death and Hades were cast into the lake of fire. This is the second death. And anyone not found written in the Book of Life was cast into the lake of fire."

In an age which asserts everyone has a right to live by his own choices without consequence, the doctrine of hell is unpopular and often rejected, even among many Christians. But Scripture consistently affirms the existence of hell. For every word Jesus spoke about heaven, He spoke three about hell. For example: "[The King] will also say to those on the left hand, 'Depart from Me, you cursed, into the everlasting fire prepared for the devil and his angels.' . . . And these will go away into everlasting punishment" (Matt. 25:41, 46).

The Bible pictures hell in horrific terms. It is a place of torment and flames (Luke 16:20–28), of "wailing and gnashing of teeth" (Matt. 13:42) where the "worm does not die and the fire is not quenched" (Mark 9:48), and of "fire and brimstone" (Rev. 14:10–11; 21:8).

It grieves me to see the rejection of Christ occurring in Western nations today. Despite the abundance of Christian churches and the widespread availability of the gospel, belief in God and obedience to Him are plummeting. I sorrow at the punishment awaiting those who turn their backs on God where knowledge of Him is so prevalent.

You, the reader of this chapter, are in a happy position. You still have time! If you have not put your trust in Jesus Christ as your Savior and come into an obedient relationship with Him, the opportunity lies open before you. It's not too late. You can still escape the rising torrent before it takes you under. But a time is coming when death will close your eyes. At that point, your eternal future will be sealed.

I urge you to turn to Christ today, at this moment! Christ Himself said, "He who believes in Him is not condemned; but he who does not believe is condemned already, because he has not believed in the name of the only begotten Son of God.... Most assuredly, I say to you, he who hears My word and believes in Him who sent Me has everlasting life, and shall not come into judgment, but has passed from death into life" (John 3:18; 5:24).

I remember the words of a song that used to be sung at church revivals when I was a boy. I still remember how I felt whenever they sang this song:

> I dreamed that the great judgment morning
> Had dawned, and the trumpet had blown;
> I dreamed that the nations had gathered
> To Judgment before the white throne;
> From the throne came a bright, shining angel
> And stood by the land and the sea,
> And swore with his hand raised to heaven,
> That time was no longer to be. . . .
> The rich man was there but his money
> Had melted and vanished away;
> A pauper he stood in the judgment,
> His debts were too heavy to pay;
> The great man was there, but his greatness
> When death came, was left far behind!
> The angel that opened the records,
> Not a trace of his greatness could find. . . .
> The gambler was there and the drunkard,
> And the man that had sold them the drink,
> With the people who sold them the license
> Together in hell did they sink.

The moral man came to the judgment,
But his self-righteous rags would not do;
The men who had crucified Jesus
Had passed off as moral men, too.
The soul that had put off salvation—
"Not tonight; I'll get saved by and by;
No time now to think of religion!"
At last, he had found time to die.
And oh, what a weeping and wailing,
As the lost were told of their fate;
They cried for the rocks and the mountains,
They prayed, but their prayer was too late.[2]

It's not too late right now! Before you take another breath or turn another page, approach the throne of grace, confess your sins, and realize that Jesus died to give you forgiveness and eternal life.

Right now, proclaim Him as the Lord of your life.

CHAPTER 29

THE BRIDGE TO ETERNITY

The Ruyi Bridge in Taizhou, China, is often considered the most beautiful bridge in the world.

It's actually three pedestrian walkways that weave and curve over one another like ribbons. Some have compared it to horizontal strands of DNA. The futuristic bridge rises 460 feet over the gorgeous Valley of the Divine Canyon. The structure is sometimes draped in clouds, giving it a celestial appearance. The floor is transparent glass, and some who walk across it describe the experience as walking across a rainbow in the sky.

Yet this beautiful bridge simply cannot compare in beauty with the thousand-year-long bridge that connects time with eternity. The Millennium is a long link in history between the Tribulation on one side and the new heaven, the new earth, and the city of New Jerusalem on the other side. It truly spans a divine canyon of hours, days, years, and centuries, and it leads us from existence on the old earth to our eternity on the new one.

The Golden Age is the way we'll transition into the eternal state. We'll be conditioned for everlasting life in heaven by our experiences during the Millennium.

Let me show you how this works out in several areas.

THE ENEMY

As we've learned, Satan will be bound and imprisoned in the bottomless pit for a thousand years (Rev. 20:1–2). But this is not his final destination.

According to Revelation 19, the Antichrist and his assistant, the False Prophet, will be cast into "the lake of fire burning with brimstone" at the end of the Tribulation (v. 20). For some reason, the Lord won't do the same with Satan. Instead, as we have seen in previous chapters, the devil will be incarcerated in a different place—the bottomless pit (20:2–3)—throughout the Millennium, then he will be set free after a thousand years for one more vain attempt to oppose Christ (vv. 7–10).

That final, diabolical attempt will fail, as Revelation 20:10 tells us, "The devil, who deceived them, was cast into the lake of fire and brimstone where the beast and false prophet are. And they will be tormented day and night forever and ever."

During the Golden Age, Satan will be bound. But during eternity, He will be in everlasting hell with no parole, no escape, no hope. Throughout eternity, he and his forces will be totally absent from our lives. Just as he wasn't present in the first two chapters of the Bible, so he isn't mentioned in the final two—Revelation 21 and 22, which describe our eternal home. Satan will never be present in our eternal future, not even for one second!

Similarly, the curse that was placed upon creation after the fall of Adam and Eve will have no more effect. That curse will be abated during the Millennium, then abolished for all eternity.

THE UNIVERSE

The millennial reign of Jesus Christ will take place on our present earth, which is surrounded by the vastness of the material universe. Genesis 1:1 says, "In the beginning God created the heavens and the earth." This original creation will continue to the end of the Millennium, but Peter tells us about its ultimate demise: "But the day of the Lord will come as a thief in the night, in which the heavens will pass away with a great noise, and the elements will melt with fervent heat; both the earth and the works that are in it will be burned up" (2 Peter 3:10).

Peter went on to say, "The heavens will be dissolved, being on fire. . . . Nevertheless we, according to His promise, look for new heavens and a new earth in which righteousness dwells" (2 Peter 3:12–13).

The apostle John took up the story at that point, telling us: "Now I saw a new heaven and a new earth, for the first heaven and the first earth had passed away" (Rev. 21:1). As I've said many times, we'll not spend eternity in some vaporous state. We'll physically live on a beautiful, huge, earthlike planet with a glorious capital—New Jerusalem—surrounded by an eternal universe of stars and heavenly bodies.

Even during the Millennium, the universe will age; the laws of entropy will still be in effect. Our current world is not endless in duration. But the new heaven and new earth will be made with eternal elements and will endure forever. If you want to read more about this, just turn to the final two chapters of the Bible.

THE CITY

In Revelation 21 and 22 you'll also find a description of that global capital: New Jerusalem. Just as the earthly city of Jerusalem will be our Lord's millennial capital, the eternal city of New Jerusalem will be His capital forever. This is "the city which has foundations, whose builder and maker is God" (Heb. 11:10), the city God has prepared for His people (11:16).

Listen to the apostle John's wide-eyed account in Revelation 21: "Then I, John, saw the holy city, New Jerusalem, coming down out of heaven from God, prepared as a bride adorned for her husband" (v. 2).

John continued, "[The angel] showed me the holy city, Jerusalem, descending out of heaven from God. It shone with the glory of God and sparkled like a precious stone . . . as clear as crystal. . . . When he measured it, he found it was a square, as wide as it was long. In fact, its length and width and height were each 1,400 miles. . . . The wall was made of jasper, and the city was pure gold" (vv. 10–11, 16, 18 NLT).

Millennial Jerusalem will be spectacular, high and lifted up, the joy of the whole earth. But it cannot compare to the glorious city of New Jerusalem, which Jesus has prepared for us. The writer of Hebrews said, "For here we have no continuing city, but we seek the one to come" (13:14).

Perhaps you're asking, "Are the descriptions of this city literal?" I certainly believe this is a literal city on an actual planet in a corporal universe. Jesus rose physically and bodily from the dead, and our human bodies will be transformed for the eternal state. We'll live in a glorious environment with work to do, people to love, praises to render, and a God to worship and enjoy forever.

THE RIVER

Do you remember how I described the millennial river that will flow from beneath the temple and irrigate the Negev Desert and turn the Dead Sea into a living paradise? This river is described in Ezekiel 47.

Well, that river is simply a precursor to the crystal river that will flow from beneath God's throne and irrigate the new earth. The last chapter of the Bible begins with these words: "And he [the angel] showed me a pure river of water of life, clear as crystal, proceeding from the throne of God and of the Lamb" (Rev. 22:1). This river will hydrate the Tree of Life park and be a joy for all who walk along its banks (vv. 1–4).

The description we're given at the beginning of the Bible's last chapter paints scenes so simple yet so sensational that any of us should be eager to walk alongside the streams, run through the parks, and eat from the fruit trees.

THE DURATION

As we've learned, many people will enter the Millennium from Tribulation days in their mortal bodies. Some will marry and have children, and life expectancy will be in the hundreds of years. Isaiah 65:20 says, "No longer will people be considered old at one hundred!" (NLT). Yet death will still occur, and those with earthly bodies will still be subject to aging.

In the new heaven and new earth, *everyone* will be immortal and imperishable. Many theologians believe we'll all appear to be in our thirties—the age of Christ when He rose again. But regardless of the appearance of our age, our lives will have no end.

The apostle John used the word *everlasting* eight times in his Gospel to describe our lives in heaven, and he used the word *eternal* nine times. For example, Jesus said in John 3:15, "Whoever believes in [Christ] should not perish but have eternal life." And "he who believes in the Son has everlasting life" (v. 36).

The eternal God has promised us life of endless duration!

We're told explicitly that there will be no death or dying in the new heaven and new earth. John wrote, "And God will wipe away every tear from their eyes; there shall be no more death, nor sorrow, nor crying. There shall be no more pain, for the former things have passed away" (Rev. 21:4). Like our Lord, we will have incorruptible bodies (1 Cor. 15:42).

THE WORSHIP

I've already described millennial worship. Remember? It will be uncorrupted, undivided, and unending. Songs will fill the air, and the very atmosphere will resound with the praises of our King. Yet worship during the earthly reign of Christ will be simply a prelude to the explosion of adoration that will fill and thrill our souls in New Jerusalem.

I want to point out a very ordinary word that appears here and there throughout the book of Revelation—*every*.

Revelation 1:7 says that when Christ comes again *every* eye will see Him. Revelation 5:9 tells us that the population of heaven will be composed of those redeemed by the blood of Christ from *every* tribe and tongue and people and nation. According to Revelation 5:13, *every* creature in heaven and on the earth and under the earth and such as are in the sea and all that is in them will sing, "Blessings and honor and glory and power be to Him who sits on the throne, and to the Lamb, forever and ever."

Twice the book of Revelation says that God will wipe *every* tear from our eyes (7:17; 21:4). Revelation 22:2 says the Tree of Life will bear fruit *every* month; and verse 12 of the same chapter says the Lord will reward *every* person for their work.

And I'll add this one: We will give Him *every* praise! If on earth we can sing, "Every day with Jesus is sweeter than the day before," how can we contain the joy when our days with Him are unceasing?

THE KING

During the coming Golden Age, Christ will rule over the nations of the earth. Though Satan will be bound, the mortals who enter from the Tribulation will still have sinful natures, and so will their descendants. By the end of the Millennium, there will again be a flash of resistance to His rule.

Not so on the new earth.

Christ will rule from His throne in New Jerusalem, yet He will be utterly accessible to His people. In Revelation 21:3, John heard a loud voice from heaven saying, "Look! God's dwelling place is now among the people, and he will dwell with them. They will be his people, and God himself will be with them and be their God" (NIV).

Revelation 22:3 says, "The throne of God and of the Lamb will be in the city, and his servants will serve him" (NIV).

Interestingly, the new earth will still be divided into nations, but all the leaders of the nations will maintain absolute allegiance to our Lord. We'll be busy serving the Lord in a billion different ways, and the new earth will be productive. The Bible says about the city of New Jerusalem: "On no day will its gates ever be shut, for there will be no night there. The glory and honor of the nations will be brought into it" (Rev. 21:25–26 NIV).

We've learned how the millennial earth will be verdant and prolific during the reign of Christ. But imagine the wealth and power awaiting us in eternity! That subject occupied Paul's mind as he wrote the book of Ephesians. He said, "And God raised us up with Christ and seated us with him in the heavenly realms in Christ Jesus, in order that in the coming ages he might show the incomparable riches of his grace" (2:6–7 NIV).

Hebrews 9:15 promises us an eternal inheritance. Peter wrote that we are called into an inheritance that can never perish, spoil, or fade, kept in heaven for us (1 Peter 1:4). We are heirs of God and coheirs with Christ (Rom. 8:17).

THE BRIDGE

Greenland sharks have the longest lifespans of any known vertebrate and can live up to 500 years. They're a fascinating fish. They don't reach sexual maturity until about 150 years, and their pups are born after a gestation period of as much as 18 years. Imagine a pregnancy lasting that long! Today there are Greenland sharks that were swimming in the oceans long before the Pilgrims sailed the *Mayflower*.

But sooner or later time runs out for even these persevering creatures. Even if we had a thousand years to live—a millennium—the final month, week, day, and hour would come at last. The Millennium is not everlasting. It's simply a thousand-year-long bridge across the final epoch in the history of this old earth. Its far side is anchored to eternal ground.

The thousand-year reign of Christ won't last a day beyond its appointed span. We'll not be staying there forever, just as we don't want to stand forever on a beautiful bridge. We understand it's a viaduct to victory, a bridge to eternity, and God's way of transitioning from human history to the eternal regions of the new heaven and new earth and New Jerusalem. Just as death is the passage to paradise, the Golden Age will lead to our glorious, everlasting, never-ending fellowship with all the saints of all the ages—and with our dear Savior, who made it all possible.

Let's look forward to the coming Golden Age, but let's also look beyond it to our eternal home! As we do, let's give all praise and glory and honor to our everlasting Lord!

CHAPTER 30

THE PROMISE
OF UTOPIA

Utopia.

That strange word was coined more than five hundred years ago by Sir Thomas More, a Roman Catholic philosopher, as the title of his fictional book describing a perfect society that existed on a remote island somewhere in the uncharted Atlantic. More invented the word *utopia* by combining the Greek term for "no" with *topos*, meaning "place."

In other words, utopia is made up—it's a nonexistent society that can be found only in our dreams.

Most literary scholars aren't overly impressed by the actual story of More's book. It's not a page-turner, nor is it a masterpiece. Yet *Utopia* has remained one of the most famous books in Western literature because of the power of its central idea: that people long for a more perfect world.

We hear it in the dreams of the poets. We read it in great stories. We see it in the paintings of famous artists featured in great museums. It's as if we as human beings instinctively understand that the paradise in the garden of Eden was our normal state. That's what we were created to enjoy, but we lost it after Adam and Eve sinned against God. Now we yearn for its restoration. We want it back.

That's the bad news.

The good news is that our often-unspoken yearning corresponds with God's plans for the future. Everywhere we turn in the Bible, we uncover prophecies and descriptions of God's true utopia—the new heaven and new earth, wherein righteousness dwells.

Importantly, these prophecies are different from those that make promises about the Millennium. When the Golden Age concludes, our eternal state will commence. That is when we will finally transition to our eternal home.

THE PROMISE OF THE NEW HEAVEN AND NEW EARTH

In Revelation 21, the apostle John described his prophetic vision of the new heaven and new earth:

> Now I saw a new heaven and a new earth, for the first heaven and the first earth had passed away. Also there was no more sea. Then I, John, saw the holy city, New Jerusalem, coming down out of heaven from God, prepared as a bride adorned for her husband. (vv. 1–2)

Talk about utopia! That word is hopelessly insufficient to describe the place God is preparing for us. It is our heavenly home—the place where Christ rules forever.

Remember, though, we won't reach that heavenly home after we pass away or even after the Rapture. Not yet. Christians who pass through the veil of death will join Jesus in paradise, which is separate from our eternal state. Then will come the Millennium, and *then*—after that period of one thousand years—we will transition with Jesus into our final, eternal home.

Notice the order of events in Revelation.

The bulk of the middle chapters in that book (Rev. 6–18) describe the unfolding events of the Tribulation, with their seven seals, seven trumpets, and seven bowls of wrath—all leading to the final climactic battle in world history: the battle of Armageddon. In the next chapter, Revelation 19, the angelic host bursts into praise as Christ returns to earth to defeat the forces of the Antichrist and rescue His people. The first part of Revelation 20 describes the millennial kingdom that Christ will establish when He returns. The last part of chapter 20 describes the great white throne judgment. This is when all who rejected Christ will be condemned.

Then we turn the page, as it were, and begin reading in Revelation 21:1 about the creation of the new heaven and new earth.

THE PURIFICATION OF THE NEW HEAVEN AND NEW EARTH

Peter described the cataclysmic moment that will take place as the Golden Age comes to an end and the eternal state is ushered in:

> The day of the Lord will come as a thief in the night, in which the heavens will pass away with a great noise, and the elements will melt with fervent heat; both the earth and the works that are in it will be burned up. Therefore, since all these things will be dissolved, what manner of persons ought you to be in holy conduct and godliness, looking for and hastening the coming of the day of God, because of which the heavens will be dissolved, being on fire, and the elements will melt with fervent heat? (2 Peter 3:10–12)

I used to understand these verses as teaching the complete destruction of the current heaven and earth—everything burned to cinders and completely remade. But as I've studied Peter's key phrases in more detail, I've come to a different conclusion. Instead of being totally annihilated, the present heaven and earth will be cleansed, glorified, and equipped for our eternal use.

Think of a blacksmith or a metalworker smelting a chunk of ore. The original material is placed in a fire of extreme heat so that all the impurities are burned away. The ore is purified. It is refined. And when it emerges from the fire, it can be fashioned into something far superior to its original form.

That's what will happen to our universe. All evidence of disease will be burned up. All evidence of disobedience will melt away. All the remnants and results of sin, sorrow, and suffering will be destroyed. Out of the smoldering ruins, God will recreate all physical reality, and He will bring forth a fresh universe—a new heaven and new earth.

THE PRINCIPLES OF THE NEW HEAVEN AND NEW EARTH

Having discussed the promise and the purification of the new heaven and the new earth, let's return to Revelation 21 to uncover some startling principles about our new universe. I want to tell you what this is all going to be like.

Among the glorious things we're told in the book of Revelation, four have struck me with particular force: the removal of the sea, the removal of sanctuaries and other physical church buildings, the total removal of suffering, and the end of separation between what is physical and what is spiritual.

THERE WILL BE NO SEA

The first thing we have to grapple with is the question of oceans. Revelation 21:1 says, "Now I saw a new heaven and a new earth, for the first heaven and the first earth had passed away. Also there was no more sea." If you're like me, that feels a little disconcerting. I live in Southern

California near the ocean, and I love watching the sun fall like a blazing orb into the Pacific in the evenings at sunset. Many of us who love the oceans cock a troubled eyebrow when we read the last phrase of verse 1.

But the Bible doesn't tell us there won't be beautiful bodies of water in our new earth. In fact, Revelation 22 describes a beautiful river, with water "clear as crystal," that will run through New Jerusalem (v. 1). Similarly, we can have confidence that the same Creator who made such impressive oceans in our current world will only increase their magnificence in the next.

What did John mean, then, when he said, "There was no more sea"? Let's remember two realities. First, for the people of the ancient world, the ocean represented chaos and fear. Genesis 1 described the earliest iteration of our world as a cosmic ocean, with "darkness . . . on the face of the deep" (v. 2). God's six days of creation brought order to that chaos. So, John noting the absence of a sea in the new creation can be understood as the absence of chaos, rather than the absence of water.

Second, the surface of our current planet is primarily water—about 71 percent. The oceans hold 97 percent of all the earth's water, but these vast wastelands of salt water are essentially uninhabitable by humans. Evidently our new world will not contain wastelands of salty seas. The composition of the planet will be so different, and the nature of our glorified bodies will be so superior, that the very ecology of the new creation will be altered.

THERE WILL BE NO SANCTUARIES

There will be no sanctuary or tabernacle or temple in the new heaven and new earth—and no churches. Revelation 21:22 says, "The Lord God Almighty and the Lamb are its temple." Why no more churches? Because God will be dwelling in the midst of His people, just as He started off doing in the garden of Eden. Therefore, there will be no need for a sanctuary to manifest His presence.

Remember, God does not dwell in buildings during this age; He dwells in His people. At present, we cannot "see" His presence as we will be able to in heaven. Instead of dwelling *in* us in the new heaven and new earth, He will dwell *among* us, in our very presence! No building or structure could improve on His tangible presence in our midst.

"Behold, the tabernacle of God is with men, and He will dwell with them, and they shall be His people. God Himself will be with them and be their God" (Rev. 21:3).

The same Jesus who healed the sick, raised the dead, fed the multitudes, died on Calvary, was raised from the dead, and who ascended into heaven will be walking among us in eternity. We will have unbroken, personal fellowship with Him forever.

THERE WILL BE NO SUFFERING

Whenever I am in pain, or meet with someone who is, my thoughts go immediately to the day described in Revelation 21:4—a day when there will be no more tears, death, sorrow, crying, or pain. All of us are touched by the pain of sickness and infirmity, both physical and emotional. Whether it touches us or someone we care about, all of us have reason to anticipate a pain-free heaven.

Think of it. Those today who are blind, deaf, lame, mute, congenitally impaired, or deformed—all will receive completely whole resurrection bodies for their eternal stay in heaven. All doctors, nurses, pharmacists, therapists, and undertakers will be out of business forever!

Similarly, verse 4 indicates that by the wiping away of tears there will be no sadness in heaven. That promise was made initially in Revelation 7:17, where John saw the Lamb wiping away all the tears from the eyes of the saints.

THERE WILL BE NO SEPARATION

That brings us to the final feature I want to mention: ultimately there will be no separation between heaven and earth. Revelation 21:4–5 says, "The former things have passed away. Then He who sat on the throne said, 'Behold, I make all things new.'"

Randy Alcorn explained it like this:

Heaven is God's home. Earth is our home. Jesus Christ, as the God-
man, forever links God and mankind, and thereby forever links
Heaven and Earth. As Ephesians 1:10 demonstrates, this idea of
Earth and Heaven becoming one is explicitly biblical. Christ will
make Earth into Heaven and Heaven into Earth. Just as the wall
that separates God and mankind is torn down in Jesus, so too the
wall that separates Heaven and Earth will be forever demolished.
There will be one universe, with all things in Heaven and on Earth
together under one head, Jesus Christ.

Alcorn continued, "God's plan is that there will be no more gulf
between the spiritual and physical worlds. There will be no divided
loyalties or divided realms. There will be one cosmos, one universe
united under one Lord—forever. This is the unstoppable plan of God.
This is where history is headed."[1]

The new heaven and new earth is the place we've always longed
for and wanted to see. One man who understood this was C. S.
Lewis, author of the Chronicles of Narnia. He used the fantasy world
of Narnia to teach us lessons about our own world and about eternal truths. In the last pages of the volume about Narnia, the stars
fell from the heavens, the old Narnia was destroyed, and the door
was shut on times past. The central characters looked around in
amazement, trying to regain their orientation. The air was unusually fresh, and there was a beauty about the landscape they couldn't
comprehend.

Lucy asked, "Peter, where is this, do you suppose?"

"I don't know," said Peter. "It reminds me of somewhere but I can't
give it a name. Could it be somewhere we once stayed for a holiday
when we were very, very small?"

"It would have to have been a jolly good holiday," said Eustace. "I
bet there isn't a country like this anywhere in our world. Look at the

colours! You couldn't get a blue like the blue on those mountains in our world."

The children began to notice that the features of this new world were very much like the features of the old Narnia, only bigger and brighter and more beautiful, as if a film had been removed from a picture. The characters looked around perplexed, for their new home looked familiar, yet so different.

Finally, Professor Digory Kirke explained it like this: "Listen, Peter. When Aslan said you could never go back to Narnia, he meant the Narnia you were thinking of. But that was not the real Narnia. That had a beginning and an end. It was only a shadow or a copy of the real Narnia which has always been here and always will be here."

Lewis continued the story, "It was the Unicorn who summed up what everyone was feeling. He stamped his right fore-hoof on the ground and neighed, and then he cried: 'I have come home at last! This is my real country! I belong here. This is the land I have been looking for all my life, though I never knew it till now. The reason why we loved the old Narnia is that it sometimes looked a little like this.'"

Our world offers a foretaste of heaven. The Millennium will be an incredible bridge, but still part of our journey home. Only in the divine utopia—the new earth, or what some call the eternal state—will our deepest longings finally be fulfilled.

CHAPTER 31

KINGDOM READY

Novelist Jennifer Willis, who is also an amateur astronomer, wrote a blog post entitled "Why We Look Up: Anticipation" to describe her experiences with stargazing.

When preparing for an evening of exploring the cosmos, she begins by reading about certain stars and choosing specific targets for observation. She studies the weather forecasts and checks all her equipment.

"Some might consider that prep work tedious," Jennifer wrote, "and the hours waiting for darkness wasted time. For me, expectation enhances the adventure. Anticipation makes everything sweeter."[1]

In this book, I've tried to provide a telescope into the future, to a Golden Age much discussed in the Bible—a millennial reign unlike any other epoch in the history of the world. I hope it's caused you to look upward to heaven in anticipation.

But these millennial blessings—which will one day be physical, literal, political, and geographical—are available to you and me right now on a spiritual, personal, emotional, and experiential level.

In talking about the ultimate blessings promised to us during the Millennium and the eternal state, the apostle Paul wrote, "We believers . . . have the Holy Spirit within us as a foretaste of future glory" (Rom. 8:23 NLT). The Holy Spirit, who is eternal and transcends time, has brought us tokens of the future.

In the book of Genesis, Jacob was an old man living in grief. His sons had gone down to Egypt to find grain, and there they met their brother Joseph, whom they thought was dead. Joseph sent them back home with an invitation for his father to come enjoy the bounty of Egypt's golden age. To reassure the old man, Joseph sent with his brothers sets of new clothing, shekels of silver, donkeys loaded with the best things of Egypt, and yet more donkeys loaded with grain and bread and other provisions.

As a result, Jacob enjoyed the blessings of Egypt before he even arrived there. How? Because his son was alive and reigning on the throne of Egypt.

Because of God's Son, who is now alive and reigning at the Father's right hand, we can enjoy the blessings of His kingdom before we even arrive in the millennial age. The Holy Spirit brings them to us. He Himself is a foretaste of all the good coming our way.

Remember what I said about the kingdom being "already but not yet"? There are some millennial qualities we can enjoy "already" while we're awaiting the "not yet." Let's wrap up these pages by exploring several of these incredible opportunities.

HOLINESS

Take the concept of holiness, for example. As we've seen, the prophet Zechariah promised that during the thousand-year reign of Christ even the bridles of the horses will have bells engraved with the words "HOLINESS TO THE LORD" (14:20). Jerusalem will be known as "My holy mountain," says the Lord in Isaiah 56:7. His habitation will be "holy and glorious" (63:15), and the Lord will teach the people of the world "the difference between the holy and the holy" (Ezek. 44:23).

Yet even now, the followers of Christ have the Holy Spirit within us—and don't disregard the adjective in His name! He is the *Holy* Spirit, and His indwelling presence within us transforms us into the image of Christ "from glory to glory" (2 Cor. 3:18). The apostle Peter told us, "as He who called you is holy, you also be holy in all your conduct" (1 Peter 1:15).

Reader's Digest carried an article that said, "Wash Your Hands Immediately after Touching These Ten Things." Want to know what they are? Money is the first thing (there's a spiritual lesson there!), followed by handrails, restaurant menus, anything in a doctor's office, animals, touchscreens, cutting boards, ink pens, anything at an airport, and even soap dispensers.[2]

If I did as the article suggested, I'd spend most of my day washing my hands! But in an intangible sense, we're surrounded by a world of corruption, defilement, foul words, impure thoughts, and lots of moral muck and mire. Just as Jesus washed Peter's feet, so we need the constant cleansing of His grace as the Holy Spirit helps us grow in daily, practical holy living.

What area of your life needs to become purer and holier? In light of all God has for you in the future, keep working diligently to live a life worthy of the Lord now. We mustn't wait for the Millennium for holiness!

PEACE

Nor should we wait until the Millennium for peace! You've read the wonderful news that for a thousand years the world will be free from wars and rumors of wars. Jesus Christ will rule over the nations, and they will beat their swords into plowshares and learn of war no more (Isa. 2:4).

But Millennium levels of peace can be ours right now through the Lord Jesus Christ. While we may have little peace in our world, we can have great peace in our hearts. How often by the bedsides of the sick or over the kitchen tables of the troubled have I quoted John 14:27: "Peace I leave with you, My peace I give to you; not as the world gives do I give to you. Let not your heart be troubled, neither let it be afraid."

All the peace Jesus will bring with Him in the future He already possesses now. And He distributes it to His children as they pray and trust Him with their burdens. While we're waiting for the kingdom that's "not yet," we can appropriate the peace of the King and kingdom who is already here. Romans 14:17 says, "For the kingdom of God is not eating and drinking, but righteousness and peace and joy in the Holy Spirit."

Psalm 119:165 says, "Great peace have those who love Your law, and nothing causes them to stumble." The apostle Paul wrote, "To be spiritually minded is life and peace" (Rom. 8:6).

I like the way Rick Stedman summed things up: "Jesus Himself, not merely a Jesus-like lifestyle, is the solution to worry, stress, and trouble. The cure for anxiety is not just to follow Jesus' way of life, but to be filled with Jesus Himself. He is our peace. His peace He will give us."[3]

VICTORY OVER SATAN

I'm sure you've rejoiced over the coming capture and imprisonment of that old serpent, the devil, who will be out of action for a thousand years on this earth. But remember, our Savior has already defeated him. We can resist the devil now, and he will flee from us (James 4:7). We can "be strong in the Lord and in the power of His might," putting on the whole armor of God to enable us to "stand against the wiles of the devil" (Eph. 6:10–11).

I never waste my time talking to Satan or rebuking him. I ask the Lord to do that on my behalf. "Lord, rebuke the devil in the name of

Jesus and by the power of His blood." When Satan was accusing the high priest Joshua in Zechariah 3, the angel simply said, "The LORD rebuke you, Satan! The LORD who has chosen Jerusalem rebuke you!" (v. 2). Jude told us that even the archangel Michael, when he was contending with the devil, "dared not bring him a reviling accusation, but said, 'The Lord rebuke you!'" (v. 9).

When you feel the devil attacking you, oppressing you, tempting you, and causing mischief in your life, remember he is a defeated foe. Put on the armor of God, resist him, and pray, "Lord, rebuke that old serpent!"

The Lord Jesus has just as much power and authority right now at this very moment as He will possess in the Millennium or throughout eternity. He is the same yesterday, today, and forever (Heb. 13:8).

LONGEVITY

I devoted an entire chapter to the subject of the long, Genesis-like lifespans of mortals who pass from the Tribulation to the Golden Age. But, my friend, even if people in "kingdom come" live the entire span of a thousand years, they have nothing on us who currently possess eternal life.

Many times in sermons and books, I've reminded you that our eternal life doesn't start when Christ returns. It begins at the moment we receive Jesus Christ as Lord and Savior.

I know the concept of eternity boggles our minds. How do we measure everlasting life? If you were to take millions of ages, billions of millennia, trillions of light-years, and quintillions of centuries— well, that would just be like the first minute of eternity. It baffles our minds, but it thrills our souls.

The Bible simply says, "He who believes in the Son has everlasting life" (John 3:36).

We have everlasting life because we serve an eternal King

(1 Tim. 1:17) who possesses eternal power (Rom. 1:20) and works toward an eternal purpose (Eph. 3:11). He offers eternal salvation (Heb. 5:9) and eternal redemption (9:12) through Jesus Christ, who offered Himself without spot to God through the eternal Spirit (9:14). He provides us with everlasting consolation (2 Thess. 2:16) through the blood of the everlasting covenant (Heb. 13:20). Because of the everlasting gospel (Rev. 14:6) we have an eternal inheritance (Heb. 9:15) and an eternal home (Eccl. 12:5) with eternal glory (2 Tim. 2:10). His kingdom is an everlasting kingdom (2 Peter 1:11).

That's even better than birthday number 969, like Methuselah!

WORSHIP

As I wrote about the worship that will occur during the Millennium, I almost thought I could hear the temple choirs and the sanctuary orchestras that will greet worshipers as they approach Jerusalem. But the deafening majesty of the royal choirs of the Millennium are no better than the raspy voice of a single saint, her hymnbook open before her, singing to the Lord during her morning devotions: "All hail the power of Jesus' name, let angels prostrate fall."

I just read about a worship service that occurred in the Polish city of Chelm, sixteen miles from the border of Ukraine. Over two thousand Ukrainian refugees showed up, and the congregation moved its services to a larger venue. The Ukrainians were weary and grieving from their continued struggle against Vladimir Putin's Russia. The service opened by singing "Amazing Grace," and every voice meant every word when they sang:

> Through many dangers, toils and snares,
> We have already come.
> T'was grace that brought us safe thus far
> And grace will lead us home.

One observer told the congregation, "Everything you do has eternal value, all the cooking, all the cleaning; and I believe the Ukrainian people can see and feel that. Although they are frightened, scared, panicked and worried, after a day or two staying in your church, they are relaxed; they are welcomed. This is the Kingdom of God."[4]

Remember, the kingdom is "already but not yet." We are God's advance team on this earth, and when we worship Him in spirit and truth, we're engaged in the highest of all kingdom activities. We can do that now!

Psalm 118:4 says, "Let those who fear the LORD now say, 'His mercy endures forever.'"

THE GOSPEL

The thousand-year reign of Christ will begin after He returns. According to Zechariah 12:10, on that day the Lord will pour out on the nation of Israel and on the inhabitants of Jerusalem the Spirit of grace and supplication. They will look on Him whom they pierced and mourn for Him as an only begotten Son. "And so all Israel shall be saved" (Rom. 11:26).

But no one has to wait until then.

The Bible says, "Behold, now is the accepted time; behold, now is the day of salvation" (2 Cor. 6:2). The prophet Isaiah said, "Seek the LORD while He may be found, call upon Him while He is near. Let the wicked forsake his way, and the unrighteous man his thoughts; let him return to the LORD, and He will have mercy on him; and to our God, for He will abundantly pardon" (55:6–7).

Perhaps you've watched actor David Suchet playing the role of the Belgian detective Hercule Poirot on television. Suchet's ability as an actor on Broadway and in film has brought him well-deserved fame and fortune. But all of that means little compared to his devotion to Jesus Christ.

Suchet told interviewer Justin Brierley how he came to faith in Christ. While filming in the United States in 1986, a random thought came to him as he soaked in the bathtub of his hotel suite. "I was thinking about my late grandfather," Suchet said. "And I suddenly started thinking about the afterlife."

His thoughts led him to get hold of a Bible and begin to investigate its claims. He had never taken Christianity seriously before. Instead, he dabbled in Eastern spirituality during the Beatles years. Suchet recalled hearing about some letters written by the apostle Paul, and he began reading the book of Romans. He decided to employ the same technique he used when reading a stage play—as though it had been written just for him.

"By the end of that letter," the actor said, "I was very moved, very emotional. I believed I had found what I had been looking for. Forget the gurus, forget everything else. I'd found a new way of being."

"Suchet went back to the beginning of the New Testament and read the Gospels of Matthew, Mark, Luke, and John—and he fell in love with Jesus. He turned to Him in faith, was baptized, and has followed Him ever since."[5]

The future is now. The coming King is available today. He loves you. He died and rose again for you. He is coming one day soon for you and me.

So, if you have never embraced Him as your Lord and Savior, do so today!

He can give you a new life, a new way of being. Confess your faults and sins to Him. Ask for forgiveness. Trust Him to give you eternal life, which can start right now. Don't lose another minute, but just now, at this moment, let the Holy Spirit fill you with a foretaste of glory divine. Let Him give you exhilaration for today and anticipation for tomorrow.

The Golden Age of Jesus is waiting to dawn in your heart.

The Jesus of the Golden Age is willing to rule and reign over your life, both now and forevermore. Let it be your story and your song, praising the Savior all the day long!

Will you join me in this?

Let's all be kingdom ready!

INDEX

SCRIPTURE INDEX

ACKNOWLEDGMENTS

This book has been one of the greatest challenges of my life, but I have not faced this challenge alone. Some of my closest and most loyal friends have helped me, and I do not wish to just acknowledge them; I wish to honor them and thank them.

Beau Sager and I have worked together for fifteen years and during that time we have released more than twenty Christian books. Beau is an incredible researcher, writer, and editor, and he wonderfully manages all things written that come out of Turning Point.

Rob Morgan is one of my closest pastoral friends. We are both pastors and authors, and when we work on projects like this together, I like to call what we do "devotional doctrine."

Sam O'Neal is an amazing hard-working editor, and we now work together on all Thomas Nelson Turning Point projects. And this year he managed to do his good work from Italy. How does that work? Sam, you are a talented one-of-a-kind friend.

When a book is finally written, Paul Joiner takes over. His marketing magic is like nothing I have witnessed in the world of books. Paul, you are the most creative person I have ever known, and I am blessed to have you as a friend.

Three years ago, David Michael Jeremiah was named president of Turning Point. What you are reading about in this page of acknowledgments is but a small part of the world he manages with excellence.

I talk to Damon Reiss on a regular basis and his weekly written reports on the progress of our books are beyond anything any publisher has ever done for us. It is obvious that you care about all of this, Damon!

Sealy Yates is my agent and has been for more than thirty years. Sealy, your consistency is one of our secrets.

This book was written as I was trying to recover from a serious spinal cord disease. I pay special tribute to my administrative assistant, Beth Anne Hewett, who worked overtime to keep us focused and on schedule.

I devote these final words to my wife Donna. She helped me set up my office in a recliner in the corner of our family room. This was a room she had just finished refurbishing, and I cluttered it up with dozens of books and papers scattered everywhere and stacked on top of each other! And she was like my servant—making certain that I had everything I needed. For the rest of my life whenever I view this book, I will remember the incredible sacrifice that was made by Donna Marilyn Jeremiah.

To God be the glory!

NOTES

INTRODUCTION

1. Alia Shoaib, "Kentucky Man Digs up Insane Treasure Trove," *Business Insider*, July 15, 2023, https://www.businessinsider.com/kentucky-man-finds-700-civil-war-coins-buried-farm-2023-7.
2. J. Dwight Pentecost, *Things to Come: A Study in Biblical Eschatology* (Grand Rapids, MI: Zondervan, 1958), 476.

CHAPTER 2

1. C. S. Lewis, *Miracles* (San Francisco, CA: HarperOne, 2009), 176.
2. Leon J. Wood, *The Bible and Future Events: An Introductory Survey of Last-Day Events* (Grand Rapids, MI: Zondervan Publishing House, 1973), 166.
3. Timothy J. Demy and Thomas Ice, *Answers to Common Questions About Heaven & Eternity* (Grand Rapids, MI: Kregel Publications, 2011), 24.
4. "After DNA Test, Maryland Man Discovers He's an African Prince," *WTHR*, May 10, 2020, https://www.wthr.com/article/features/trending-today/after-dna-test-maryland-man-discovers-hes-african-prince/531-c3405c8b-1789–431a-9a3f-14a8405c411e.

CHAPTER 3

1. Anna Hansen, "World's Largest Puzzle Awaits Missing Piece at Pardeeville Funeral Home," *Portage Daily Register*, February 15, 2023, https://wiscnews.com/news/community/portagedailyregister/world-s-largest-puzzle-awaits-missing-piece-at-pardeeville-funeral-home/article_5fe53563-cb4a-5883-afe9-aca5c927a4be.html.
2. J. Dwight Pentecost, *Things to Come: A Study in Biblical Eschatology* (Grand Rapids, MI: Zondervan, 1958), 476.
3. Tim LaHaye and Ed Hindson, eds., *The Popular Encyclopedia of Bible Prophecy* (Eugene, OR: Harvest House Publishers, 2004), 235.
4. From unpublished notes by Alva J. McClain, Winona Lake, IN: Grace Seminary, n.d.), 14.
5. Visual Journalism Team, "Your Complete Guide to the King's Coronation," *BBC*, May 6, 2023, https://www.bbc.com/news/uk-65342840.

CHAPTER 4

1. Dale Van Atta, *With Honor: Melvin Laird in War, Peace, and Politics* (Madison, WI: The University of Wisconsin Press, 2008), 470.

2. Henry Steele Commager, *The Study and Teaching of History* (New York, NY: Merrell Publishers, 1980), 74.

3. George Eldon Ladd, *Gospel of the Kingdom* (Grand Rapids, MI: Eerdmans, 2000), 16–17, 21.

4. J. C. Ryle, "Matthew 6:9-15," *Expository Thoughts on Matthew* (Edinburgh, Banner of Truth Trust, 1856), https://ccel.org/ccel/ryle/matthew/matthew.vii.ii.html, quoted in Curtis Rose, *The Lord's Prayer* (Castle Rock, CO: Renew Publication, 2014), location 267, Kindle.

5. Thomas Watson, "The Lord's Prayer," from *A Body of Practical Divinity: Consisting of Above 176 Sermons on the Lesser Catechism* (London: Thomas Parkhurst, 1692), location 1140, Kindle.

6. J. Vernon McGee, *Revelation, vol. 3, Revelation 14-22* (Nashville, TN: Thomas Nelson, 1991).

7. Mark Batterson, *Praying Circles Around Your Future* (Grand Rapids, MI: Zondervan, 2018), 20, 60.

CHAPTER 5

1. Brian Kruse, Jackie Anderson, and Leslie V. Simon, "Fire Ant Bites," StatPearls, last modified, August 7, 2023, https://www.ncbi.nlm.nih.gov/books/NBK470576/.

2. Katie Hunt, "'We Knew This Day Would Come': One of World's Most Invasive Species Reaches Europe," *CNN*, September 11, 2023, https://www.cnn.com/2023/09/11/europe/invasive-red-fire-ant-europe-italy-scn/index.html.

3. J. Dwight Pentecost, *Things to Come* (Grand Rapids, MI: Zondervan, 1958), 489.

4. Tim LaHaye and Ed Hindson, *The Essential Guide to Bible Prophecy* (Eugene, OR: Harvest House Publishers, 2012), 151.

5. Randy Alcorn, *Heaven* (Wheaton, IL: Tyndale House Publishers, Inc., 2004), 105–106.

6. "Restoration of Notre-Dame's Smoke-Damaged Stained Glass Starts," *Reuters*, September 3, 2022, https://www.rappler.com/world/europe/restoration-notre-dame-cathedral-stained-glass-starts/.

CHAPTER 6

1. Kathy Gilsinan, "72 Minutes Until the End of the World?" *Politico Magazine*, April 29, 2024, https://www.politico.com/news/magazine/2024/04/29/the- frighteningly-fast-path-to -nuclear-armageddon-00154591.

2. "New Study on US-Russia Nuclear War: 91.5 Million Casualties in First Few Hours," Campaign News," *ICAN*, September 18, 2019, https://www.icanw.org/new_study_on_us_russia _nuclear_war.

CHAPTER 7

1. Robert St. John, *Tongue of the Prophets: The Life Story of Ben Yehuda* (Noble, OK: Balfour Books, 2013), location 1215–1227, Kindle.

2. Teddy Kollek, *Jerusalem* (Washington D.C.: Washington Institute for Near East Policy, 1990), 19–20.

3. Elhanan Leib Lewinsky, "Jerusalem: Famous Quotations," Jewish Virtual Library, accessed May 13, 2024, https://www.jewishvirtuallibrary.org/famous-quotations-on-jerusalem.

4. Randall Price, *Jerusalem in Prophecy: God's Stage for the Final Drama* (Eugene, OR: Harvest House, 1991), 74.

5. Frederick Buechner, *Whistling in the Dark: An ABC Theologized* (San Francisco: Harper & Row, 1988), quoted in *A Little Bit of Heaven* (Tulsa, OK: Honor Books, 1995), 118.

6. *World Happiness Report*, accessed June 24, 2024, https://worldhappiness.report/.

7. Dan Senor and Saul Singer, *The Genius of Israel* (New York, NY: Avid Reader Press, 2023), 92.

8. Joe Lieberman, *The Gift of Rest: Rediscovering the Beauty of the Sabbath* (New York, NY: Howard Books, 2011), opening note, 34, 221.

CHAPTER 8

1. George L. Klein, *The New American Commentary: Volume 21b–Zechariah* (Nashville, TN: B&H Publishing Group, 2008), 413–414.
2. Nathaniel West, *The Thousand Years in Both Testaments* (Chicago: Fleming H. Revell, 1880), quoted in John F. Walvoord, *The Millennial Kingdom: A Basic Text in Premillennial Theology* (Grand Rapids, MI: Zondervan Academic, 1983), 320.
3. "Moroccan Man Finds Faith After Earthquake," SAT-7 International, April 11, 2024, https://sat7.org/moroccan-man-finds-faith-after-earthquake/.

CHAPTER 9

1. Elizabeth II, Queen, "Christmas Broadcast 2011," *Their Majesties' Work as Prince of Wales and Duchess of Cornwall*, November 17, 2015, https://www.royal.uk/christmas-broadcast-2011.
2. Robert Strauss, quoted in "People, Apr. 17, 1978," *Time*, April 17, 1978, https://time.com/archive/6849825/people-apr-17-1978/.
3. David C. Ward, "'Now He Belongs to the Ages': The Assassination of Abraham Lincoln," *Smithsonian* (blog), accessed April 23, 2024, https://npg.si.edu/blog/%E2%80%9Cnow-he-belongs-ages%E2%80%9D-assassination-abraham-lincoln.
4. Carme Colomina, "The World in 2024: Ten Issues That Will Shape the International Agenda," Barcelona Centre for International Affairs, December 2023, https://www.cidob.org/en/publications/publication_series/notes_internacionals/299/the_world_in_2024_ten_issues_that_will_shape_the_international_agenda.
5. Ria Gupta, "7 Stunning Thrones to See Around the World," Conde Nest Traveler, October 22, 2022, https://www.cntraveller.in/story/7 stunning thrones to see around the world/.

CHAPTER 10

1. Biography.Com Editors and Sara Kettler, "William, Prince of Wales," Biography, March 15, 2024, https://www.biography.com/royalty/prince-william.
2. Arnold G. Fruchtenbaum, *The Footsteps of the Messiah: A Study of the Sequence of Prophetic Events* (San Antonio, TX: Ariel Ministries, 2020), 447.
3. Luke Dormehl, "Today in Apple History: Apple Co-Founder Quits and Cashes in His Stake for $800," Cult of Mac, April 12, 2024, https://www.cultofmac.com/475927/ron-wayne-quits-apple/.
4. "10 Facts About Michelangelo's Statue of David in Florence, Italy," *Context* (blog), accessed June 3, 2024, https://www.contexttravel.com/blog/articles/ten-facts-about-the-statue-of-david.

CHAPTER 11

1. "The World's Most Secure Buildings: ADX Florence Prison," *IDENTIV* (blog), July 20, 2022, https://www.identiv.com/resources/blog/the-worlds-most-secure-buildings-adx-florence-prison.
2. "New Species of Amazon Anaconda, World's Largest Snake, Discovered," *Reuters*, March 1, 2024, https://www.reuters.com/world/americas/new-species-amazon-anaconda-worlds-largest-snake-discovered-2024–03–01/; Jesse O'Neill, "Anaconda Species Thought to Be Largest in the World Discovered During Will Smith Documentary Shoot," *New York Post*, February 26, 2024, https://nypost.com/2024/02/26/world-news/new-species-of-giant-anaconda-discovered-during-filming-of-will-smith-docuseries/.

3. Thomas A. Tarrants, "Hindrances to Discipleship: The Devil," C. S. Lewis Institute, June 4, 2012, https://www.cslewisinstitute.org/resources/hindrances-to-discipleshipthe-devil/.

4. René Pache, *The Return of Jesus Christ* (Chicago, IL: Moody, 1955), 395.

5. Paul Bond, "Satan Is Getting Hot as Hell in American Pop Culture," *Newsweek*, March 28, 2023, https://www.newsweek.com/satan-getting-hot-hell-american-pop-culture-1790669.

6. Martin Luther, "A Mighty Fortress," Hymnary.org, accessed June 24, 2024, https://hymnary.org/text/a_mighty_fortress_is_our_god_a_bulwark.

CHAPTER 12

1. Ray Brewer, "Unexpected Journey led to Lifetime of Coaching, Caring for Troubled Teenagers," *Las Vegas Sun*, May 21, 2023, https://lasvegassun.com/news/2023/may/21/unexpected-journey-led-to-lifetime-of-coaching-car/.

2. "Godly Talk—The Last Words of Early Church Martyrs," Christian Refuge, accessed March 22, 2024, https://christianrefuge.org/godly-talk-the-last-words-of-early-church-martyrs/.

3. Randy Alcorn, *Heaven* (Wheaton, IL: Tyndale, 2004), 226.

4. Henry M. Morris, *The Revelation Record* (Wheaton, IL: Tyndale, 1983), 412.

5. D. Michael Abrashoff, *It's Your Ship* (New York, NY: Grand Central Publishing, 2002), 21.

CHAPTER 13

1. Gary Stoller, "Unparalleled Beauty on One of America's Most Treacherous Highways," *Forbes*, October 10, 2023, https://www.forbes.com/sites/garystoller/2023/10/10/unparalleled-beauty-on-americas-most-treacherous-highway/?sh=394ac11c1ce0.

2. J. C. Ryle, "What Is True Practical Holiness?" excerpted from Holiness: *Its Nature, Hindrances, Difficulties, and Roots* (Chicago, IL: Moody Publishers, 2010), C. S. Lewis Institute, December 3, 2016, https://www.cslewisinstitute.org/resources/what-is-true-practical-holiness/.

CHAPTER 14

1. Jessica Baker, "AGE: I'm the Oldest Woman in the World but I Have NO Health Problems . . . Now Scientists Think I May Hold the Key to Immorality," *The US Sun*, October 24, 2023, https://www.the-sun.com/health/9402264/oldest-woman-world-maria-branyas-key-immortality-spain/.

2. John Piper, "Why Did the First Humans Live for So Long?" Desiring God, April 30, 2021, https://www.desiringgod.org/interviews/why-did-the-first-humans-live-for-so-long.

3. Sara Berg, "What Doctors Wish Patients Knew About Falling U.S. Life Expectancy," American Medical Association, March 10, 2023, https://www.ama-assn.org/delivering-care/public-health/what-doctors-wish-patients-knew-about-falling-us-life-expectancy.

4. Adapted from unpublished notes by Alva J. McClain (Winona Lake, IN: Grace Seminary, n.d.), 7.

5. Charlotte Alter, "The Man Who Thinks He Can Live Forever," *Time*, September 20, 2023, https://time.com/6315607/bryan-johnsons-quest-for-immortality/.

CHAPTER 15

1. "Sphere," Google, accessed June 14, 2024, https://g.co/kgs/yF9q6wT.

2. Taylor Lane, "Here's the Sphere, by the Numbers," *Las Vegas Review-Journal*, August 2, 2023, https://www.reviewjournal.com/entertainment/heres-the-sphere-by-the-numbers-2881041/.

3. Linda Geddes, "The Dark Town that Built a Giant Mirror to Deflect the Sun," *BBC*, March 13, 2017, https://www.bbc.com/future/article/20170314-the-town-that-built-a-mirror-to-catch-the-sun.

4. Omar Memon, "Double Sunrise: History's Longest Ever Commercial Air Service," Simple Flying, April 19, 2024, https://simpleflying.com/double-sunrise-historys-longest-ever-commercial-air-service/.

CHAPTER 16

1. Eduardo Medina, "Sheriff Releases Body Camera Footage in Police Killing of Airman in His Home," *New York Times*, May 9, 2024, https://www.nytimes.com/2024/05/09/us/roger-fortson-police-shooting-florida.html?searchResultPosition=1.
2. Dan Krauth, "Squatter Standoff Captured on Camera in Queens," *ABC 7*, April 18, 2024, https://abc7ny.com/squatters-standoff-queens-new-york-city/14540298/.
3. Cara Tabachnick, "Hit in DNA Database Exonerates Man 47 Years After Wrongful Rape Conviction," *CBS News*, September 5, 2023, https://www.cbsnews.com/news/leonard-mack-exonerated-47-years-after-wrongful-rape-conviction/.

CHAPTER 17

1. Vladimir Isachenkov, Dasha Litvinova, Yuras Karmanau, and Jim Heintz, "Russia Attacks Ukraine as Defiant Putin Warns US, NATO," *Associated Press*, February 23, 2022, https://apnews.com/article/russia-ukraine-europe-russia-moscow-kyiv-626a8c5ec22217bacb24ece60fac4fe1.
2. Helene Cooper, Thomas Gibbons-Neff, Eric Schmitt, and Julian E. Barnes, "Troop Deaths and Injuries in Ukraine War Near 500,000, U.S. Officials Say," *New York Times*, August 18, 2023, https://www.nytimes.com/2023/08/18/us/politics/ukraine-russia-war-casualties.html.
3. "Ukraine Emergency," UNHCR, accessed March 26, 2024, https://www.unrefugees.org/emergencies/ukraine/.
4. Chris Hedges, "What Every Person Should Know About War," *New York Times*, July 6, 2023, https://www.nytimes.com/2003/07/06/books/chapters/what-every-person-should-know-about-war.html.
5. C. S. Lewis, "Reflections: Truths Ancient and Simple," C. S. Lewis Institute, June 1, 2017, https://www.cslewisinstitute.org/resources/reflections-june-2017/.
6. John Stuart Mill, "The Contest in America," *Fraser's Magazine*, February 1862.
7. M. R. DeHaan, *The Great Society* (Grand Rapids, MI: Radio Bible Class, 1965), 7–8.
8. W. A. Criswell, *Expository Sermons on Revelation,* vol.5 (Grand Rapids, MI: Zondervan, 1966), 790.
9. Hollis Godfrey, *The Man Who Ended War* (Boston, MA: Little, Brown, and Company, 1908), 1.

CHAPTER 18

1. David E. Hamilton, "Herbert Hoover: Campaigns and Elections," UVA Miller Center, accessed March 6, 2024, https://millercenter.org/president/hoover/campaigns-and-elections.
2. "Presidential Campaign Slogans," PresidentsUSA.net, accessed March 6, 2024, https://www.presidentsusa.net/campaignslogans.html.
3. Richard Schlesinger, "Doris Buffett Goes for Broke to Help City," *CBS News*, December 4, 2009, http://www.cbsnews.com/stories/2009/12/04/eveningnews/main5893628.shtml.
4. Mark Hitchcock, *The End* (Carol Stream, IL: Tyndale House Publishers, 2012), 428.
5. John N. Oswalt, *The Book of Isaiah: Chapters 40–66* (Grand Rapids, MI: Eerdmans, 1998), 507.
6. Cathy Free, "Iowa Teen Grew 7,000 Pounds of Veggies, Then Gave Them All Away," *Washington Post*, November 14, 2023, https://www.washingtonpost.com/lifestyle/2023/11/14/iowa-teen-farmer-donate-garden/.

CHAPTER 19

1. Sandra Boodman, "Medical Mysteries: A Surgeon's Ominous Pain and a Question of Grilled Meat," *Washington Post*, July 8, 2023, https://www.washingtonpost.com/wellness/2023/07/08/medical-mystery-pain-grilled-meat/.
2. "The Top 10 Causes of Death," *World Health Organization*, December 9, 2020, https://www.who.int/news-room/fact-sheets/detail/the-top-10-causes-of-death.
3. "Leading Causes of Death," Center for Disease Control and Prevention, last updated May 2, 2024, https://www.cdc.gov/nchs/fastats/leading-causes-of-death.htm.
4. "Something for Thanksgiving" in *The Bible Society Record* (November 1953), 144.

CHAPTER 20

1. John F. Helliwell and others, *World Happiness Report*, March 20, 2023, https://worldhappiness.report/ed/2023/executive-summary/.
2. Bård Amundsen, "What Makes Us Happy? A New Global Study Provides Answers," Sciencenorway.no, October 21, 2023, https://www.sciencenorway.no/happiness-psychology/what-makes-us-happy-a-new-global-study-provides-answers/2268287.
3. A. W. Tozer, *Who Put Jesus on the Cross?* (Camp Hill, PA: WingSpread Publishers, 1976), Kindle.
4. C. S. Lewis to Sheldon Vanauken, *A Severe Mercy* (San Francisco, CA: HarperSanFrancisco, 1992), 189.
5. Randy Alcorn, *Happiness* (Carol Stream, IL: Tyndale House Publications, 2015), viii, 22, 491.

CHAPTER 21

1. Zoe Sottile and Andy Rose, "Mountain Lion Claws Man's Head While He Sits in Hot Tub, Officials Say," *CNN Travel*, March 29, 2023, https://www.cnn.com/2023/03/27/us/mountain-lion-colorado-hot-tub-attack-trnd/index.html.
2. John F. Walvoord and Roy B. Zuck, eds., *The Bible Knowledge Commentary: Old Testament* (Colorado Springs, CO: David C. Cook, 1983), 1057.
3. John Wesley, *The Beauties of the Rev. J. Wesley, M.A.* (Philadelphia, PA: Jonathan Pounder, 1817), 236.
4. "An Inseparable Bond—The Impact of Puppy Wishes," Make-A-Wish, accessed March 21, 2024, https://wish.org/akwa/inseparable-bond-impact-puppy-wishes.

CHAPTER 22

1. Arnold G. Fruchtenbaum, *The Footsteps of the Messiah: A Study of the Sequence of Prophetic Events* (San Antonio, TX: Ariel Press, 1982), 505.
2. Fred Lambert, "Tesla's Next Factory is Going to Be in Austin, Texas, and It's Going to Happen Quickly," Electrek, May 15, 2020, https://electrek.co/2020/05/15/tesla-factory-austin-texas/.

CHAPTER 23

1. Cécile Lemoine, "In Jerusalem, the 'Red Heifer' Worries Religious and Political Leaders," *LaCroix International*, April 25, 2024, https://international.la-croix.com/world/in-jerusalem-the-red-heifer-worries-religious-and-political-leaders. See also Mersiha Gadzo, "What Do Texan Red Heifers Have to Do with Al-Aqsa and Jewish Temple?" *Aljazeera*, April 9, 2024, https://www.aljazeera.com/news/2024/4/9/what-do-texan-red-heifers-have-to-do-with-al-aqsa-and-a-jewish-temple.
2. Chris Livesay, "What These Red Cows from Texas Have to Do with War and Peace in the

Middle East," *CBS News*, https://www.cbsnews.com/news/israel-war-hamas-red-heifers
-from-texas-jerusalem-jewish-temple-al-aqsa/.

3. J. Dwight Pentecost, *Things to Come* (Grand Rapids, MI: Zondervan, 1958), 525.

4. Arno Gaebelein, *The Prophet Ezekiel* (New York, NY: Our Hope, 1918), 312.

5. John F. Walvoord, *Prophecy Knowledge Handbook* (Wheaton, IL: Victor Books, 1990), 202.

6. Thomas D. Ice, "Why Sacrifices in the Millennium," *Liberty University Article Archives* 60 (May 2009), https://digitalcommons.liberty.edu/cgi/viewcontent.cgi?article=1059&context=pretrib_arch.

7. Charles Lee Feinberg, *The Prophecy of Ezekiel* (Eugene, OR: Wipf and Stock, 2003), 254–255.

8. Ice, "Why Sacrifices in the Millennium."

9. "Instruments of Death Become Symbols of Eternal Life," Preaching Today, accessed June 10, 2024, https://www.preachingtoday.com/illustrations/2019/april/instruments-of-death-become-symbols-of-eternal-life.html.

10. Charlotte Elliott, "Just As I Am," https://hymnary.org/text/just_as_i_am_without_one_plea.

CHAPTER 24

1. "The Most Unsafe Place I've Been in My Life," Southwestern Baptist Theological Seminary, November 3, 2022, https://swbts.edu/news/the-most-unsafe-place-ive-been-in-my-life-southwestern-student-recalls-lessons-from-the-underground-church/.

2. "Largest Simultaneous Sing-Along (Multiple Venues)," Guinness World Records, accessed May 30, 2024, https://www.guinnessworldrecords.com/world-records/largest-simultaneous-sing-along-multiple-venues.

3. A. W. Tozer, *The Knowledge of the Holy* (Nashville, TN: HarperCollins, 1978), 3.

4. Joan Huyser-Honig, "Keith Getty on Writing Hymns for the Church Universal," Calvin Institute of Christian Worship, September 1, 2006, https://worship.calvin.edu/resources/resource-library/keith-getty-on-writing-hymns-for-the-church-universal/.

CHAPTER 25

1. "Australian Gets Life Term for Nursing Home Fires," *San Diego Tribune*, July 31, 2013, https://www.sandiegouniontribune.com/sdut-australian-gets-life-term-for-nursing-home-fires-2013jul31-story.html.

2. George Eldon Ladd, *The Meaning of the Millennium: Four Views* (Downers Grove, IL: IVP Academic, 1977), 40.

3. J. Dwight Pentecost, *Things to Come* (Grand Rapids, MI: Zondervan, 1958), 538.

4. Tim Chaddick, *The Truth About Lies* (Colorado Springs, CO: David C. Cook, 2015), 19.

5. Chaddick, *The Truth About Lies*, 21–25.

CHAPTER 26

1. Based on personal conversation and correspondence, used with permission.

2. Louis Casiano, "NYC Art 'Portal' to Dublin to Close Temporarily Following Bad Behavior, Including Nudity, Mischief," *Fox News*, May 14, 2024, https://www.foxnews.com/lifestyle/nyc-art-portal-dublin-close-temporarily-following-bad-behavior-including-nudity-mischief.

CHAPTER 27

1. David K. Li, "Murderer Released After Being Deemed Too Old to Kill Again, Kills Again," *NBC News*, July 19, 2019, https://www.nbcnews.com/news/us-news/murderer-released-after-being-deemed-too-old-kill-again-kills-n1031736.

2. J. Vernon McGee, *Reveling Through Revelation, Part II* (Pasadena, CA: Thru the Bible, 1974), 74–75.

3. Charles R. Swindoll, *Insights on Revelation* (Carol Stream, IL: Tyndale House Publishers, Inc., 2014), 288.

4. Warren W. Wiersbe, *Be Victorious* (Colorado Springs, CO: David C. Cook, 1985), 142.

5. Craig S. Keener, *The NIV Application Commentary: Revelation* (Grand Rapids, MI: Zondervan, 2000), 482.

6. Jeannie Ortega Law, "Hollywood Actor Says Playing the Devil Showed Him How Blessed by God He Really Is," *The Christian Post*, June 10, 2023, https://www.christianpost.com/news/hollywood-actor-says-playing-devil-showed-him-how-blessed-he-is.html.

7. Adam Staten, "Christian Actor Neal McDonough Was Hesitant to Play the Devil But Wife's Words Convinced Him," God Updates, June 19, 2023, https://www.godupdates.com/christian-actor-neal-mcdonough-plays-the-devil/.

8. "How Playing the Devil in the Shift Brought Neal McDonough Closer to God," February 21, 2024, Movie Guide, https://www.movieguide.org/news-articles/playing-the-devil-brought-neal-mcdonough-closer-to-god.html.

CHAPTER 28

1. Don Siegelman, *Stealing Our Democracy* (Montgomery, AL: NewSouth Books, 2020), Chapter 1.

2. Yumbert P. Rodeheaver, *Rodeheaver's Gospel Solos and Duets* (Winona Lake, IN: The Rodeheaver Hall-Mack Co., 1925).

CHAPTER 30

1. Randy Alcorn, *Heaven* (Wheaton, IL: Tyndale House Publishers, Inc., 2004), 101.

CHAPTER 31

1. Jennifer Willis, "Why We Look Up: Anticipation," *Sky and Telescope* (blog), June 6, 2024, https://skyandtelescope.org/astronomy-blogs/why-we-look-up-anticipation/.

2. Emily DiNuzzo, "Wash Your Hands Immediately After Touching These 10 Things," *Reader's Digest*, January 31, 2024, https://www.rd.com/list/wash-hands-after-touching-these-things/.

3. Rick Stedman, *Praying the Promises of Jesus* (Eugene, OR: Harvest House Publishers, 2016), 84.

4. Caroline Anderson, "Thousands of Ukrainian Christians Find Solace in Polish Baptist Church," IMB, March 11, 2022, https://www.imb.org/2022/03/11/thousands-ukrainian-christians-find-solace-polish-baptist-church/.

5. Justin Brierley, *The Surprising Rebirth of Belief in God* (Carol Stream, IL: Tyndale House, 2023), 97–99.

ABOUT THE AUTHOR

DR. DAVID JEREMIAH is the founder of Turning Point, an international ministry committed to providing Christians with sound Bible teaching through radio and television, the internet, live events, and resource materials and books. He is the author of more than fifty books, including *Where Do We Go from Here?*, *Forward*, *The World of the End*, and *The Great Disappearance*.

Dr. Jeremiah serves as the senior pastor of Shadow Mountain Community Church in El Cajon, California. He and his wife, Donna, have four grown children and twelve grandchildren.

stay connected to the teaching of

DR. DAVID JEREMIAH

· · · · · · · ·

Publishing | Radio | Television | Online